Architect's
Essentials of
Negotiation

Architect's Essentials of Negotiation

Second Edition

Ava J. Abramowitz, Esq., Hon. AIA

WILEY

John Wiley & Sons, Inc.

Published by John Wiley & Sons, Inc., Hoboken, New Jersey.
Published simultaneously in Canada.

For general information about our other products and services, please contact our Customer Care Department within the United States at (800) 762-2974, outside the United States at (317) 572-3993, or fax (317) 572-4002.

Wiley also publishes its books in a variety of electronic formats. Some content that appears in print may not be available in electronic books. For more information about Wiley products, visit our web site at www.wiley.com.

Library of Congress Cataloging-in-Publication Data:

Abramowitz, Ava J.
    Architect's essentials of negotiation / by Ava J. Abramowitz. – 2nd ed.
      p. cm.
    Revision of: Architect's essentials of contract negotiation. 2002.
    Includes index.
      ISBN 978-0-470-42688-3 (pbk.)
    1. Architectural contracts.   2. Negotiation in business.   I. Abramowitz, Ava J. Architect's essentials of contract negotiation.   II. Title.
    NA1996.A24 2009
    720.68′4–dc22
                                                    2008045530

10   9   8   7   6   5   4   3   2   1

Contents

3
The Purpose of Contracts 45

4
Power and Leverage: How to Get It and Keep It 89

5
Preparation Tips 127

Introduction

When John Czarnecki, senior editor at Wiley, invited me to discuss the possibility of a second edition of this book, I was thrilled. So much has changed since 2001, when I wrote the first edition of the *Architect's Essentials of Contract Negotiation*. Today, if you gather a group of architects together, new acronyms roll off their tongues, and you will hear them discuss such things as Integrated Project Delivery (IPD), Building Information Modeling (BIM), Sustainability (capital "S" if they think it's an ethical obligation for the architect; lowercase "s" if they think it just makes smart business sense for their clients), global practice, and how to deal with increasingly strong client representatives—substantial issues today, just preparing to loom as issues back then.

Oh, yes, some things stay the same. "The Five Challenges of Architect Negotiation," a seminar I devised a while back, is still a draw. It explores the five fears so many architects seem to have—the fear of clients, the fear of risk, the fear of confrontation, the fear of leaving money on the table, and the fear of just plain old losing. Those challenges are just as riveting in this century as they were in the last. "You're going to update the book?" said an architect friend of mine, as he was walking to fill his fourth cup of coffee. "Keep the old section on fees. Don't change a word." He ordered his cup and turned back toward me. "On second thought, can you expand the section on fees, please? It is just so tough out there."

I nodded. It *is* tough out there, and it looks as if it may get tougher. I don't want to start this book on a downer, but the reality is, as I write this, the economy is troubled. And that affects everyone's willingness to risk. Owners are less willing to invest in new buildings when they are uncertain about who will fill them. Contractors are less eager to give guaranteed maximum prices (GMPs) when future commodity prices are anyone's guess. And support systems are beginning to crack. Banks seem more interested in securing their bottom lines than helping anyone else grow theirs. Insurance is relatively cheap, but multi-year policies for all but the smallest firms are a thing of the past. Architects are wary and watchful. As a result, many are less open to developing new skills, even when they know that new skills are called for. This is especially so when the old skills still seem to work—maybe not perfectly, but acceptably. Promises of greater achievements in a time of increasing unknowns are too easily met with "if it ain't broke. . . ."

But it may be broke. Organizations everywhere reengineered themselves in the 1980s and 1990s. They became leaner, many meaner, and most internally more efficient. Companies in design and construction, though, have come late to the table. More usually, they have continued to design and build the way their mentors did before. Oh, I know computer-aided design and drafting (CADD) came in, and that freed architects from pencils and slide rules, and design-build hit the scene, but the process essentially remained and remains the same for most involved. The Owner hires the Architect and signs a contract. The Architect designs the building. The design is put out for bid and negotiation. Contractors bid, and ultimately the Contractor is selected. The Owner hires the Contractor and signs a contract with him. The three are in a triangle—a love triangle if all works out; a Bermuda triangle if it doesn't. Then, finger pointing is all too often the norm, maybe even (hired) guns a-blazing. Everyone—especially the Owner—is exhausted by the resulting noise and accompanying waste. The process is just too expensive, the wear and tear too great.

That's why so many owners are flirting with IPD and BIM. They see them as a way to reengineer a process that has become too costly and time-consuming. They want the savings that smarter hand-offs would engender. They want the improved peace and productivity that substantive collaboration can produce. Their mantra is simple: Down with silo thinking; up with team building. "Yes," they say with certainty, "that's the wave of the future. Get on board while the getting is good."

They may be right in their instincts and thought. Magic can occur in teams as creative members collaborate and devise greater ideas. But to produce that magic, especially in a group setting, requires a different set of interpersonal skills than most people have been taught in school. No contract can force it; no computer program can dictate it. Thankfully, though, negotiation and collaborative skills can be learned and modeled. This book has the acquisition of those skills as its goal.

This book can be read three ways:

1. *It can be read cover to cover, and it is indeed cumulative.* How do you set a project up for success? How do you use the law to increase the odds of that success? How do you negotiate for it? How can you use your contracts for success? Can you still strive for success even when things go wrong?

2. *Or, it can be read solely as a guide to negotiation.* Chapters 4, 5, 6, 7, 9, and 10 provide you with process, preparation, communication, collaboration, and dispute resolution skills—all with the intent of empowering you at the negotiation table.

3. *Or, it can be read as a guide to contract management.* Chapters 1, 2, 3, 8, and 10 introduce you to tough legal concepts, hopefully in an easily accessible way, so that you can use them for the benefit of your client.

What about me, you ask? Why can't I use this book to look out for Number One? Because if looking out for you as Number One is on the top of your list, you guarantee your needs won't rank high on anybody else's list. People don't like working with self-dealers. They shun ego-driven people who demand leadership roles but can't fill them gracefully. People want to work with partners who are easy to work with, and, if you are focusing on you first, your collaborators will understandably feel overlooked.

This book is not tied to your past. On the contrary, this book is a strong advocate for your future. It is rooted in the belief that architects can design their practices as consciously and as well as they design their projects. It believes in assertive practice and is dedicated to the advancement of assertive practitioners, for it is assertive practitioners who will face the future, redefining how architecture is delivered in the process.

What is this phenomenon—the assertive practitioner? Have you ever met a colleague who whined about how awful it was on the street? Or dealt with a colleague who displayed more ego than sense? An assertive practitioner avoids either end of the spectrum. Clothed in a solid sense of self, these architects have the ability to recognize and then look beyond their own personal needs, so they can more clearly recognize and focus on the needs of the Other. (I use the term "Other" to signify that the person with whom you are negotiating is not you—not an enemy, not a friend, just not you.) With that twin understanding of needs, they free themselves to collaborate.

Assertive practitioners do not bemoan others' perceptions of their value. They provide value instead. They do so by:

➤ Committing themselves to using design to help clients meet their business objectives

➤ Having an insatiable curiosity about the expertise and design and business needs of those with whom they negotiate—whether they are clients, their clients' clients, their partners or employees, or the contractors and consultants with whom they work everyday

➤ Having a cornucopia of design and business skills that they work daily to keep current and valuable

➤ Quietly believing in themselves and their capacity to use design to serve

➤ Knowing that risk and reward go hand in hand, and loving them both

➤ Knowing that empathy without assertiveness and assertiveness without empathy don't help anyone

➤ Believing in front-end alignment and no-surprise design, and striving to achieve both

➤ Listening solely with the intent of learning

➤ Worrying not about their liability, but about helping their clients manage risk, and

➤ Knowing categorically that if they look out for their client's needs, they will take care of their own needs in the process.

It is assertive practitioners to whom laypeople look when they think "architects." It is they who are respected because of their professionalism and trusted because of their unerring competence, candor, and concern. It is they for whom people pay big bucks.

Being an assertive practitioner is not easy, but it is not hard either. This book will lead you to it, using negotiation as the hook. I also hope that this book will help make your professional life easier. The stakes are so high in design and construction, no matter what measurement system is used, that it is sometimes hard to step back and experience fully what is going on. But the more you use the communication behaviors in Chapter 6, the easier that will become.

A few administrative tasks, if I may. When I refer to "the client" (or "the developer" or "the Other"), I invariably write "the client . . . they," and not "the client . . . he or she." There is a reason for this. Most clients are made up of groups. In the commercial setting, there is a board. Even when there is none, and you are dealing with the chief executive officer (CEO) only, there still is a group to be contended with, made up of the chief operating officer (COO), the chief financial officer (CFO), the general counsel, the user, whoever—there is always more than one person to respond to. In the residential setting, you have a husband and wife, and even if the client is single, you still have to deal with everyone in the client's kitchen cabinet. So clients are always referred to in the plural, because, ten to one, more than one person will make up the role.

Second, in order not to add words unnecessarily to this book, all documents referred to by letter and number are American Institute of Architects (AIA) standard documents. If they are not, the organization initiating the documents will be identified. You should know, though, that the AIA is coming out with a new series of documents, as this book is being published. Some of those documents are a logical step from the old B141, others a giant step into the world of IPD. This book is not intended to analyze them or to tell you how to modify them. As an assertive practitioner, that is your responsibility, and I won't take it from you. But I will give you an approach to help you negotiate them, as any document, no matter who drafted it, is open to negotiation.

Third, I have changed the book since the first edition to meet changing times and have expanded the section on negotiating fees. I have added a chapter on collaboration and team building, and I have increased the number of what I call sidebars to address issues that demand attention—all with the intent of making this book more used and more useful.

Fourth, I have changed the title from the *Architect's Essentials of Contract Negotiation* to the *Architect's Essentials of Negotiation* because I want architects to embrace negotiation, and that means the book has to be read. You will learn in Chapter 6 that how you say what you say is often more important in a negotiation than the information you want to deliver. That is why I am changing the name of the book.

There are probably some 150,000 or so architects in the United States, some practicing, some not. Most will never review a contract in their professional career. Some won't because they work in large firms and never see a contract. Others won't because they work in tiny firms and provide services on a handshake. And, still others won't because they are holding nontraditional positions that do not necessitate their signing a contract. These architects see a book entitled the *Architect's Essentials of Contract Negotiation*, and they feel entitled to pass: After all, from their point of view, the title says "irrelevant-to-me."

Yet nothing could be further from the truth. Architects negotiate all the time, and usually about design issues. Not having the requisite negotiation skills creates so many unnecessary problems for them and their Other. I mean, think about it. Today, every smart law student graduates having taken at least one course in negotiation. And every smart MBA student graduates having taken at least one course in negotiation. Only architects graduate from school *never* having taken a course in negotiation. In most architecture schools, it's not even an option. Then they enter the workforce and confront negotiation-trained lawyers and MBAs. No wonder so many architects fear negotiation. If I were untrained in the art, I would be scared, too.

There has to be a way to level the playing field. My hope is that changing the title will encourage more architecture professors to use the book as a text, and lead more architects to pick it up and say, "Wow! This is just what I need."

This book is intended to level the playing field in yet another way. While the title still says "Architect's Essentials," the book is not for architects alone. Any design professional will benefit from it. Clients and contractors can benefit too—which only stands to reason. Design and construction, to work well, are essentially collaborative endeavors. If all the parties speak the same language, have the same negotiation approaches and the same communication skills, it stands to reason the endeavor can be implemented more efficiently, with fewer problems.

In fact, I became an owner's representative because of this book. A prospective building owner had read it and tracked me down. "Will you put my building together for me? I want the architect, the engineer, the contractor, and me to end up at the finish line on time, on budget, with no claims and a building we can be proud of. I don't want to go through the hell of bad design and construction that I hear about." I, of course, said yes. How could I not? How did it work out, you ask? I spent a long time with the architect and the contractor breaking bad habits, including the refusal to share their expertise for fear of liability. And I spent a long time with them and the owner translating design- and construction-speak into English, so the owner could learn what questions to ask, so he could make a reasoned decision. Suffice to say, the building was built, and all the parties lived happily ever after.

Finally, please know that I have a distinct view as to the attributes of an expert negotiator. Their styles may vary. Their strategies may differ. They may be outcome-oriented. They may be problem solvers. Invariably, though, to be classified as expert in my book, a quality negotiator reaches agreements, those agreements are implemented successfully, and the Other is willing, if not eager, to negotiate with them again. I hold to this standard as it incorporates fully my view of professionalism. Why else do we serve if not to have both our clients and ourselves succeed? Why else are we in business if not to enjoy repeat business? It is my hope that between that philosophy and this book, all your negotiations will be more productive ones.

Ava J. Abramowitz

A Word from an Owner

Thank God for the Internet! That's how I found this enthusiastic and lively book when I set out a few years back to build a dream home for my family. I'd had a fast-paced career in law, banking, and public service but had never before commissioned a major construction project. Because I'd heard so many anecdotes about residential, commercial, and, especially, government construction projects spinning out of control and turning out badly for all involved, I figured I'd better do my homework. I was determined that I not become a modern-day Mr. Blandings.

Though directed primarily toward design professionals, the *Architect's Essentials of Negotiation* is a worthwhile read for anyone involved in a construction project, whether as architect, contractor, or owner. A successful construction project requires, above all, constant cooperation, coordination, and teamwork, or, as Ms. Abramowitz puts it, "partnering" among the owner, architect, and contractor. In theory, most understand the need for "partnering," but, in practice, few architects, owners, or contractors consciously do much to ensure it. And that, perhaps, is why the construction field is sufficiently notorious to attract Hollywood's attention.

In order to make sure the partnering process works and the building is actually built, the parties need to negotiate at the outset and agree on the terms of their engagement. Ms. Abramowitz presents thoughtful and well-researched recommendations for preparing the parties for their negotiations. She clearly explains why it is in no one's interest to be either a "soft" or "hard" negotiator, but rather in everyone's interest to be a "principled negotiator" who seeks to solve problems and to create options for mutual gains. Being a principled negotiator, like being a team player, requires one to subordinate some personal aspirations in order for the common goal to succeed or the building to actually be built.

In my own project, I followed the book's advice to hold regular "partnering" meetings with the architects and contractors. By meeting regularly before we began the project and by continuing those meetings throughout the construction process, we were able to keep responsibilities and expectations clear, make crucial decisions on trade-offs, limit surprises, and generally head off problems before they occurred. While the process was by no means perfect, and while at certain times my wife and I may well have felt like Jim and Muriel Blandings, we nonetheless managed to minimize misunderstandings, cost overruns, and delays. Having read the first edition of this book, we knew that problems were normal and, rather than shying away from them, we spoke up and resolved them early and head-on.

"Partnering" does mean that the owner will have to pay the architect and contractor for their extra time spent planning, coordinating, and communicating. But in the long run, those extra fees probably produce a savings by preventing misapprehensions and mistakes. And principled negotiating does mean that the owner must recognize that the architect and contractor are in business to do well and, yes, to make a profit. All buildings cost more than their owners would like. The key is that owners are apt to get the most value for their money when they step up to bat, pay for partnering, and give their team the authority, responsibility, and budget needed to succeed.

I thank Ava Abramowitz for again sharing her passion in this second edition of a very fine book, which I recommend with wholehearted enthusiasm and confidence to owners, contractors, and architects alike.

Peter G. Fitzgerald
U.S. Senator, Illinois (1999–2005)
Chairman, Chain Bridge Bank, N.A.
McLean, Virginia

A Word from an Architect

I've been in this profession for more than 50 years and head of the Gensler firm for more than 44 years. I truly wish I had had an opportunity to read the *Architect's Essentials of Negotiation* years ago. It would certainly have assisted me as I negotiated the thousands of contracts with which I've been involved.

I first met Ava Abramowitz in 1987, at the height of a liability crisis when no large firm could buy affordable professional liability insurance. At the time, she had begun counseling large firms like my own to come to grips with risk and learn how to manage it well and profitably. Then, as now, she was ahead of the field in understanding how success for either an individual architect or an architecture firm requires skills in the practice as well as the design aspects of the profession.

One of the primary factors in achieving this success is simply starting the project in the right way. No project can be successful unless it is properly structured from the beginning, with clearly stated goals and identified challenges. The idea of starting a project off right is so critical, and yet so often misunderstood. As design professionals, architects are eager to start the design process and move forward as quickly as possible in the arena in which they are most comfortable. In today's world, however, everyone involved with the project must first understand, and then reach consensus on, the scope, schedule, budget, and required services. The negotiation and crafting of the contract are key to determining the scope and services the project team will provide.

While many design professionals receive very little formal education and training in the area of contract negotiation, they still must be able to negotiate and resolve contractual issues. Whether as an owner of a design firm or an individual staff member in a firm, every design professional needs to understand the obligations committed to under the terms of the negotiated contract. The owner must understand the liabilities and risks required of the firm by the contract negotiations phase, and identify the best way to reach closure on the contract issues.

Many professionals fear and often loathe the contract negotiation phase, but if properly handled, it is an opportunity to begin to forge a quality client-architect relationship. This step allows the architect to explain to the client both the relevance of the design to the client's specific business challenges, and the value the architect brings to resolving these issues. Avoiding this part of the project process can only serve to hinder a strong kickoff. It is during this negotiation phase that many important questions can arise that will help to more carefully define the project and, in turn, the contract requirements.

I have learned from experience on many projects that, as a result of the discussion and analysis that occur during contract negotiations, the client's original concept and services required for the project often undergo modifications, even before the contract is resolved.

One of the critical issues that comes through loud and clear in this book is the need for architects to develop communication skills. We all want to be skilled negotiators, and we want to learn ways to build trust that will endure for the entire project process. Ava gives us options and methods for reaching agreement in a variety of ways, providing practical examples, techniques, approaches, and tips to help the architect find a personal negotiation style.

To negotiate a successful contract and effectively solve problems, the architect must also learn both to ask questions and to be an active, flexible listener. During the exploration phase, the architect establishes common ground with the client, which in most cases will reflect almost everything required in the contract. Then it is necessary to focus only on those areas in which there is an initial lack of agreement. The *Architect's Essentials of Negotiation* explains complex aspects of negotiation, clarification, and finalization of the contract, breaking the process down into a series of simple steps and discussing those areas that are uncomfortable for many designers.

Here again, Ava provides us with clear examples on how to come to a true "yes" when negotiating a contract, recognizing that there are both legal issues and service or scope issues that must be resolved. Her book provides design professionals with excellent guidelines to help them move through the process toward a well-negotiated contract. This book also discusses how to be an expert long-term negotiator, since an architectural contract doesn't just cover the design or documents or construction phase of the project. The contract has relevancy during the period after substantial completion, which in many cases may last 10 years or more.

Ultimately, what everyone wants is for clients to get the project they want in the most cost-efficient, claims-avoidant manner. The great thing to realize is that being fair and ethical is not only the right way to act, it is also the best way to reach the desired contract results. Contracts need not be one-sided, since both sides must be protected. The terms of the contract should provide not only legal protection for the architect but also adequate fees to allow successful project completion, while yielding a fair and equitable profit. Clearly, architects need to know the law because, as we all know, knowledge is power. Furthermore, understanding the concept of interlocking exposure, capability, responsibility, and power is essential to a successful contract.

Ava Abramowitz has written a book that should be an essential part of every architectural professional's library and a must-read for every student taking professional practice courses. If an architect reads and studies this book, the result should be a more fair and equitable contract. But the real gain will be the knowledge and skills to properly start a project and develop a client relationship that will, in the end, bring forth wonderfully designed projects.

M. Arthur Gensler Jr., FAIA, FIIDA, RIBA
Chairman, Gensler

A Word from a Construction Lawyer

As the author, Ava Abramowitz, points out in Chapter 1 of the *Architect's Essentials of Negotiation*, negotiating is something we do every day of our lives. It is not something reserved exclusively for lawyers or big business or government. The fact that negotiating is an integral part of all of our lives, however, does not mean that most of us understand it well or engage in it successfully. In fact, our experience often is quite to the contrary. And our lack of negotiating skills may lead to frustration and anxiety, as well as to poor results.

It may seem odd that a lawyer who generally represents owners, developers, and lenders is writing a foreword to a book for architects. While I occasionally represent other members of the development community, including design professionals, construction managers, and trade contractors, it is true that they do not make up a major part of my practice. Why, then, is an individual who has written volumes on owners' and lenders' issues recommending this book? And as importantly, why should you bother to listen to what I say?

Before I answer those questions, I need to digress and thank Ava for providing me with this opportunity, knowing she risks the confusion of her audience and the taint to her book, associating it with an owner's perspective. While I realize that this is not too great a risk—how many people read a foreword after all?—I am grateful for the platform, however small. Upon rereading this book in its new edition, I am more persuaded than ever that it not only should be essential reading but also should be required implementation in just about every negotiating setting. Here's why.

Despite the book's name, beginning with the words, "Architect's Essentials," it easily is applicable to many other negotiating situations. However, because the construction industry is in dire need of the assistance that this book provides, I am delighted Ava chose to direct her comments to this practice area. Supporting the urgency of this need are the frightening statistics provided by the National Institute of Standards and Technology (NIST) in its *Cost Analysis of Inadequate Interoperability in the U.S. Capital Facilities Industry*. That mouthful of a study concluded that in 2002 alone the construction industry lost at least $16.8 billion because of inadequate and redundant interactions—and that was a conservative estimate! As if that were not enough to get one's attention, the U.S. Department of Commerce reported that unlike every other non-farm industry classification, which has improved each year, since 1964 productivity in the construction industry has decreased year after disappointing year after dismal year.

"What does this have to do with elements of contract negotiation?" I hear people asking. The answer is "a lot." Among the inefficiencies driving these extraordinary costs of construction are the communication barriers often inherent in the traditional construction process. Parties rarely share information fully and with all those affected by it. The lack of contractual incentives to communicate with one another is a major impediment to improved performance. Opportunities are lost because stakeholders fail to understand related responsibilities and to coordinate with each other on a routine basis.

The news is not all negative, however. The NIST report concluded that significant improvement would result if delivery models tied individual rewards to project success. Among NIST's solutions to the challenges faced by the construction industry is precisely what is at the core of this book. As Ava eloquently phrases it in Chapter 3, contracts are not divisive purveyors of risk and liability but "the last best, relatively low-stake opportunity that architects and their clients have to align themselves for project success. . . ." The best way to achieve success may vary from contract to contract, but the shared value of what's best for the project does not. This is not only good for the project and the project's owner, it also is enlightened self-interest when opportunities for compensation are tied to project success. This is contrary to the insistence on personal success, which raises only rancor, suspicion, and barriers among the parties.

We are lucky to be practicing at a time when many collaborative models of association are evolving and in use. We can choose from among Building Information Modeling, Integrated Project Delivery, and Lean Construction, to name several of the possible delivery systems being advanced today. But none of these approaches will ensure success unless the parties are prepared to embrace the responsibilities that are under their control and to exchange information freely. And here, again, Ava's book explains the benefits of that approach.

Accepting appropriate responsibility results in additional advantages. It helps those architects who are willing to accept logical allocations of responsibility to expand their services—and therefore their compensation. It also helps architects to become the masters of their own destinies, which ultimately results in less, rather than greater risk, by being able to manage those stated obligations. Once again, a collective approach to achieving project goals and proper assignment of duties can lead to individual fulfillment.

Upon reflection, perhaps it is not so odd that Ava asked an owner's lawyer to write a foreword to her book. It supports the collaborative notion she advances in her book. And it recognizes that each project belongs to its owner. That does not mean that the owner is the omnipotent and omniscient master of all and that the architect cannot and should not have a meaningful impact on the project. It simply means that the architect should be realistic in assessing his or her role and then be effective within the context of that role. It is a philosophy bound to result in happier outcomes for all.

Owners, of course, have many responsibilities of their own to fulfill. A primary one is to pay for the project. And while some owners spend their time thinking of ways to avoid making payments, the good ones know that the project benefits when everyone makes money. After all, what good does it do if the contractor and architect are looking for ways to cut corners, hide problems, and manipulate change orders because their compensation is inadequate for the job? And owners need to be forthcoming about their desires and what they know about the project, as well. Knowledge may be power, but in this case, everyone's power is increased when it is shared.

The publication of this new edition, and the opportunity to revise its foreword, offered me the pleasure of rereading many of the book's principles. One obvious but often ignored point is that it helps no one to take an "us versus them" approach to anything. Ava, as the successful advocate and negotiator that she is, knows that to suggest otherwise would not advance her client's—or any client's—interests. All project participants benefit from this reminder.

The book breaks down the stereotypes of what makes a successful negotiator and replaces them with concrete tools for reaching successful conclusions. These tools are as valuable to owners, contractors, and vendors, and their counsel, as they are to design professionals and their lawyers. In fact, shortly after Ava sent me the first galley of this book, it became a practical and useful primer for someone unrelated to the construction industry.

I was approached by a young attorney who practices intellectual property law, seeking advice. She was having a particularly difficult time resolving an issue and was frustrated because, as she saw it, her client's position was completely "fair." She could not understand why the other parties could not or would not appreciate that. I did not need to search far for a helpful response. I pointed to the portions of this book that explain that certain terms are "irritators" and, as such, neither advance the process or the parties' goals. In fact, irritators block momentum and divert attention from the substantive issue being confronted.

For those of you who have not yet read this book, let me explain. Irritators are words or phrases avoided by skilled negotiators, but often used by those less thoughtful. Why is the word "fair" an irritator? Because, by definition, if your position is "fair," then the other side's position must be "unfair." Very few participants are prepared to view themselves that way. And so it happens that the focus of the discussion is shifted to an individual's personal attributes from the parties' intended point.

Our discussion revealed the sad reality that many lawyers are not taught effective negotiating skills in law school. More to the point, their tutelage often is limited to the misunderstanding that a successful negotiation is one that obliterates the opponent's position. Even the choice of the word "opponent" is evidence of the failed approach to negotiation that many in our profession share.

My colleague is a very good lawyer now, even better for having learned the skills contained in this book. No matter what their backgrounds, lawyers, as well as architects, owners, contractors, lenders, and whoever else is engaged in negotiation, will benefit from a close reading. The skills and principles espoused in this book are universal and can be applied to achieve whatever the goal—that of a successful project, business, relationship, or task of any kind.

Read this book. Keep it handy. Refer to it often, and recommend it to others. Thank you, Ava, for producing a clear, comprehensible, and comprehensive road map to a construction project's success.

Lynn R. Axelroth, Esq.
Formerly, Managing Partner and Chair,
Construction Law Practice Group
Ballard Spahr Andrews & Ingersoll, LLP

Why You Want to Read This Book

Do you toss and turn the night before an important negotiation? Do you enter into a negotiation afraid you will lose? Does facing one more negotiation make you want to volunteer to do anything but that? If so, this book is for you. It is intended, in plain words, to give architects everywhere and the parties with whom they work the keys needed to negotiate and profit from negotiation. Or maybe you're an architect who loves to negotiate and are just looking for some new ways to win. This book is for you also. You'll find lots of tips in it and, I venture to say, a new idea or two.

Or maybe you're like the architect friend I was accompanying on a construction site when we bumped into his client. The client was upset about something—nothing big—and I watched the two work out the client's dilemma. The architect acceded to some items, including one that surprised me. He agreed to do some additional services at no cost to the client. And he stood pat on one item (he didn't want to change a design feature). The client left the negotiation seemingly happy. "It's hard to negotiate on the fly, isn't it?" I asked, guessing my friend felt forced to agree to provide the free services. "Huh?" he responded. "What negotiation? I wasn't negotiating. We were just talking." If you're like my friend, this book is for you, too. It will help you recognize when you are negotiating and help you find the breathing space you need to think on your feet. If you're not used to negotiating, though, a few of the concepts may seem difficult to grasp at first, but rest assured, all of them are accessible. So, get yourself a cup of coffee, settle back, and enjoy.

First, some basic insights. You already know how to negotiate. You wouldn't be where you are today if you didn't. How else could you get through a day? You negotiate with your spouse ("What do you want for dinner?"). You negotiate with your colleagues ("Any chance you can help me with this report?"). You negotiate with strangers ("Excuse me, but I was first in line."). You negotiate with children ("Finish your homework, and you can watch TV."). So, the issue isn't learning how to negotiate. You already do that, thank you. The issue is learning how to negotiate better.

Second, someone may have told you that you have to be a lawyer to negotiate effectively. If that were true, you would be lost already. As a lawyer myself, I say, "Bananas!" Not being a lawyer may even help you be a better negotiator, especially if you put your design skills to good use. Architects are problem solvers, and solving problems is what negotiation is all about. Furthermore, if you are reading this, you probably never wanted to be a lawyer. If you had, you would have gone to law school. In fact, you might not even like lawyers. That is okay, too. Negotiating, especially negotiating owner-architect agreements, has as much to do with design and construction logic as with legal reasoning—or it should for you, in the future, after you have read this book.

Third, negotiating can be fun for both you and the "Other," a term I use to reference the other person with whom you are negotiating. This is true only if you use negotiation, not to align words on paper, but to align energies for project success. Project negotiation—whether the negotiation involves you with an owner, a contractor, a zoning official, or whomever—provides you the opportunity to focus with the Other on what is necessary for project success. This is true even with respect to negotiating owner-drafted agreements. Contract negotiations provide you and the owner the last best chance to finalize expectations and to make sure that both of you will be working equally hard on the same project to the same end.

Now, you may be thinking, "That's easy for her to say. She's not an architect." That is quite true. I am a lawyer; furthermore, I was brought up learning how to negotiate. Most architects are not taught how to negotiate, in no small part because the National Architectural Accrediting Board and the National Council of Architectural Registration Boards historically have not required negotiation to be taught. But the need is there.

This first came home to me when I was deputy general counsel at the American Institute of Architects (AIA). At that time, I would often walk to work with a colleague, Jim Franklin (now FAIA), who lived around the corner. One morning I told him the story of my niece, Beatrice, who was seven at the time. She had called the night before, crying uncontrollably and beyond consolation. Her mother had refused her request to hold an overnight at her house. Now this was a real loss to her. Since Beatrice at that time was afraid to leave her mother, she never went on overnights, and not being allowed to have an overnight in her own home meant that she could not be part of her peer group. She just could not stop crying. Finally I said to her, "Beatrice, stop crying immediately. One, I don't have the power to reverse your mother, so all your tears are in vain. And, two, you are crying prematurely. You have no idea why your mother said no. Maybe she didn't want it *that* Saturday night; maybe she wanted it *in three weeks.* Maybe she didn't want *10* girls; maybe she wanted only *five* girls. You have no basis for crying, none whatsoever. Now, go wash your face, brush your hair, go back to your mother, and—not accusingly in any way whatsoever—simply ask, 'Mama, about that overnight: Why didn't you want it?' Find out what your mother's concerns are, give me a call, and we'll figure out a negotiating strategy." Five minutes later the phone rang again. "It's in two weeks, on a Saturday night, six girls plus me."

Jim was somewhat horrified and very jealous. He said to me, "This is unfair. No one ever taught me how to negotiate!" And I looked at him and said, "How do you get through *life* not knowing how to negotiate? Architects have to negotiate everything—not only their salary each year, but also design with owners, school boards, contractors, everybody, all the time. How can you function without knowing how to negotiate?" Right then and there, I silently promised myself that someday I would write this book.

And here it is. This book is my "thank you" to a profession that has made the world a better place. It is meant to give architects, to give *you*, the skills you need to negotiate wisely and well with owners, contractors, friends, and even enemies. It is designed to give you the tips, tools, and opportunities to view and do negotiations comfortably and in a different light.

How to Use This Book

Now, how should you use this book for maximum impact? You will read new ideas that may make you question your existing way of doing things, what you know from others and from life, even how you do business. And, of course, you may question the ideas themselves. Question, by all means, question all that you read here. The best negotiators aren't afraid to question everything, so you shouldn't be either. And accept only those ideas that make sense to you personally. You are *you*. Only you know what you are facing both personally and professionally, and only you can judge the usefulness of the ideas presented here.

This book has wide margins and space for you to jot down your thoughts. Feel free to mark it up and make it yours. You will also find exercises throughout this book designed to give you a chance to apply your new knowledge and skills. Do them, not in a haphazard way, but thoughtfully, so you can try new skills on for size in the privacy of your own home. Then, when you take what you have learned onto the construction site, don't try to implement every new idea at once. Pick the one skill you most want to work on, and focus on acquiring that one skill until you absorb it comfortably into your essence. Then, choose another. Under no circumstances should you try to change everything about how you negotiate all at once. You are not that much of a negotiating mess, but you will be if you take the "adopt everything" approach. You won't be listening to the Other. You'll be thinking, "What should I do next?" or worse, "Why did I do that?" So promise yourself, try just one new skill at a time. Master it, and move on to another.

To make maximum use of this book, must you read it cover to cover? No. Each chapter can be read independently, and each chapter is indexed so you can easily access the book that way. You can even use it as a reference tool, looking up key words and starting from there. At the same time, however, you should know that the book was written cumulatively, so that Chapter 2 builds on Chapter 1, and so on. This was done purposely to maximize the ease of learning new skills.

Let me show you what I mean. In the next chapter, you will be learning about what claims data have to teach you, the owner, and the project team that will help you front-end align your projects and become a better negotiator. Chapter 3 translates tough legal concepts into design and construction so you can negotiate as an architect and not as an ersatz lawyer. You are introduced to negotiation concepts for the first time in Chapter 4. What is negotiation? How does the negotiation process work when it works well and when it does not? Does it make a difference if the "Other" is an owner? A contractor? Someone you like? Someone who makes you exceedingly uncomfortable? In Chapter 5, you will read how expert negotiators prepare for negotiations, including what they do to get the fees they want. Chapter 6 lets you in on research into how skilled negotiators communicate. What do they do—and do differently from negotiators who are merely good—to make them and their results so special? How can you pick up those skills and make them yours? Chapter 7 teaches how to work effectively in groups. Chapter 8 applies what you learned in the first seven chapters to some of the most egregious owner-drafted contract language and some of the most common problems. Chapter 9 discusses dispute resolution, just in case the first eight chapters don't quite work for you. The final chapter pulls it all together, as final chapters should, giving you the tips you need to incorporate your new knowledge into practice. I have even included an appendix of other sources of information on negotiation, so you don't have to rely on this one book for all the answers.

Let me also tell you what this book isn't. It isn't an exhaustive compilation of all the most onerous owner-drafted language edited for reasonable acceptability. No one can ever presage what creative lawyers will do, nor can anyone anticipate all future owner needs in an ever-changing construction world. Besides, every architect's and engineer's insurer has a book just like that available for the asking. More important, it wouldn't be helpful to write such a book: It would be too prescriptive, and neither you nor your practice is a cut-and-paste effort. Worse, over time, it could become a standard of care, a set of rules for you to adhere to, even if they were not in your or your clients' interests. So don't think of this book as a prescription for you to follow or this year's formula for success. In the negotiation process, as in professional life, success comes from creative critical thinking, not from adhering religiously to someone else's set of rules. You will have to think about what and how you want to negotiate, to become a successful negotiator. The purpose of this book is to help you with your thinking.

Please don't think the preceding paragraph is just the usual lawyer's disclaimer. I learned the dangers of unwittingly setting a national standard of care when I served as legal counsel to AIA's *Handbook* Review Committee for both the eleventh and twelfth editions of *The Architect's Handbook of Professional Practice*. An architect called me up during a recess of an arduous trial. Opposing counsel had just tried to impeach him using the tenth edition of the AIA *Handbook*. "Nobody does it that way anymore," the architect wailed. "But I'm the one who looked like a fool." As a consequence, we took great pains in both those editions never to set a standard of care. Issues were raised. Issues were discussed. The impact of the various resolutions on the designer, owner, and contractor were explored, but all decisions were left to the parties. That way the *Handbook* could be made equally useful to an architect in a large-firm setting as to the sole practitioner.

I've taken similar pains here. As a result, you will never read in this book "the architect must...." You have the power within you to design your own practice. This Honorary AIA is not going to steal that power from you.

Nor are there any rules dictating good client behavior. And even if there were, if your clients are like some I've met, they probably don't think that *any* rules apply to them. Clients come in all different shapes and sizes. Some are nice people; some are not. Some are smart; some are not. Some know about the realities of design and construction; some do not, and so on and so on. This book starts you out wherever you find your client.[1] And I've written it with the gamut of client types in mind. So, you are going to want to develop your client selection skills (a skill you will read more about in Chapter 2 on front-end alignment) as much as you are going to want to develop your client negotiation skills. In the interim, if your words fail you, feel free to give a copy of this book to your client. I say the same things to owners (and engineers, contractors, and lawyers) as I say to you.

Now, a bit more about me, so you can put everything I say into perspective. You already know that I am a lawyer and that I am committed to the success of your profession. Three more confessions—one you'll enjoy, two you may not. Here's the one you will like: I am smitten by most of the architects I have had the pleasure of working with these past many years. Architects, by and large, are creative people committed to doing good. I learned this first as deputy general counsel for The American Institute of Architects and later as vice president of Victor O. Schinnerer & Company, Inc., counseling architects on negotiation and risk management strategies. After nearly 25 years, I can assure you that architect negotiating skills may be lax, but architect commitment to project success is not.

Now for the two other confessions—the ones you may like less. First, I am also an owner. In the last ten years, I have had the opportunity to oversee thirteen projects, some large, some small. All with

---

[1] It also applies whatever shape you find the contractor in.

challenges, all with difficulties, all with varying degrees of success. Most built. One not, and even that was a success of sorts. (It was an adventurous commercial building that went well during the design stages, but was terminated in the construction documents phase due to a change in client corporate strategy.) In the course of doing these projects, I have interviewed lots of architects in the sales setting. I have sat across the table from architects and negotiated. I have worked with architects as the Client. Through this hands-on experience, coupled with the nearly 25 years working directly for the profession, I have watched thousands of architects, engineers, contractors, and owners negotiate. These experiences have stayed with me and form the human construct of this book.

Now for my second confession. I am an unabashed believer in what I call "assertive practice." (If you read the Introduction, you will already know this.) *Assertive practice is an approach to architecture that combines creativity and risk taking in a way that provides clients value and puts architects in control of their practices.* It stems from the belief that people have power over their practice lives, if they only choose to exercise it. I know there are meanies out there who will try to throw roadblocks in your path. I know the market is competitive, and, as John F. Kennedy once said, "Life is unfair." Excuses, excuses. You can still position yourself and go for your gold, however you define gold.

If this sounds Pollyanna-ish, I assure you, if you knew me personally, you would be thinking no such thing. I know life is gritty. That is not the point. The point is that society values people who provide value, and, if you are not one of those valued, I say, don't whine about it—whining never helps. Face it. Evaluate what you need to increase your value, and increase your value.

That is a key rubric of assertive practice. Assertive practitioners don't whine. As I said to the AIA board of directors in the early 1990s, the AIA has to stand for more than "Ain't It Awful." Increasingly, it does. Today, more and more AIA architects subscribe to the tenets of assertive practice. Assertive practitioners do not bemoan the rise of construction managers; they improve their construction administration skills and provide construction management (CM) services themselves. They do not complain about interior designers taking interiors work from them; they expand their practices to provide those services, often hiring interior designers in the process. Simply put, assertive practitioners keep their skill levels high and their knowledge levels even higher. They design their practices with one eye on the market's needs and demands and the other on their own needs and demands. They provide their clients value so that they, in turn, are themselves valued. They take control over their value and over their responsibility for maintaining it.

There are corollaries to these key tenets, and they surface throughout the book, but the primary two are these: One, *assertive practitioners make friends with risk.* They know that in our society people who take on reasonable risks and manage them reasonably make money; people who shy from risk do not. Risk and reward. In architecture, they go hand in hand, in no small part because help in managing risk is one of the values clients expect the architect to provide. "Can you help me bring this project in on time and on budget?" "If things go wrong, will you be there, looking out for me and my project?" For many owners today, if you can't help them manage the reasonable risks of design and construction, they will find an architect who can.

Notice I write "reasonable risks." Assertive practitioners know which risks they can reasonably handle and which they cannot. They have a cadre of consultants available to them to fill their competency gaps. They respect what others bring to the table, and they know how to help maximize everyone's contribution, including the owner's and the contractor's, so that a symphony is orchestrated and not a cacophony of mere sound. Simply put, assertive practitioners may not be easy people; they have boundaries. But they are easy to work with because they are skilled (and work hard) at stepping up to the design plate, both facilitating the group process of design and construction and achieving client satisfaction.

They are also easy to work with because they do not look at the world through the prism of liability. Prisms tend to distort things, and the prism of liability is no different. Assertive architects know that their best defense against engendering liability is not arguing about words but focusing on action: in other words, assertively managing the risk. After all, a well-managed risk reduces the probability of harm. *If you can prevent a harm so that there is no injury, no liability can result.*

Assertive practitioners get paid for their abilities to manage risk. It may be a tragedy to the profession that design expertise does not always link to personal success, but the reality of design is that owners expect architects to be able to design well. That's a given. They want more. The purpose of this book is to help you provide that "more."

Now for the second corollary of assertive practice: *Assertive practitioners believe in "no-surprise design,"* and they work hard to put that belief into action. What do I mean by "no-surprise design"? Before I answer that question, I want you to think, not about the negotiation process, but about the design process. Think back to the best design experiences you have had with your clients. Remember the ones where, when you showed your developed designs, the client said, "That's exactly what I wanted!" The ones where, when the building was built, the client looked at it and you and said, "I'm so glad I selected you to design the building." Ask yourself: What happened to make those client statements possible? Was it a matter of pure chemistry? Perhaps. But if you have a long track record of those positive design experiences and many repeat clients, I submit those successes did not just happen. You worked *with* your client to make them happen. And you worked hard because you know that repeated success is not a matter of luck. Nor is it an issue of chemistry or magic. It is a matter of hard work, coupled with solid skill development and application. It is the result of "no-surprise design."

Now then, what is "no-surprise design"? Research into the methods of high-level consultants (and negotiators) shows one characteristic that all these professionals share: At any point in the negotiation, these people have a very good idea of what their clients need and expect, and how their clients will react to the proposals they make and the actions they take. As a result, their ideas, proposals, *and* actions never surprise their clients. Each step they take proceeds smoothly and, from the client's perspective, seamlessly from the step before.

How do these consultants achieve such consonance with their clients? How do they know what clients are thinking? How can they be so certain of their clients' reaction? It's not just from their contract negotiation abilities, although those are one important component of their success. No, top consultants see negotiation as an ongoing process. From the very first moment, they engage their clients strategically and continuously in those communication behaviors that produce mutual understanding and accord. They keep their focus on their clients and their clients' problems as their clients define them. They actively create a comfortable arena where hard concepts can be discussed openly and resolved efficiently and amicably. As a consequence, they earn the trust of their clients so that, even when there is a glitch—as there invariably is in even the best of projects—their clients know that the consultants' primary concern will be the enduring interests of the client.

I have one more thing to tell you. As strong as my commitment is to assertive practice, I took steps in the first edition to protect you from my idiosyncrasies. I asked wiser souls than I to review this book for error. My good friends gave me their time unstintingly, and I thank them profusely again today for their wisdom and their goodwill: Harold L. Adams, FAIA, RIBA, JIA, former chairman of RTKL Associates Inc.; Robert A. Odermatt, FAIA, of The Odermatt Group; John M. Laping, FAIA, of The Kideney Partnership; Philip G. Bernstein, FAIA, formerly of Cesar Pelli's office and now a vice president at Autodesk and still an instructor at Yale University's School of Architecture; Deborah S. Ballati, Esquire, of Farella, Braun and Martel and president-elect of the American College of Construction Lawyers; Michael C. Loulakis, Esquire, of Capital Project Strategies, LLC, well known for his work on partnering and on design-build contracts; and Howard G. Goldberg, Esquire, of Goldberg, Pike & Besche, P.C., and a founding Fellow of the American College of Construction Lawyers. They did much to expand the breadth and depth of this book.

Thank you again for help with the first edition to the AIA, the American Bar Association, the American Arbitration Association, and Victor O. Schinnerer & Company, Inc., for permitting me access to and use of materials that I developed (or helped develop) while I was working with them. Special thanks also again to Huthwaite, Inc., and its former leader, Tariq Zaidi, for giving me permission to use its intellectual property for the benefit of the design professions.

This edition also glows with the wisdom of my friends and colleagues. I thank David S. Haviland, Professor Emeritus from Rensselaer Polytechnic Institute; James P. Cramer of the Greenway Group, Inc.; Boyce Appel of Appel Associates; Robert C. Bordone, Esquire, of the Harvard University Law School and its Negotiation Project; Frances Railey of the insurance broker Ames & Gough, Inc.; and Andrew Caruso, Assoc. AIA, LEED AP of Gensler, for their ideas and input. I must also thank M. Arthur Gensler, Jr., FAIA, FIIDA, RIBA, chairman of Gensler; the Hon. Peter G. Fitzgerald; and Lynn R. Axelroth, Esquire, Ballard Spahr Andrews & Ingersoll, LLP, as well as Scott Simpson, FAIA, LEED AP of Kling Stubbins for giving this book the human context that make books on negotiation come to life. Finally, I doff my hat to Martha M. Hamilton and Kate Schnable for this new edition as they bled over each new word with me, keeping my confidence up when I could no longer see the track.

And, most of all, I thank my husband, Neil Rackham, for introducing me to his seminal research on negotiations, persuasion, and sales. Neil first became interested in measuring how people interacted while studying for his doctorate in England. With the help of public grants, he developed a system and used it to measure interactions between teachers and students and later therapists and patients, all with the goal of determining which types of behaviors were effective and which were not. From those studies it was an easy leap to study negotiators in action. Over time he became convinced that so much was lost in the interactions that preceded the negotiation that he turned his attention to sales and persuasion. That was an even easier leap. Unlike negotiators, salespeople loved being watched. From those studies, he produced *SPIN*® *Selling*, a study of 35,000 sales calls, which became a *New York Times* bestseller and later a *Business Week* bestseller, too. If not for Neil, his 10 books, three of which are cited herein, and his willingness to review my many drafts, this book would not be what it is.

Now, on to negotiating essentials.

Front-End Alignment

The Prerequisite to a Successful Project and a Solid Contract

2

Victor O. Schinnerer & Company, Inc., started the "teach-architects/engineers (A/Es) risk management" business back in the early 1960s; by the time I joined them, ideas that were once considered radical had become conventional wisdom: "The project is the owner's, not yours." "You make recommendations. The owner makes decisions." "A strong contract provides critical protection for you and your client." And so on. One day a group of us asked, "What if something else or something additional to conventional wisdom is necessary to provide architects and engineers with claims-free practices? Worse, what if we are wrong? What if something altogether different is required? What then?" Fortunately, Schinnerer was in the position to find out, and find out they did.

Before I describe the research and share with you the results of Schinnerer's two-year research effort (capably implemented by David S. Haviland, then professor of architecture at Rensselaer Polytechnic

Institute), ask yourself, "When does a construction project start to go bad?" If you are like many architects, you are probably thinking things turn south some time after the contract is signed, most probably during construction administration, when third parties—that is, contractors—implement your designs. (If you are like many lawyers, you are probably thinking that trouble starts after the parties try to ignore a dispute that has arisen or attempt to resolve it without the benefit of legal counsel. Go figure.) But Haviland's research suggests that construction projects get into trouble much earlier, well before you call in the insurance and legal troops to help you deal with the problem, and perhaps even before construction starts. In fact, the project may already be in trouble when you sit down to negotiate your contract.

The results of Haviland's study indicate that, while many factors can precipitate or prevent claims, a combination of several factors, when "aligned" by parties at the front end of project development, can ward off claims. Hence, the importance of what I call *front-end alignment* in making construction negotiations a tad easier. It is the best claims preventer around.

The Study

In order to make maximum use of the findings, you need to understand how Haviland went about the study. Schinnerer made available to Haviland nearly 40 years of insurance applications and claims files. In order to go beneath the data and eliminate any insurer bias, Haviland stratified this database to come up with a core group of architecture, engineering, and A/E firms that would receive an 18-page questionnaire examining management practices and claims experience. (From here on, lest you think I am writing only about architects, I use the term A/E to describe the firm findings, as did Haviland. However, the findings did not differ that much by design expertise.)

To select the core group, Haviland identified 1,800 policyholders continuously insured with Schinnerer from 1981 through 1991—a rather rough-and-tumble economic period. He preliminarily divided that group into three subgroups: architects, engineers, and combined A/E firms. He further stratified them by the size of the firm (small, medium-small, medium-large, and large), and by the firm's claims experience (high, medium, low loss, or no loss, as compared to similar firms of that type and size).

Expecting to produce findings with statistical significance, out of these 1,800 firms Haviland selected a balanced sample of 72 A/E firms to complete the questionnaire. The questionnaire asked the respondents to identify which of 99 management practices they engaged in during the 10-year study period. Among the practices it covered were various project delivery approaches; criteria for the selection of the architect, engineer, and contractor; types of services provided; types of form agreements used; construction contracting practices; compensation methods and their adequacy; responsibilities for establishing project parameters; client characteristics and practices; selection of and practices employed by project staff and consultants, and approaches to planning, marketing, and risk management.

In addition, Haviland developed a list of 138 factors that, in theory, caused or prevented claims. Some of these factors reflected conventional wisdom. (A strong contract will help prevent claims. So will exacting a limit of liability from the owner.) Others sprang from the collective gut of a bunch of us at Schinnerer who worked with Haviland on the questionnaire. (High firm turnover helps to create claims. Recessions bring about claims.) Ultimately, Haviland created a questionnaire that asked the 72 firms to rate each of 138 factors on whether, in their opinion and experience, each factor prevented or ameliorated claims, caused or aggravated claims, or did both. The answers to these questions would allow Haviland to assess the impact of the insured's management practices and business opportunities, as reported in their insurance applications, on claims production.[1]

The Findings

The report concluded that no one factor or practice warded off or caused claims. Rather, Haviland found that a number of factors came into play with each claim or potential claim, many at the very outset of the project, when the owner and key players assembled the team. Haviland identified the 40 most-often-mentioned factors—20 *claims preventers* and 20 *claims starters*. Table 2.1 delineates the 40 factors architects and engineers identified as the top claims preventers and starters.

---

[1] I thank Schinnerer and Haviland for allowing me to plumb the raw data. However, the analyses and conclusions here are mine alone, as are any mistakes.

Table 2.1

The 40 Factors

	Top 20 Claims Preventers	Prevention Value (highest = 5)	Top 20 Claims Starters	Starter Value (highest = 5)
1	Site responsibilities are clear and coordinated.*	4.32	Site responsibilities are not clear and coordinated.*	4.10
2	Firm turns down projects with uncompensated risks.*	4.27	Client differences are not resolved immediately.	3.90
3	Construction administration services are in the contract.*	4.26	Construction schedule and budget are not tied to scope.*	3.85
4	Project staff in the firm are experienced.*	4.21	Client's project representative is inexperienced.*	3.74
5	Firm has substantial experience with project type.*	4.21	Firm accepts projects with uncompensated risks.*	3.74
6	Scope, schedule, and budget are determined at the outset.*	4.20	Infrequent site observation.*	3.63
7	Firm's PM** is experienced in managing projects.*	4.11	Client has difficulty making decisions.*	3.60
8	Client differences are resolved immediately.*	4.10	Key issues are resolved after agreement signed.*	3.56
9	Firm's values and orientation are stable over time.*	4.08	Firm has high professional staff turnover rate.*	3.53
10	Client's project representative is experienced.*	4.07	Consultant project staff are not very experienced.*	3.52

(Continued)

Table 2.1
(Continued)

	Top 20 Claims Preventers	Prevention Value (highest = 5)	Top 20 Claims Starters	Starter Value (highest = 5)
11	Systematic review of construction documents.	4.06	Firm's PM is inexperienced in managing projects.*	3.50
12	Firm has past experience with the client.*	4.03	Construction contract administration services are not in contract.*	3.48
13	Key issues are resolved before agreement is signed.*	4.02	Project agreements are not well coordinated.*	3.46
14	Project staff have experience with project type.*	4.02	The project is fast-tracked.*	3.41
15	Staff are assigned to the project on a continuous basis.*	3.98	The construction budget is inflexible.*	3.40
16	Firm's PM has experience with project type.*	3.97	There is a high volume of change orders.	3.39
17	Firm's leadership/ ownership is stable over time.*	3.97	The construction schedule is inflexible.*	3.39
18	Construction schedule and budget are appropriate to scope.*	3.95	Client decisions are not systematically documented.	3.35
19	The client makes decisions firmly and on time.	3.95	Consultant's PM is not very experienced.*	3.35
20	Systematic materials and product investigation.	3.95	The client is a committee.*	3.31

* Indicates pre-project factors. These can be addressed and managed before a contract is signed.

**PM refers to project manager.

The table entries constitute an interesting list, don't they? Many of the staples are missing. For example, no one lists having a good contract as a claims preventer. Worse, no one mentions having a great lawyer as the key to claims-free practice. Despite these clear errors of judgment on the part of the architecture and engineering professions (you *are* chuckling, aren't you?), a very clear picture emerges when you analyze this list. Juxtapose the top 20 claims preventers (or ameliorators) against the top 20 claims starters (or aggravators) and analyze them for commonalities. Now put that analysis up against the backdrop of the full study, and look what you will find.

First, the study found that 25 percent of the 72 firms were free of claims over the 10-year period. Let's stop right there and savor that information. The penchant for self-victimization on the part of some in the profession notwithstanding, the study clearly found that *a firm can go claims-free* for at least as long as the 10-year study period. That is pretty amazing in a country as litigious as ours. The study also found that a number of factors are present in all of the claims-free insured firms. Even more revealing, these factors can be, even have to be, *secured before the contract is negotiated*. They reflect an alignment of the project participants as to their objectives and ability to work effectively together at the outset of the project, and it is this front-end alignment that allows the project to be completed without any claims.

Isn't that interesting? While nowhere in the top 40 preventers/aggravators is the existence of a contract listed as a factor in preventing or producing claims, aligning the core stuff that needs to be in a contract is. With this in mind, look again at the list of factors that claims-free firms strived to secure. They are these factors, and they make up the core necessities of effective front-end alignment and also of sound design and construction contract documents:

> ➤ The owner chooses experienced, capable participants.
> ➤ The owner chooses committed participants who work well together.
> ➤ The owner allocates the risks and responsibilities to the party most capable of handling them, and does not seek to retain all the benefits and none of the risks. Further, the owner provides each party with the authority and economic means to handle assigned risks and responsibilities well.
> ➤ The owner makes necessary decisions promptly and is open to resolving disputes as soon as they arise.

Personally, I found this quite surprising. As important as the architect is to design, as critical as the contractor is to construction, it is the owner who can make or break the project. That makes sense, if you think about it, and claims data back it up. Nearly 60 percent of the claims brought against architects are brought directly by their own clients. So, the more capable an architect is at attracting and retaining as clients those owners who are smart about team building, the greater the probabilities of a claims-free project.

If David Haviland were writing this chapter, he would be quick to point out that, while significant, these findings must be interpreted in context. First, the respondent group, while representative, is a small sampling of a large profession. Second, the data are not comprehensive. Third, the findings have not been blind-tested. Nonetheless, he would agree, they teach an important lesson: Before any contract is negotiated, the owner and the architect need to open discussions—preferably with all the other key project participants—about the project and engage in advance planning to manage project risk.

Let's now look at some of the other factors that are important to project success. Again, you will see that many of them revolve around team building, which puts a premium on your developing strong negotiation and communication skills.

The Role of Experience

If one factor reverberates throughout the study, it is experience. Experienced parties are a core predicate to project success. Experience is as necessary for the owner and the owner's key staff as it is for the architect, the engineer, the contractor, and the subcontractor. To be blunt, inexperienced people tend to cause problems because they usually have unrealistic expectations and make unreasonable demands. The more power inexperienced parties have in the project's hegemony, the more problems they can cause.

What kind of experience is needed? A certain level of competence must be present. Beyond that, the parties must be familiar with both the project type and the project delivery system (e.g., *design-bid-build*, *design-build*, or *Integrated Project Delivery* [IPD]). Without this expertise, they will be handicapped in foreseeing problems and taking remedial steps.

Additionally, the parties must be comfortable with the contract and its division of labor. They must be able to work effectively, both as individuals and as a team. The research suggests that when parties have previously worked together effectively, the project benefits. This may be because they know what to expect of each other and have developed a level of trust. Parties are less prone to finger pointing when they have had proven working relationships that they wish to maintain.

Does this mean that inexperienced parties need not apply? Of course not. But they must recognize their inexperience as a limitation and take measures to remedy their lack of real experience. They must also be open to the advice and insights of others. So, if you are an architect inexperienced in a certain aspect of a project, or if you are experienced but find yourself working with an inexperienced owner, consultant, contractor, or subcontractor, help yourself by devising a strategy to fill the experience void.

One strategy available to you, if the inexperience is your own, is to form a strategic alliance with an architect or other professional who can fill the void. That alliance can take the shape of informal mentoring, or it can be fully and formally ensconced in a subconsultant contract. If the inexperience is your client's, you might want to suggest that you both engage in "partnering" as a means to enhance the project's success.

By partnering, I do not mean the touchy-feely process by which all the parties work to build trust *after* the construction contract is signed. Rather, I have in mind a highly substantive and interactive method in which all the parties to the design and construction processes—experienced and not—get together at the outset, often with a partnering facilitator, and delineate project goals and objectives. Working together, the parties strategize ways to reduce risk, open channels of communication, and agree on the steps to be taken to resolve disputes. This helps them maximize the attainment of the participants' individual and collective goals, and hence, the probability of project success. Partnering works best when performed *before* any contracts are signed, so that the contracts can incorporate the results of and commitment to the partnering process.

Partnering

Every project my husband and I do is partnered. The architect is retained on Day One, and as soon as schematics are sufficiently underway to have a project to discuss, we bring the contractor on board. At that time, we detail our project goals and objectives (sometimes with the help of a facilitator, depending on project complexity). We identify inconsistencies (my husband and I invariably disagree on something) and ultimately resolve them, always with the active involvement of the architect and contractor. As a group, we explore trade-offs (time? money? quality? scope?), and we make policy decisions so the architect, the contractor, and we ourselves are all marching to the same drummer. ("On this project, quality is more important than time.") We spend a lot of time surfacing special problems and pinning down risk-management strategies. The session does not end until there is shared understanding of our—that is, the owner's—goals and a consensus that (a) those goals can be met by the architect and the contractor *and* (b) what steps everyone needs to take to meet those goals. This consensus is incorporated into everyone's contract, (e.g., "The architect will strive to design a building that will assist the owner in achieving. . . .").

We also work out partnering schedules, as we believe everyone needs to meet face-to-face throughout the project, so that issues can be addressed before they become problems. These schedules also are incorporated into everyone's contract, including the fee necessary for all parties to work together as partners as the project runs its course. Everyone works hard at these meetings. We concentrate on raising issues early and resolving them

(continues)

(*continued*)

thoroughly. It never matters who raises what issues, and everyone brings individual expertise to bear on the issue's resolution. When the building is done, a dedication party is held for everyone who helped design or erect the building and their families. Key participants to the design and construction process sign their names on the signing board, which is dated and tucked safely inside the maintenance room so that in years to come everyone will know who made the building what it is today.

The Owner's Role

If the claims-free A/E firms in the Haviland study had anything in common, it was the ability to make an intelligent choice about the owner they wished to work with. While each participant in a construction project has the power to make or break the project, owners play a unique role, because they select the project's design and construction teams, and because their expectations are the ones to be satisfied.

The design professionals who participated in the study observed that successful owners shared these attributes:

- ➤ They were experienced with the project type and the delivery process.
- ➤ They were clear in their goals, objectives, project parameters, and constraints.
- ➤ They were willing to compensate the A/E firm appropriately for the scope of work to be done.
- ➤ They were flexible in their approaches to the various issues that arose.
- ➤ They made decisions firmly and on time.
- ➤ They were open to resolving disputes immediately.

In other words, the owner was pivotal in and an active contributor to the success of the project.

These owner attributes warrant your special attention. Today, too many owners are asking their lawyers for contracts that give them rights without responsibilities and rewards without risks. One contract I read had the architect developing the owners' goals and objectives, so frightened were the owners of sticking their own necks out. The study makes clear that this one-sided approach to the project endangers its chances of success. It is the owner's project, yes, and it is the owner who has to be a proactive participant in project formation and implementation, else the owner has little chance of getting a project that will meet the owner's needs.

This means that owners must take on certain responsibilities. They must determine the scope, quality, time frame, budget, and the objectives of the project. After all, no other participant in the construction process is in a position to know the owner's objectives. The owner also must make timely decisions to keep the project on track[2] and must give the other participants sufficient support and guidance to permit them to meet their responsibilities. That support invariably means paying an appropriate fee for the work as much as it means timely feedback.

It may be hard for inexperienced owners to see that providing appropriate fees and feedback is in their interests, but the study shows this to be the case. For firms participating in the study, selection based primarily on (lowest) price or fee produced

---

[2] And the architect and contractor have to give the owner everything the owner needs to make a timely and wise decision that the owner and everyone else can live with. Partnering leaves no room for posturing or game playing.

more claims and, to a lesser extent, higher losses from those claims.

Similarly, the study indicated that the nature of the owner's feedback can influence the project. It seems that negative feedback (e.g., anger and adversarial posturing) does little to contribute to keeping the project on schedule and tends to produce more claims, but not higher losses from those claims. In other words, if one transfers the adversarial system used in the courtroom and replicates it on the construction site, lawyers win; clients don't.

I tell owners and their lawyers this all the time. It is the owner who receives the ultimate rewards of the construction project. Maximizing those rewards over the long run requires the owner to step up to bat in all the design and construction innings, with an openness and flexibility that encourage problems to surface and get resolved quickly. Owner passivity or adversarial posturing, put simply, is self-defeating and invariably increases project expense.

On Passivity

The one building my husband and I didn't do was to be a green building, geothermally heated, built into the bank of a hill, with sod on its roof and sides. During one of the partnering sessions, I shared my fear that the building would leak, and asked the architect to bring in a waterproofing consultant. I later told a fellow construction lawyer about the partnering session. He asked why I did it that way. After all, he pointed out, it was cheaper for me to have the building leak, sue the architect and contractor, and have their insurance companies pay for the fix. This strategy is the antithesis of front-end alignment, but clearly, if that lawyer is any indication, there are those who subscribe to planned passivity as a risk-management device. You will want to know if your client is one of them before you accept the project. Assertive practitioners know life is very short. So do good clients.

Front-End Alignment

Stability of the Firm

Six of the top 40 factors that A/E firms identified with claims prevention relate to stability. The firms ranked a high turnover rate of the professional staff as the number 9 aggravator of claims. The more stable a firm's leadership and staff, the less likely claims will occur. This follows logically if we assume that experience and a commitment to the project are two key claims preventers. Too high a level of turnover defeats both. While the study looked only at the A/E firms' experience, the issue of stability would logically seem to have equal application to the other construction participants, including the owner.

Likewise, the stability of firm finances is a factor in claims prevention. The tightness of money may stretch a firm more than any project can afford. The extra mile most owners want the A/E firm or the contractor to walk may just not be walkable, financially speaking. No one knows that better than you. It is why you need adequate fees—to deliver the project the owner wants delivered.

If you become aware that your client's (or consultant's or the contractor's) staff is turning over at an increasing rate or having financial problems, you may want to raise the issue immediately and explain how firm instability might affect the project. Depending on the politics of the project, you may want to raise it directly with the owner, or you may want to address it internally first. Either way, you can then brainstorm potential options to manage those risks until a viable solution is found and implemented, and everyone's staff stabilizes.

In the same way, whenever a construction party's conduct is increasing the risk of claims or disputes, you can bring that conduct to that party's and the client's attention. There is no reason not to do so—although *how* you do so is an issue you will want to consciously work out before you act. In design and construction, one party's challenge can all too easily become another party's catastrophe. Stable firms, self-aware and in constant communication with each other, can more quickly identify and manage risk, without acrimony and recriminations.

Other Factors

Is your client asking you whether to go design-award-build or design-build? Are you unsure how to advise? The data show that five factors are more important claims preventers than the specific type of delivery approach selected. The first factor is experience with the particular project delivery approach selected. As we said earlier, experienced people succeed, more often than not, because they can anticipate and address problems faster and better than those who are new to the situation. This is one reason why everyone should think twice before proposing unique delivery systems (or unique contracts) with which few people on either side are familiar.

The second factor is allowing the A/E firm to be involved in the selection of the contractor, or the construction manager (CM), if there is to be one. Since construction contract documents are never complete, construction will go more smoothly if the contractor (or CM) can work effectively with the architect to bring the construction documents to life.

That is why so many claims-free firms volunteer a list of good contractors (or CMs) from which the owner may invite bids. Some of these firms charge a lower fee for construction contract administration services when the contractor (or CM) is selected from their "recommended" list; alternatively, they charge a surcharge for construction contract administration when they are not.

Using qualifications to select the contractor, rather than bid price alone, is the third factor. The data suggest that contractors selected on the basis of qualifications perform better. The federal government and some states are beginning to recognize the value of qualifications in the contractor selection process. The U.S. Army Corps of Engineers, for example, is increasingly using a "best value" approach to contractor selection. The Corps decides which contractor skills and qualifications are necessary, assigns a weight to each of the qualifications, and makes its selection accordingly. Immediate cost is invariably a measure in contractor selection, but it no longer needs to be the controlling one.[3]

A fourth factor is whether the project involves a CM. The data show that the presence of a CM increased the number of claims for the studied firms

---

[3] Several organizations, including the Associated General Contractors of America (AGC) and AIA, have produced suggested contractor qualification criteria available for modification based on the owner's value system. For example, owners interested in maintaining a safe site may want to ask all bidders to reveal their "workers' compensation modification factor." (Just in case you are wondering, we retain all contractors based on a series of values and qualifications. Price alone is never the controlling factor—quality is, because we think life-cycle costs first, including maintenance costs, and short-term costs last.)

and, albeit to a lesser extent, losses from those claims. This is not an anti-CM statement. Often having a CM can make all the difference. However, in many projects, CMs are brought in too late to have their ideas and expertise incorporated into the A/E's thinking. When that happens, all the CM can do is "undo" the design that was bid on, under the guise of "value engineering."[4] In fact, according to CNA/Schinnerer data, the later in the process value engineering is introduced, the more likely that it will cause a claim. Even when CMs are brought into the project early, they are additional parties with their own ideas and objectives for the project. This adds one more set of risks that needs to be managed.

The fifth and final factor is having adequate time to perform the job. Undue speed can cause problems. There is nothing inherently wrong with fast-tracking a project. But fast-tracking, without the careful detailing of an agreed-upon program and scope of work, can be dangerous. Designs implemented at one stage may prove to be insufficient at a later stage. This is especially true if the parties' understanding of the project objectives or design parameters changes over time.

Why is this all-important to you and your client? A project works best when reasoned decisions about process are made before the contract is signed. Data are one key to solid decision making, which brings us to the next point.

---

[4] Value engineering has little to do with engineering, and even less to do with value. Claims data suggest that, when entered into after the project's bid has been accepted, value engineering is done too late and serves only to cheapen the building and attract claims.

Implementable Contracts

As I mentioned earlier in this chapter, having a contract is not mentioned anywhere in the key factors, but a review of the 40 issues identified as claims starters or preventers reveals that an astonishing 85 percent of them can be discovered before the project begins, and more than half of these can be addressed in the negotiating process. It follows that, to enhance the potential for a claims-free project, each of these issues would best be resolved before anyone puts pen to paper to draft the contracts. Once these issues are resolved, their resolution can be incorporated into the contracts. This incorporation will ensure that the contracts are implementable and provide clear, coordinated, consistent, and realistic predictions of what will happen, whether all goes well or not.

This is easier to say than do. People today tend to look out solely for their own parochial interests. We lawyers, for example, are trained and ethically required to zealously protect our client's parochial interests. Front-end alignment, however, requires that all parties look out first for the project's interests. This should mean that, at the outset of a project, all parties, including their lawyers, will want to behave less like adversaries and more like business consultants, turning their attention away from contract language and toward the design and construction processes and the division of labor. That way, project risks and responsibilities have a better chance of being assigned to the party most capable of managing them, and the activities and fees of all can be orchestrated for coordinated success.

Haviland's study also recognizes the inherent dangers in letting difficult issues lie dormant

—hence, the emphasis on decision making up front and dispute resolution later. You will want to learn how to recognize early warning signs of project distress so that you can help your client recognize when a dispute is in the offing. Disputes stand a better chance of being resolved when they are approached quietly and quickly. We'll say more about this in Chapter 9 on dispute resolution.

The Role of Full A/E Services

The study data show that A/E firms, claims-free or not, place great importance on providing full construction contract administration (CCA) services. They see this as a significant claims preventer.

The reason for this is obvious. An A/E with CCA responsibilities, if on-site at the appropriate moments, will be in a position to facilitate the construction process, by helping catch mistakes, answering questions, and interpreting drawings. Moreover, since some design work is best left to the field, that work can be completed by the A/E during construction in a way that is consistent with the overall project goals. Under most standard documents, unless an owner's representative is retained, the A/E with CCA responsibilities is the key person on-site serving as the express agent of the owner, charged with looking out for the project's best interests.

With today's bundling and unbundling of A/E services, it is possible to have more than one A/E firm providing services. The owner should make sure that some A/E firm is providing CCA services to the project. If not, the owner should be advised of the potential impact of this arrangement on the project, to prevent unrealistic expectations concerning the A/E's role.

How to Use Front-End Alignment in Practice

We've covered a lot of ground here, but what, if anything, does front-end alignment have to do with learning negotiation skills? You will be learning in Chapter 4 that negotiating success is contingent on you and the Other building common ground. What better common ground is there in the world of design and construction than project success? And, what better method is there to build project success than discussing front-end alignment, pinning down issues early, and then following through accordingly?

Now reexamine this chapter with that in mind. Do you see how effective use of the front-end alignment process can help both you and the owner build common ground? Struggles around who should do what or when are much easier to address and resolve when there is no dispute around the goal and definition of project success. Building that common ground should make design negotiation and contract negotiation that much easier.

I use the word "build" purposely. Common ground doesn't just happen. You have to consciously work at building it. And the more you know about the project and the Other, the easier it is to build. That's why focusing on front-end alignment long before you begin contract negotiations is such an important step in building common ground that will help not only with negotiations, but also with the inevitable difficulties of contract implementation.

But, as important as securing strong front-end alignment is, the critical first step in building common ground is selecting your client. I know: Some of you want to tell me that life is tough on the street, and it is the client who selects you, especially in down markets. In part, that may be true, but it isn't the whole story. Haven't you ever thrown away an interview after meeting a client and realizing that the two of you wouldn't work well together? You drop your energy level. You stop looking at the person with interest. You start creating problems, sometimes wittingly, sometimes not. Instead, make client selection a conscious decision, because the better you are at client selection, the greater your chances are of having a claims-free practice.

One final point: In Chapter 3, you will learn the legal elements of a contract. What I don't say there, however, is that, in our market society, the law allows you to walk away from a contract unilaterally and for any reason, including the fact that you just don't feel like implementing it. It's not a crime, but you do have to pay damages, giving the Other the benefit of the bargain, as if you had performed. Typically, architects don't do that, which is one of the many reasons society respects them so. They stick, even under the tyranny of a bad client. To avoid that tyranny, to maintain your breach-free reputation, and to maximize the benefits of front-end alignment, choose your clients well.

Here are some things to find out about your client before you sign on the dotted line. Some you'll discover during the "sales" process, some, during the negotiation process. Knowing the answers to all will help you build the common ground so necessary for project success.

➤ *Know your client's history with architecture because that history is going to become your present.* If your client has worked with architects before, and thought them all incompetent, it is unlikely your judgment will be trusted. If your client loved working with architects and thinks they can do no wrong, then you are just as challenged. If you are human, you make mistakes. If your client has never worked with an architect, you will have to figure out gambits to boost their experience quotient. You will also have to be open to learning together how to make architecture accessible and nonthreatening, even fun, for that client. So explore that history, early and openly, and identify steps, strategies, whatever you can do to make this encounter productive for the client. Then budget for those steps, so you can deliver on the shared understanding.

➤ *Know your client's management structure.* Owners retain architects to help them manage their risks. One aspect of that risk is the owner's management structure. Find out early, when push comes to shove, who's going to do the shoving. Who in the owner's world has the need for the project? Who has influence over it? Who has power over the project? Over you? Who controls the money, and, if that person is not the one with the need, what does that mean for the design and construction process? Make that structure work for both you and the owner by keeping your eye on the what's-best-for-the-project ball. And don't forget to discuss benefits of owner-architect-contractor meetings, and incorporate the resulting costs into the budget. (You will be picking up the collaboration and team-building skills to do so later in the book.)

➤ *Suss out client attitude.* Every architect knows there are trade-offs to be made in the course of a project. Make sure your client knows that. Making the trade-offs between quality, scope, money, and time is not easy, and it just gets harder for the owner the longer the project goes on. The more you are sensitive and responsive to the trade-off issues facing the client, the easier it is for your client to trust you.

➤ *Find out early the owner's value system and concept of good design.* If theirs is not compatible with yours, do yourself and the client a favor: Walk away. There are lots of clients out there. You can find one that you are right for and who is right for you. Otherwise, respect the client's choices. After all, it is the client's building, not yours. And be prepared for clients changing their minds over the course of the project, as the problems inherent in design and construction become more real to them.

Take money, for example. At the start of many projects, money will be an issue, but in the design honeymoon period for most owners, if there is a trade-off to be made between money and either scope or quality, scope or quality will win—at least in the beginning. As time and dollars tick away, money will increasingly become an issue.

Not all architects understand this, perhaps because not all have taken courses in construction and building finance. One architect cavalierly challenged me during a meeting when I included the amount charged for reimbursables as an architect's cost. "That's just reimbursables. Not my fee. They don't count against budget." Hello out there. The owner has but one pocket, and, though some architects may differentiate their fees from reimbursables, or their fees from construction costs, or their fees from unanticipatable, market-driven increases in costs, rest assured, the owner doesn't. It's all money to the owner, and it is all coming out of the owner's hide. So find out your owner's limits, and budget under them, so the foreseeable but unanticipatable doesn't throw anyone for a loop.

➤ *Which brings me to solvency.* You just read in this chapter that your firm's financial stability is a claims-preventing factor. So is the client's. If your client is 100 percent capable of affording the project the day they sign the construction project, but only just, then that client is for all intents and purposes insolvent. Where are they going to get the money for the first unexpected change? The second? How are their finances going to affect your cash flow? Discuss this early with the client so you can save both of you from the Tweedledum and Tweedledee of claims—you for your fees, the client for your negligence.

➤ *Know your client's reputation, both in the business world and in the community.* Your client's reputation is a key lubricant that enables the project to proceed smoothly. The better the reputation, the easier it is to attract quality consultants and constructors. The better your client's reputation, the easier it is to get community and governmental support for the project. Clients with bad reputations, or good clients with projects that have bad reputations, such as facilities people don't want in their backyard, carry with them inherent frictions. Ask yourself if you have the skills to manage that grit, and, if you do, make sure you budget with the owner for all the meetings and delay it will cause.

➤ *Know your client's reputation with respect to dispute resolution.* I met one architect who decided to take as a client an owner who had a fierce reputation for stiffing architects, charging them all with negligence to avoid the final payments. The architect addressed the client's reputation up front with the client and its implications for hiring anyone good to work on the project. The two came to this deal: The owner and architect would meet every Friday. The architect would present progress made over the week and then bill for the next week. The owner would pay or not pay, depending on owner satisfaction with the services rendered over the week. If the owner chose not to pay, the architect would walk, drawings in hand, with no other liability on either party's side. They finished the project together.

➤ *Chemistry*. It is chemistry that is going to get you through your first crisis. It is how you handle that crisis that will get you through the next, but without chemistry before you start the project, you'll never make it through that first problem. As much as you may want the project, take time to find out whether you also want the client. And don't think you will change the client after you "marry." That never works. Not in marriage and certainly not on the construction site.

Finally, add your own "look out fors." As you do more and different kinds of projects, you will find some client types with whom you excel and some with whom you do not. For example, committee clients have a horrendous reputation in the A/E insurance world. Committee members each think the building is theirs. Each has a separate vision to protect, a distinct ideal. Everyone is worried about money. No one is responsible for the budget, or so it seems. And the membership changes over time, tossing the group and the architect backward to revisit ground long ago covered. Yet despite all these characteristics, some architects pick up committee management skills and excel with them. If you're not one of those architects, add committee clients to your "look out for" list until you develop committee management skills.

But revisit that list from time to time. You're changing, picking up new skills, and developing new ideas of what you want for your practice. Don't let anything as static as a list written on paper take control over your thought process.

Your negotiation skills will aid you in your client selection skills because they require you to focus on the Other as a person, not as a problem. And that's another reason why this chapter should make your future negotiations less fraught with tension. You will be learning in later chapters that even expert negotiators get stuck from time to time, and, when they do, they do not panic. They seek out objective data to help them get to a better place. This entire chapter is full of objective data. Oh, I know, it is based on the surveys of architects and engineers, but I share this data with owners and contractors who routinely assure me of its resonance.[5] Planned projects with experienced people who are unafraid of the process and revel in each other's expertise have the best chance of producing claims-free projects. Now the data belong to you. Use them freely on your projects and with your clients and colleagues.

---

[5] So, by all means, share this chapter with your clients. Better yet, give them their own copy of the book. There are no secrets in it.

The Purpose of Contracts

3

If your experience is similar to that of most architects, you were first introduced to contracts in one mandatory course during your last year in school. A professor—sometimes a lawyer, sometimes an architect, and often retired—stood in front of the class and walked you through the old B141 (now the new B101-2007) word by word, painstakingly etching into your brain the myriad horrors that can befall an unwary practitioner. Anxious and drained, you left the class swearing that, when you had your own firm, the first thing you'd do is find a partner willing to negotiate all contracts for you.

Or perhaps your introduction came from an insurance company dedicated to the proposition that you should sign nothing uninsurable and to its corollary, that whatever deviation the owner wants from the standard contract is probably uninsurable. Thus, the insurance company told you to send all contracts its way so it could protect you from your clients and yourself, reinforcing the myth that most architects are naïve, and few have good business sense. In the process, the insurance company drummed into your head that architecture is a liability-harassed profession. And it taught you to become dependent on it—good for the insurer, but not necessarily good for you.

If either of these experiences rings true for you, then contract negotiation is probably something you approach with caution or even dread. Rest assured, there is no reason for contracts to be that difficult. The first step to negotiating contracts successfully is to cut through the fears you have been so carefully taught: the fear of clients, of words, of uninsurability, and of architect frailty. To do that, you have to first reorient your understanding of the purpose of contracts from that of a defensive practitioner to that of an assertive one. In other words, as we saw in Chapter 1, as an assertive practitioner, you will want to take control of risks, so you can manage them, and they don't manage you. With that new perspective solidly supporting you, no contract, no client, and no insurance company should daunt you.

As it is true that contracts are creatures of law, let's talk about the law right off, so we can learn it, understand it, and set it aside. Then we will be free to think about contracts in terms of architecture, assertive practice, and client service.

The Difference between Contracts and Torts

Lawyers will tell you that there are two legal theories under which most architects are sued: *contracts* and *torts*. *These two legal theories are quite different in both purpose and result.* Understanding those differences will empower you when you negotiate.

Contracts make commercial life predictable. Contract law is what permits our market economy to thrive. Contract law is what allows each and every one of us to buy a product or service safely from a stranger. It tells us what our rights are before we hand over our money, and what our rights and obligations are if everything goes well or if it does not. Even when you don't sign a formal contract, contract law is still in operation.

Think about it. What are your rights if you buy a television and it does not work? You know, and you never went to law school. You can:

1. Exchange the TV set for another.
2. Get the store to fix it.
3. Get your money back.

Nothing else. No emotional distress. No pain and suffering. You can't walk into the breaching store and demand $2 million, saying, "I'm scarred for life. You made me miss *Seinfeld*." All you can get is economic damages for economic loss. And both you and the seller know the terms before you buy the set. You recognize that, all things being equal, if one of you breaches a contract, the court will give the other one the benefit of the bargain had the contract not been breached. In fact, both of you can calculate the probability and consequences of a loss, in determining whether to sell or buy the television and how much to charge and pay for it. Now, ask yourself: Would you buy a set from a stranger if there were no contract law? Would you sell a set to a stranger if there were no contract law? Could we have a robust market economy without contract law? Without question, the answer to all is no. *Contract law is what makes business, any business, predictable, including the business of architecture.* And that predictability is what makes any business, again including the business of architecture, doable. Without it, the risk of business is just too high.

If contract law makes commercial life predictable, what then is the purpose of tort law? *Tort law makes our daily life predictable*, and, ultimately, as you will see, it makes the *practice* of architecture doable. Traditional tort law requires each and every person over the age of seven[1] "to act as a reasonable, prudent person would act, facing the same or similar facts and circumstances." Tort law sets a standard of care for us all. It *imposes* a "promise" on each of us, that, as a matter of law, we will act reasonably and prudently. That's it—no more, no less. Perfection is not required. Experimentation is not forbidden. Error is not illegal. All we must be, by law, is reasonable and prudent under the facts and circumstance facing us.

Could we live any other way? Not likely. Our society is too heterogeneous and too complex for any lesser standard of care to rule. Think about it: We are a country of immigrants. Who would venture into the street if people could act as unreasonably as they wanted? We rely on our neighbors and

---

[1] According to William L. Prosser, the authority on tort law, "some courts have attempted to fix a minimum age, below which the child is held to be incapable of all negligence. Although other limits have been set, those most commonly accepted are taken over from the arbitrary rules of the criminal law, as to the age at which children are capable of crime. Below the age of seven, the child is arbitrarily held to be incapable of any negligence; between seven and fourteen he is presumed to be incapable, but may be shown to be capable; from fourteen to twenty-one he is presumed to be capable, but the contrary may be shown." W. Prosser, *Handbook of the Law of Torts* 155-56 (4th ed. 1971).

The Purpose of Contracts

even strangers to be reasonable. We expect it. We demand it. That is why when someone does something egregiously outside the norm, we rationalize that the person must be crazy. Or else, there is no explanation. No way to justify, to accept wayward unreasonableness. And, if we aren't treated reasonably by another person, as tort law prescribes, and are injured as a result, we expect the law to make us whole, to compensate us, so as to undo the tort's damages to the extent money can ameliorate an injury.

But is society demanding too much when it requires each of us to be reasonable 24 hours a day? To pay for the consequences of our negligence? Usually not, because people, by and large, are not negligent.

In point of fact, we try as hard as we can to be reasonable, and usually it is easy. There are circumstances, however, when knowing what is reasonable and prudent is problematic at best. You are driving and come upon a red light in the middle of the day? You stop. It is unreasonable to do otherwise. But, what do you do when it is the middle of the day and you are taking your crying two-year-old to the hospital because you cannot get her 105.1° fever down? A tough decision, and you choose the wisest, most reasonable, safest way to go, all things considered, knowing that usually you choose well. So, can you live with tort law? Sure. You're reasonable, and you expect others to be reasonable in return. Can you live without it? Not a chance.

So contracts and torts have different purposes and different remedies. It used to be, in the olden days, that courts everywhere distinguished 100 percent between contracts and torts. If you brought a breach of contract case, you and the Other had to both be parties to the contract—that is, "in privity" with each other—and you could get economic damages only—that is, the economic benefit of the contract had it been successfully implemented. If you brought a tort case, you had to prove the Other had a duty to you and that the Other's unreasonableness in fulfilling that duty caused you personal injury or property damage. Hence, a contractor who sued an architect for delay damages would be told, "Being an architect, my duty is to the owner only. If the owner's wanting a certain item caused you delay damages, that is between you and the owner. My job is to look out solely for the owner, not for you." The bottom line was that a contractor could not sue an architect, either for breach of contract—no privity—or for negligence—no duty. The contractor could look only to the owner for recompense.

As of 2008, most courts still adhere to this interpretation, but over the last 30 years, a growing minority has not. They reckon that the success of the building enterprise is so interdependent, the parties' interreliance so necessary, that each party owes every other party a duty of reasonable prudence and care. Hence, these courts combine contract law and tort law to create a new theory of *economic damages*, a theory that permits contractor recovery against an architect. I label this theory *ConTort*. These courts look to the contracts of all the parties to see, first, what duties are owed and, second, the reasonably foreseeable results of delivering or not delivering those duties. The courts then evaluate how reasonably those duties were completed, and assess damages if unreasonable conduct (a tort concept) resulted in economic damages to another (a contract concept), even though no contractual duty to that Other was ever contemplated. Architects practicing in those jurisdictions can find themselves in a double bind. If they look out zealously for the rights of their owner, they can be blindsided by a suit from the owner's contractor for economic damages caused by that same zealousness.

An example: Let us say that, 35 days after contractor selection, the contractor comes up with a complex but seemingly attractive substitution. He argues for it, saying, "value engineering." The owner wants to save money and directs the architect to look into it. The architect does, but the contractor's substitution is so complex that it takes the architect 60 days to arrive at a recommendation. He turns it down. The contractor screams foul. "The architect's 60 days was excessive. The substitution was not that complex. I held things up, expecting, indeed relying, on a speedier review. Now I will have to order material that is no longer as easy, as cheap, or as available to get. The architect should pay for all the costs caused by his unreasonable delay." In an economic damages (ConTort) jurisdiction, the contractor would have a shot at recovering in court, the value to the owner of the 60-day review notwithstanding.

Put your personal bias as an architect and your affection for architecture aside: Is an economic damages court wrong in this day and age? Another example. In non-ConTort damages jurisdictions, the contract documents are meant to describe for the owner alone the building that will result. Contractors are not to rely on them as a cookbook, as they know no contract documents can ever be pretested and, hence, debugged. But in economic damages (ConTort) jurisdictions, a contractor can recover from the architect if the contractor's reliance on negligently prepared contract documents causes the contractor economic injury. Which jurisdiction produces the most just, the most fair, result? The answer to that depends on whether you are an owner, an architect, or a contractor.

Can we learn something by looking at other professions? The lawyers' code of ethics, for example, expects lawyers to look out for the interests of their clients "zealously." Do owners want a zealous architect when a merely reasonable one would do? Given the increasingly complex and sometimes forceful demands of owners, should an architect owe a contractor an equal duty? If yes, what duty? If not, does the architect owe the contractor anything? Do owners want to pay architects enough money to produce contract documents complete enough that the contractor can justifiably rely on them? Are architects sufficiently knowledgeable about construction that they can take on that responsibility? Should they be? Assuming architect fluency with construction, would an owner pay what it takes to have "complete" contract documents? Could an owner afford them? Is that a wise demand, given the realities of the market and the evolving demands of the construction site? Does the answer to all these questions change as increasingly collaborative methods of project delivery, such as Integrated Project Delivery (IPD) with Building Information Modeling (BIM), are used?[2]

Most courts have answered these questions by restricting the allegiance of the architect to the owner alone, but in time this may change, should

---

[2] The AIA has published two sets of documents in support of IPD projects, including the A295-2008 family of documents and the C195-2008 single purpose entity document. The latter is expected to have additional, associated documents published later.

more courts become enamored with ConTort law. To protect you and the Owner, there is wisdom in addressing these policy issues with the owner before the contract is signed, and in developing and implementing risk-management techniques, such as partnering, to help the project run smoothly.

The Architect's Standard of Care

If being reasonable and prudent is the standard of care for each of us as ordinary citizens, what exactly is the standard of care for architects? Does society demand more from its professionals than reason and prudence? Does it figure that, after five or six years of school, three years or more of internship, and one rigorous, multipart examination, architects should produce perfection? Certainly not. Architects, like all professionals, are held to the *professional standard of care*, which means that they must act as other reasonably prudent professional architects would act facing the same or similar facts and circumstances. And the people you are working with know that. They depend on it. That is why an owner is willing to build your designs, and people are willing to inhabit them. They are relying on your having been reasonably prudent in developing those designs. In other words, to the extent contract law makes the *business* of architecture doable, tort law makes the *practice* of architecture doable.

Sounds clear enough, but the one question I am always asked is this: If, to be "non-negligent," an architect has to act reasonably and prudently as other reasonable, prudent architects would act facing the same or similar circumstances, who sets the standard of care? This question has always confused me, because, in the deepest sense, architects are in control of their own standard of care—as is every profession.

Take it apart. What comprises the standard of care? Where do architects look to decide what is reasonable and prudent under the facts and circumstances facing them? These resources come quickly to mind:

- ➤ Codes and standards
- ➤ Licensing laws
- ➤ The profession at large
- ➤ The AIA
- ➤ Your firm
- ➤ Your marketing
- ➤ Your contract and all its project requirements
- ➤ Your conduct
- ➤ Case law

And, if you think about it, in no small part, each is within your control. Let's examine each of these in turn.

- ➤ *Codes and standards.* Architects contribute directly to the codes and standards in their states by participating on local boards and their national counterparts. AIA, for example, has a very active codes and standards committee. Additionally, every time architects seek and obtain a variance for a project, they are personally amending their local code to meet their project's unique needs.
- ➤ *Licensing laws.* Architects make up each state's licensing board. There may be a public member or two on each board, but for the most part, when the majority rules, the majority

are architects. Even when state legislatures step in, architects have power, as they are the people with the knowledge the legislators need to enact laws. The more and better the information architects have, the more active they are in, and the more witting they are about, government affairs, the more and better their influence and power.

➤ *The profession.* Every profession sets standards for itself through its codes of ethics and its monographs and learned treatises—that is a leading characteristic of being a learned profession. And who makes up the profession of architecture? You do.

➤ *The AIA.* Whether you belong to the American Institute of Architects or not, the market looks to the AIA to determine what a reasonable architect should do. That should be motive enough for every architect to join and get involved in the Institute. Why should you allow others to define without you what is reasonable for you?

➤ *Your firm.* Does your firm have an internal operations handbook? A model specifications loose-leaf notebook? A quality-control manual? If so, the firm is setting its own unique standard of care for the architects employed by it.

➤ *Your marketing.* Have you ever thought of your brochure as a treatise setting a standard of care for your firm? Probably not, if only because standard AIA owner-architect contracts contain clauses that are intended to override the brochure's promises. But one brochure I read said, "When you work with us, we promise, you will be happy," setting its firm's clients' expectations way beyond its control. Whether or not the promises inferred by your client from your brochures are incorporated in the final contract, your clients carry them close to their chests throughout the project, obliquely demanding your compliance with them. And who has final say over your brochures? You do.

➤ *Your contract.* When you sign a contract, each promise you make, each duty you take on, each responsibility you accept helps define your standard of care for that project. Your client will expect you to perform to the letter of that "standard of care," as will a judge or jury, should the project fail. You are fully in control of your contracts. Whether the contracts you sign are AIA standard contracts or owner-drafted contracts, no one forces you to sign them. Whether to commit to a contract is one decision fully of your making and yours alone.[3]

➤ *Your conduct.* Your firm's contracts may be exact, your brochures thoughtful, your in-house manuals totally up to date, but your conduct and the conduct of any of your partners, employees, and other agents can undo all that exactitude. They can even change the

---

[3] Can you opt out of doing something in your contract? Sure, but an obligation may be implied by the relationship of the parties. Take it out of architecture completely. An accountant contracts with a client and in the engagement letter specifically says that "it is not the accountant's responsibility to discover embezzlements." Thus, the accountant has no contractual responsibility to do so, but the accountant can still be held liable if he or she fails to discover an embezzlement by failing otherwise to conform to the auditing standards of the accountant's profession.

standard of care on you. For example, architects don't usually guarantee construction results, because they have no power over constructors, but should a person in your firm say to the client, "I promise you, our roofs don't leak," the client can infer a leakproof roof has been guaranteed. And who has control over the conduct of architects?

> *Case law.* I know you're going to tell me judges and juries make case law, not architects. That is true, but where do they look for what is reasonable and prudent? First, they look to the items we just listed and demonstrated are within your control. And on whom do judges and juries rely when they are stuck? On expert witnesses—*on architects* who testify to whether, in their expert opinion, the defendant architect acted within the scope of conduct that reason and prudence allow.

So there you have it: A standard of care more or less defined by you and your colleagues. And it does not change, and most probably never will change, as long as lawyers are held to the reasonable, prudent lawyers' standard of care. What then is the problem? Not the standard, I submit, but the challenge of deciding what is reasonable, given the ever-increasing complexity of projects and the demands and needs of the people who build them. It is figuring out "the facts and circumstances facing you" that gives architects pause, because no matter how excellent the architect, each project is a one-of-a-kind, never-been-tested experiment in art and technology. That a building comes together in the end is one of the wonders of architecture.

With that in mind, we can now translate these two concepts—*contract law makes commercial life predictable* and *tort law makes life predictable*—more completely into architectural concepts. What do they mean for you when you negotiate your next project? What do they mean for your clients, consultants, and all the contractors?

The Contractor's Standard of Care

If the standard of care for an architect is reasonable prudence, and, if both the architect and the owner expect the contractor to be reasonable and prudent, is the law's standard of care for contractors reasonable prudence, also? No, typically contractors sign a contract that holds them to a different standard of care.

Contractors guarantee that they will perform in strict conformance with the contract documents.[4] Regardless, when contractors reach agreement with their owners, they imply a promise that, if the owner gives them total control over the construction site—over the men and women who will be constructing the building and over the means, methods, sequences, techniques, and safety precautions of construction—they will deliver the described building on time and within budget, with it adhering to the contract documents. Their owners and the law will hold them to that promise, so if their work is not in compliance with the construction documents, and some injury happens as a result, the fact that they conformed to industry practices in building the project will not absolve them. This contractual standard of care is quite different from that of the architect, who has, as a defense, compliance with the profession's standard of care, even if the building fails to achieve a desired result.

Now test yourself on your understanding: Where do the two very different standards of care leave an owner who has (1) a leaky roof, (2) an architect whose designs and conduct were reasonable and prudent, and (3) a contractor who strictly complied with each and every aspect of the contract

---

[4] Some jurisdictions require the contractor to perform in *substantial* compliance with the contract documents. They do this, in part, to avoid economic waste, that being given a higher priority than either the specifications or the demands of the owner and architect.

documents? If you answered "in the lurch," you well understand the difference between architects' and contractors' standards of care.

You also understand why some owners prefer design-build or better yet IPD. They view the single source of responsibility that design-build provides and the total collaboration that IPD calls for as a means to avoid the legal hassle of deciding who is responsible for what. After all, under both project delivery systems, at least in theory, everybody's fingerprints should be everywhere. These owners reason that, because of that collaboration, the finger pointing of traditional lawsuits would be to no avail. Instead of assessing blame, these owners are hoping that everybody will simply chip in and solve the problem together.

Design-build claims are too few and the resulting law too sparse to assess definitively the validity of these owners' thinking. We know even less about IPD law, but in the complicated world of design and construction, the allure of design-build's single-source responsibility and IPD's total collaboration is beguiling.

They mean, first, that each of you will be reading each other's contracts looking for the promises each of you makes and the duties each of you agrees to. Second, they mean that—regardless of whether your state is a pure contract/pure tort law jurisdiction or a ConTort jurisdiction—each of you will be expecting the other to fulfill those duties reasonably and prudently and as promised.

Reexamine the preceding paragraphs on standard of care, and think about them again. Their implications are both comforting and unnerving: comforting because a well-negotiated family of contracts will put all the players on the same page, sharing the same vision and definition of project success; unnerving because, while society may not expect more of you than you can reasonably provide, your clients may have higher expectations of you. Your expectations of yourself may be even higher still. If unrealistic expectations are not openly addressed, they may cause both you and your client problems over the course of the project. And therein lies the value of well-negotiated contracts.

How Liable Are You?

A Short Course on Direct, Vicarious, and Joint and Several Liability

Can you stand just a few more legal concepts? Lawyers routinely toss around three more when discussing liability. Let's translate them into English first and then into Architecture. As we noted earlier, in our society, we are responsible for our own actions. No one has a right to be negligent. Each of us has a right, as well as a duty and responsibility, to be reasonable and prudent every day of our lives. If we are not reasonably prudent—and that's the standard of care—then we are *directly liable* for any foreseeable injury that results from our negligence.

What I just wrote probably evoked a yawn. Everybody knows that. It's why we exercise prudence in all that we do. But do you know you are also *indirectly liable* for the negligence of your children, your employees, and your agents—anybody who is under your supervision and control? Now you may be thinking, "My children aren't under my supervision and control. Whose children are?" I won't quibble about that, but society exacts that indirect liability from each of us, as a way of increasing the chances of an injury-free society. The more society holds *principals* responsible for the authorized acts of their *agents*, theory goes, the more likely it is that principals will think about what authority they are delegating and watch how their agents are carrying it out. It does have a logic to it.

Lawyers label that indirect liability as *vicarious liability*. Translating it into Architecture, it means the owner can sue you—the architect, as principal, in tort for the negligence of your "servants [translate that into employees] and agents"; and, if the court finds that their negligence caused the owner injury, you will be held vicariously liable for that negligence. You, in turn, can sue your employee or agent for their negligence, but that rarely happens, as employees and agents are usually judgment-proof: that is, too poor to be worth the effort.

Does the same logic apply to architect-consultant relationships? No. Consultants are not employees or agents or someone you control. Consultants are independent entities. Indeed, you hired them for their independent expertise and judgment, and you want and expect them to exercise it. So you're not going to be vicariously liable for consultants under *agency law* in the same sense that you are for one of your employees. Rather, you will be directly liable for them under *contract law*. The law empowers you to enter into contracts and agree to be responsible for the negligent acts and omissions of others, even though the law would not otherwise hold you responsible for the conduct of that other person. Your signing a contract delegating some of your responsibilities to a consultant makes you vicariously liable under contract law if those duties were negligently performed. Hence, the owner can ask under contract law that you be held liable for the negligence of your consultant, even though you were not negligent, and thus the owner has no grounds to sue you in tort.

There is also something else called *joint and several liability*, and that occurs whenever a court cannot tell where your negligence stopped and the other's negligence started. Here, the court, for all intents and purposes, says to both parties, "We are not wasting one more penny of taxpayers' resources trying to work out this private dispute. Both of you are 100 percent liable. You sort it out, but whatever you decide, the person who sued you will get all the money owed from you—either alone or together."

I hear you asking, "What if the *owner* hires the consultant to provide the services that the architect usually delegates? Is the architect vicariously liable in the same way?" No. The consultant is not your consultant; the consultant is the owner's consultant. That is the legal answer under contract law. But you're not performing legal services when you're designing. You're being an architect, right? And what services involving consultants do architects provide, regardless of who does the hiring of the consultant? Coordination. Exactly.

So even though you don't have a contract with the owner's consultant, you are going to be coordinating that consultant's services with your services and everybody else's. Now you have a real architecture issue facing you that could translate into legal liability. If you don't make sure that owner-retained consultants deliver their documents to you in ample time for you to coordinate their services with yours, *you might have coordination responsibility but none of the power* (or merely insufficient power) to effectively coordinate consultant services. As a result, something may negligently fall through the cracks, and whose negligence caused what injury may become an issue. Welcome to the world of joint and several liability. And, if the owner's consultant is judgment-proof, or just "gone," you may find yourself jointly and severally liable for that negligence and totally on your own.

The Purpose of Design and Construction Contracts

There are high stakes in contract negotiation, and those stakes do not revolve merely around insurability and fee. On the contrary, negotiating a contract is the last, best, relatively low-stakes opportunity that architects and their clients have to align themselves for project success—whether that client is the owner or a contractor. While the terms you negotiate will vary depending on your client, the contract is still the time to align the parties for project success. However, for the purposes of this discussion, I will assume throughout the book that your client is the owner.

Why "low-stakes opportunity"? Should negotiations fail, all you have to lose is the commission (assuming you have not started project delivery without a contract). Not your reputation due to a project gone awry. Not your insurance deductible because of a claim. Not unpaid services for lack of a contract. Indeed, you just may find yourself much better off for losing that project.

Accordingly, for you as an architect, a contract should never be just about negotiating words or coming to "yes" about legal terms. Rather, a contract serves many purposes, every one of which is in your interests and can be made to serve you, the owner, and the project. Let's take them one by one:

> *At its most basic, a contract makes the progress of the project predictable.* It is the "legal schematic" that describes how the project will go, if it proceeds well, or if it does not. This view of a contract as a legal schematic is true for every party to the building enterprise, not just for you. So all parties benefit from a contract that defines the construction process. That fact will empower you throughout the negotiation because you can use it as a tool to negotiate project-friendly terms.

> *More broadly, a contract helps the parties achieve their strategic objectives.* Architects, perhaps due to their schooling, don't always understand this. They believe owners retain them to design a building, and, if the building is well designed and, later, the construction is well administered, they have done a good job. Not so. That is not enough for most of today's owners. As one owner said to me, "Architects don't get it. To them, the project stops when it is built. To me, it is still going on. I need a building as a tool to help me solve a problem. Design is never my goal unto itself." Contract negotiation affords both the owner and you the opportunity to lay out your individual strategic goals. It gives you both the chance to understand each other and decide whether you really want to, and can, work together. Again, as we will see in the next chapters, this realization can empower you during the negotiation process.

➤ *A contract affords both parties the opportunity to set realistic expectations of the Other.* In order to be an effective tool that allows a project to be predictable, a contract must be grounded in realistic expectations. Negotiation is the time to work out project scope, budget, roles, quality, quantities, process and procedures, and timing. Now is the time for both parties to discuss and understand the implications of what they can and cannot do.

➤ *A well-negotiated contract assigns an exposure to the party in the best position to manage the risk, and then gives that party all the responsibility and power they need to handle the exposure successfully, including fee.* Intuitively, this makes sense. There is no sound reason to assign an exposure to someone not capable of handling it, or to give anyone insufficient resources to manage a risk. Project success doesn't result from hedging. Nor does design excellence. Claims do. Contract negotiations provide the parties the chance to align scope, strategy, systems, and budget to enhance the possibilities of success.

➤ *Contracts can provide the framework that can facilitate future negotiations.* Because the owner and architect continue to negotiate the design of the project after the contract is signed, negotiation doesn't end with the initial contract. It is an ongoing process throughout the project. Many neophytes in design and construction, including nonconstruction lawyers, don't understand that once a contract is signed, an entirely new series of negotiations begins, from what the design should look like to how it should be configured. And let us not forget change orders, which become a fact of life as the owner sees the building for the first time and gets a better sense of what they really want. A contract with too tight an intellectual framework can disadvantage the parties, no matter what the project. A framework that is too loose can be just as problematic.

➤ *Contracts help solidify the working relations the parties will need to succeed.* In addition to securing implementable language, contracts help secure working relationships. As we will see in Chapter 5, expert negotiators leave the table with three things: (1) an agreement similarly understood by both parties, (2) an agreement that can be successfully implemented, and (3) a willingness by the other party to negotiate with them again. Design contracts need all three of these attributes secured, as design and construction will inevitably involve continuing negotiations. If a contract is fought too hard or adversarially, a troubled project is probably not far behind.

What Contracts Don't Do

Simply put, contracts don't ensure success. That is not their purpose. Most lawyers don't draft them with that goal in mind. They're thinking how to protect "my" client if all goes asunder. That's why so much of a contract focuses on termination. Architects and engineers implicitly know this, which is probably why, as noted in the Chapter 2, those responding to Haviland's questionnaire did not consider having a contract to be either a claims preventer or a claims aggravator.

That view makes sense. In most cases, contracts don't cause claims. People do. I say "in most cases" because a "bad" contract that assigns responsibilities without competence or gives responsibility without power can confuse the parties and the design and construction processes so badly that a claim will logically result. But most contracts aren't bad, just inartful. Nor will a perfectly arrayed contract guarantee project success if it is implemented contentiously.

That's why developing strong negotiation skills is so crucial to assertive practitioners. They know that the wrangling over words is complete when the contract is signed, but that the parlaying of ideas and the uncovering of problems have just begun. Handling the resulting issues without negotiating expertise is a sure-fire road map to project disappointment or even breakdown.

> *Contracts are a private law—a law written by two parties that our public courts will enforce.* I put this purpose of contracts at the end because it is the least important of all the purposes of contracts, for one reason and one reason alone: Most projects succeed. It is the rare project indeed that ends up in court or even becomes the object of litigation. But when a contract does land in court, it is invariably enforced.

Though it is true that most projects succeed, that is never a reason for negotiating a sloppy or unimplementable contract. Doing that just increases your chances that your contract will be one of the few that ends up in court. Nor should you use the fact that insurers estimate that some 95 percent of the projects in America will go claims-free to convince yourself into signing what you believe is an unconscionable contract. Courts are in power to enforce legal contracts. They look for ways to enforce contracts, to give the parties the benefit of their private law. They may agree that you were dumb to sign an egregiously one-sided contract, but in America, if you are competent to sign a contract, you have a legal right to sign a dumb one, and enforce it the courts will.[5]

Four Key Concepts

But enough about overarching contract goals and the law. Let's get real. You don't wake up thinking, "What legal duty can I breach today?" You go to the office with a list of architecture to-do's in mind, hoping that you will accomplish each efficiently and effectively. You think architecture, so let's talk architecture. That is your strength, your passion, and your area of expertise. And when you view contracts through your architect lens, the contract negotiation arena will shine brighter and lighter.

How do you decide which to-do's—which duties—you are willing to take on, for isn't a to-do "a duty" but by a lesser name? Look at your tomorrow's to-do list: Aren't most of the items on it action promises you made to people? And aren't those people depending on you for the completion of each action promise? Most assuredly. Now ask yourself, "How did these promises get there? How do I decide which items I agreed to do?"

I submit that if you're like most architects I've worked with, you intuitively run through four key concepts before you agree to take on any challenges you put on your to-do list: *exposure*, *capability*, *responsibility*, and *power*. You suss out these

---

[5] Is there no way out of an egregiously bad contract? There are a few circumstances that permit a contract to be rejected, such as fraud, impossibility, or extreme unconscionability. All are really tough to prove to a court's satisfaction. Isn't it easier to just not sign the contract in the first place?

four quickly and, usually, well. Only when your thinking is haphazard or wrongheaded do you have problems. The aim of this section is to help you make that mental process conscious and profitable, both in the short and long run. In this way, all things being equal, you'll take on duties that you can succeed at and profit by.

Let's take these concepts one by one.

Exposure

Life is full of risks. That's what makes life a challenge. That's what makes it interesting. Whether to take on any one risk, however, is a highly personal decision, and it depends in no small part on how *you* personally evaluate the risk. Each of us has our own "risk-o-meter." Some of us enjoy grappling with the unknown. Others of us do not. What is risky for one person may not be for another. Hence, if you are like most people, a necessary prologue for determining whether to take on a risk is answering the question: "How risky is the exposure to me personally?"

Answering that question may not be easy. It requires technical and empirical knowledge about the contours of the problem facing you. The more you know about the risk contours, the less risky the exposure is, or can be made to be, for you. Conversely, the less you know, the harder to assess the risk, lessen it, and decide whether to take it on.

One caveat: When you are thinking through risk, it is important not to think of possibilities, but only of probabilities. Is it possible that anything you touch can go wrong? Sure. Is it probable? No. But if you make decisions based merely on possibilities, the risks of wrongdoing can overwhelm you, and you can immobilize yourself all too easily. In a society where risk is related to reward, nothing is less in the architect's interest than to avoid those risks that are mere remote possibilities.

So think exposure instead. How probable is it that something will go wrong? The higher the probability, the greater the exposure, the more intense is the need for risk-management strategies and, more likely than not, the higher the potential reward when you succeed.

Capability

No matter how technically proficient your analysis of the exposure, you really can't answer the question "How risky is this exposure to me personally?" without also taking into account your own capabilities. Now is the time to openly assess your own strengths and weaknesses. Sometimes it is easy: If you have never designed a hospital, for example, a request to design one poses inherent risks. Sometimes it is harder: Once you have successfully designed a hospital, designing a second hospital will be less risky by virtue of your experience from the first one. Even if you failed in the design of the first, the second will be less risky, *if* you learned from the failure.

But *how much* less risky? That's the issue. Accordingly, "How risky is this exposure to me?" is a moving target, one that has to be addressed *each time* you come upon an exposure, in light of that exposure and your own increasing knowledge and skills.

Responsibility

Once you have analyzed the exposure and assessed your capabilities to manage it, you now have to decide two issues. First, you are going to want to decide whether to shoulder the responsibility of managing the exposure. If you do, then you next must decide what other responsibilities you need assigned to you, to manage the exposure's risks effectively. In the best of all possible worlds, both of these issues would be consciously addressed, so that any responsibility you take on is one you wittingly want and agree to take on.

An example: Designing a "green" opera house may involve you in being responsible for services not traditionally offered by architects. It may also require you to retain a slew of consultants whom architects traditionally do not retain, if only because of lack of need. You would have to identify which services are necessary for project success—traditional or not—and decide whether you want to deliver them. Then you would have to identify the responsibilities you want assigned to you and your consultants so you can provide the necessary services.

Now make a business decision. Given your assessment so far, decide whether you want to take on the project at all. Does it advance your practice? Your business plan? Does it have "gut sign-off"? Decide for yourself, or else others define your practice for you. Assertive practitioners don't give that self-definition power away, not to anyone.

Power

Your work isn't over yet. Once you have been assigned the responsibility for managing the risk, you will also want to be given all the power you need to pull off the responsibility you agreed to take on. There are two aspects of power you will need.

First is authority—the ability to supervise, control, or coordinate your own and others' activities, depending on the scope of the authority given. There is nothing worse than being responsible for something over which you have no authority. (Try coordinating the services of an engineer with yours when you have no authority to require the engineer's drawings on a day certain.)

On Stretching

When I lectured about risk for the AIA, and later for Schinnerer, I used to say that, in the best of all possible worlds, no one would take on a risk without being personally 100 percent capable of managing it well the very minute it was assumed. I don't believe that anymore, for if it were true, life would be a bore. Boredom, in turn, would engender sloppy thinking, mediocre design, and a whole slew of other more deadly sins. We are made to stretch. The issue is how far, how often, and how much do we stretch, as well as how do we go about involving the owner in the process?

To a large extent, answers to "how far, how often, and how much?" reside in the architect alone. Those of us whose risk-o-meter has a high set point might be eager to take on a project where we are 80 percent capable, as long as we can align ourselves with others who have the expertise we lack. Those of us with a lower threshold for risk might want to be more certain of our capacity to perform before we accept new challenges.

How one goes about taking on a "stretching risk," however, is *not* an issue for the architect alone. One of the key tenets of both contract negotiation and risk management is to remember that the project is your client's project, not yours. That means you will want your clients to know about your experience—or lack of it—with their project. After all, as it is the client's project and the client's risk, clients will have to determine for themselves whether you should have the opportunity to stretch on their project. This is not a losing battle for the newcomer—some clients may want the new ideas and new solutions that freshness and nonexperience bring—but it is a battle that will have to be fought. You ethically owe your client competence, and, absent full competence, owners will want information about what you know and don't know and how you will fill that void.

Fortunately, by and large for architects, most risks facing architects do not encompass either ethical or moral issues, just business decisions. That frees you up to decide on a risk-by-risk basis which exposures you want to take on and which you do not, without your conscience or the judgment of others affecting your decision-making process.

Second is fee. The money the client provides empowers you to deliver the service you promised the client. Without adequate fee, you will be hard-pressed to deliver the amount and quality of service the project demands. In other words, fee is not merely compensation for services rendered; it is the fuel owners give you that enables you to deliver their projects. While an insufficient fee won't excuse negligence any more than an excessive fee will guarantee success, it's the sufficiency of the fee that will increase both your and your client's chances of getting the project of the client's dreams and managing the exposures inherent in the process.

How do these four concepts—exposure, capability, responsibility, and power—work together to facilitate contracts negotiation? You will see this more fully in later chapters, but here is a précis. When you read a contract, ask yourself, paragraph by paragraph, section by section:

➤ What is the exposure inherent in the duty I am being asked to take on? Is it one I want to accept?

➤ Who is the person most capable of taking on the exposure? Is it me? Am I capable of handling it by myself now? If not, what do I have to do to make myself capable of managing the risk?

> Who has (or should have) the responsibility for managing the exposure? If it's me, are the duties laid out in the contract clear and sufficient enough for me to manage the exposure? Do I need more responsibilities? Which ones?

> Who has the power to make sure each responsibility is carried out effectively? If it's me, do I have enough authority to pull off those responsibilities? Enough fee? Will my authorities be correctly included in other parties' contracts?

Assertive Practice

Why must you decide *both* which exposures you want to take on *and* which responsibilities you must accept to manage the exposure? And why must both be settled before you even begin to think about fee?

Remember, we are talking about negotiating as an assertive practitioner—as an architect who believes that you can design your practice as effectively as you can design a building. Assertive practitioners consciously choose which risks they want to take on and which they do not. They do not slide into projects they are truly ambivalent about. They figure they owe themselves and their clients more than that. They make conscious decisions, so they are not so busy fooling around with small "filler" projects, taken on only for their bread-and-butter appeal, that they aren't free for their passion when that project opportunity comes their way.

Rest assured, it is not the risk alone that usually makes assertive practitioners walk away. They know that in our society people who take on reasonable risks and manage them reasonably make money. People who run from risk do not. They reason that, if they want the rewards that come from managing risk, they must steel themselves to make friends with risk.

That's how assertive practitioners succeed for themselves and their clients. They analyze what the project needs and what skills they bring to bear. They then consciously decide whether the project meshes with their business goals and objectives. Once they determine it does, they actively seek out the necessary responsibility to meet the part of the exposure's demands they want to take on. This analysis of risk and responsibility is the first step in giving them confidence so they can well meet the exposure's demands. Only then do they take the critical, but second, step to building in project success: thinking hard about authority and fee. With the project's demands thoroughly thought through, they are in the best position to help the owner make sure that resources, risks, responsibilities, and powers are correctly aligned for project success.

Once you think through those issues, your negotiations will no longer focus on words and what's best for you versus what's best for the owner. Rather, you will be in the position to negotiate every aspect of the contract, including fee, from the vantage of *what's best for the project*.

In helping the owner think through what's best for the project, you will find yourself increasingly urging the owner to assign each exposure to the entity most capable of managing the risk and then to give that entity all the responsibility and power required to pull off that exposure effectively. Sometimes that analysis will dictate that a new consultant be brought onto the design team. Sometimes it will mean a construction budget is increased or a project's scope is decreased. Whatever it means, the bottom line is that the more thoroughly an exposure is thought through and planned for, the greater the chance of a successfully implemented project.

Analyzing contract clauses this way also gives you a greater opportunity for building your client's trust. Clients will see you thinking every issue through, not from your own self-interest, but from the vantage point of "what's best for the project." And, I ask you, what more can an owner negotiating in good faith want?

Will thinking through a project this openly with an owner hurt you? Will it cause the owner not to trust you? To question your every step? Research on what an owner wants and needs from consultants in order to trust them suggests not.

Huthwaite, Inc., a research think tank on persuasion and sales, studied the issue of trust and found that clients need three things from their consultants in order to trust them: competence, candor, and concern.

Competence was usually expected from recognized professionals, and, when not presumed by the client, most consultants spent time proving it in their proposals and presentations. Candor and concern were harder to establish and proved to be the deciding difference. Simply saying, "I am being candid, I am being concerned," had the opposite effect, however. Clients tended to be put off by consultants who aggressively asserted themselves, questioning their integrity and client-centeredness. These attributes of candor and concern had to be more subtly proved. Indeed, they were best inferred from consultant conduct and attitude. Successful consultants show candor and concern by sitting on the client's side of the table and seeing the project and its challenges through the client's eyes.

Addressing the four key concepts of exposure, capability, responsibility, and power with the owner gives you the very opportunity owners need to ascertain whether you are worthy of trust. Keeping your eye rigorously focused on project success in every statement you make, every question you ask, can assertively prove how candid and concerned you are.

If mnemonics help you remember the four key concepts, try this: Capability, Authority/power, Responsibility, and Exposure equal CARE, and that is what clients want and what architecture is all about.

Managing Risk

You may have noticed that I do not list "liability" as a key concept, nor do I mention it anywhere. Why not? Liability is a retro-concept determined long after the fact by people who were not around when decisions were made. During contract negotiation, you are in the here and now. You need to decide things, to discuss issues, to evoke competence, candor, and concern for the client. *Discussing any issue from a liability perspective will defeat your best efforts before you begin.*

Think about it. When you talk about your liability, what are you really worried about? *Your* pocketbook, *your* licensing issues, *your* deductible, *your* reputation. And whom are you concerned about? Most certainly not the owner, and the owner knows it. Drip, drip, drip. You water the owner's seedbed of doubt. In no time, owners won't trust you at all. Why should they? You have made it eminently clear: They come second.

So don't start from a liability premise. It won't help you. Nothing has yet happened. At this point there is no one to blame. Thinking liability now is premature. In fact, it is downright irrelevant. It just does not help you assertively think through a problem. And, it can even hurt. It can stop you from addressing issues in your true role as a problem-solving architect and start you thinking like a lawyer—and an untrained one to boot.

Instead of worrying about liability, think risk management. That's what owners need from you—help in managing their risks. Remember, who owns the project? The owner. Who owns its rewards? The owner. Who owns its risk? The owner. And are most owners trained and capable of managing the risks inherent in the building enterprise? Assuredly not. So, if you can help the owner assertively address and resolve those risks before anything bad happens, you will be worth every penny the owner pays you. Probably more.

Thinking in terms of risk management has fringe benefits, too. Besides increasing your probabilities of having a claims-free project, you also increase your value and, in the process, your chances of getting repeat business and a reference worth having. And you decrease your liability in the process.

Consider it: When you talk liability, it isn't because something bad has happened; it is because your learning and expertise suggest there's a high likelihood that something bad will happen. Instead of being afraid, instead of wasting your energies fretting, instead of wishing the problem would just go away, risk management gives you the chance to act and assertively address that "something" *before* things go wrong. Owners will love you for it.

Five Ways to Manage Risk

When I served as deputy general counsel of the AIA in the 1980s, architects were facing a liability crisis. Claims were out of sight, and for many of them so was insurance. On top of that, in many parts of the nation, architects were facing a severe recession. Work simply was hard to come by. Often architects would call with problems they were having deciding whether to take on certain exposures. As one explained to me, "It's take it or leave it time. My client just crossed his hands and said, 'There are other architects out there dying for this job.' What choice do I have?" Take it or leave it. No other options. And he wasn't alone. It was a rare architect who, in the midst of a crisis, could think of other options.

At the time, the AIA *Handbook* Committee gave me this challenge: Develop options for the architect to reduce the chances of taking on bad work and increase the chances that good work can be negotiated. I took up the challenge with some trepidation. It's easy for a lawyer to say, "Take (or don't take) on a risk. . . . If I were you. . . ." But no lawyer is you, and I certainly wasn't all architects. Moreover, a recession was engulfing the profession, and recessions mean, after all, that anxiety about getting business can lead to bad risk-taking practices. No one wanted options developed that resulted in that.

I identified five options to manage risk that became part of the eleventh and later the twelfth edition of *The Architect's Handbook of Professional Practice.*[6] Today in this falling economy, all that thinking is again critically important. See if these five options work for you as well as they have for others of your colleagues these last many years. And don't be surprised to find that, as you and the owner pin down which exposures you will handle which way, the more you become conversant with these five options, the easier your negotiations become. Here are the five ways to manage risk:

- ➤ Take it
- ➤ Leave it
- ➤ Abate it
- ➤ Allocate it
- ➤ Transfer it

Let's explore each in turn.

Take It

Most architects pride themselves on being generalists capable of doing most projects. That may be,

---

[6] See, for example, the twelfth edition's Chapter 3.32, "Managing Project Risks and Opportunities" (AIA: Washington, DC, 1994), rewritten and ascribed to others in the most recently published fourteenth edition of the *Handbook.*

but it doesn't necessarily mean you want to do *all* projects. If you are like most architects I have had the honor to work with, you want only good projects, that is, projects where you can provide a bona fide service, quality design, and (usually) make money in the process. That's to the good, because owners who realize you are offering them measurable value are, by and large, easier to negotiate with. So, if it's the right project and you are confident you can handle it safely, accept the risk.

A caveat: Just because you are trained to do it and have done it before doesn't mean you have to do it now. One of the most famous firms for design excellence in the commercial setting lost its shirt designing a single-family residence for the chairman of the board of one of its biggest business clients. It can happen.

Leave It

You can always walk away from a risk. And there will be risks worth walking away from, even in projects you can design in your sleep. You have a bad sense about the owner. The owner plays such hardball that you doubt there is the necessary chemistry you both will need to see you through the project's rough times. Or the project isn't challenging enough, or will not enhance, and may even hurt, the firm's reputation. As we learned in Chapter 2, developing client selection skills is a key component of risk management and design excellence. Being prepared to walk away not only keeps you clear of projects that will go wrong, it also gives you a stronger negotiating position to argue for the kind of corrective actions that can reduce risk and let the project succeed.

This was brought home to me in the late 1980s, when architects first lost their coverage for asbestos abatement. (It has since been restored.) Most quickly stopped doing anything that had anything to do with asbestos, or they demanded their clients sign hold harmless clauses or otherwise limit their liability. One Tennessee architect thought otherwise. He reasoned that, if he could make himself an expert in asbestos abatement, he could make money developing abatement plans—heaps of it. And he could make even more money and better manage his risks if his own people did the abatement. That way he could ensure himself that every safety precaution spec-ed was being taken. So he set up two companies: one to design and one to build. He then took his money to the bank.

Were the architects who rejected the asbestos exposure wrong and the ones who decided to develop an expertise in it right? *Taking on an exposure is not a moral decision.* It is a question of assessing reasoned and reasonable odds. Stay or walk away: just decide. Then, whatever you decide to do, go for it.

Abate It

That is, make the exposure less risky to you personally. How does one do that? Hit the books. Take a class. Call an expert for advice. In other words, beef up your skills to match the risk. Remember, while professionals are not expected to know everything, they are expected to know what they don't know. And to know where to go to find out. Taking steps to fill your knowledge gaps will make even the risky exposure more accessible.

Filling your skill gaps is also good business. There is no better way to stave off the competition than to have knowledge and know-how superior to theirs.

Allocate It

More likely than not, the most common way you manage special architecture-connected risks is to allocate them to a consultant more capable of handling the risk than you are. That's what you do when you pull together your design team. You select other professionals you have confidence in and assign them all the responsibilities and powers they need to manage a risk they can handle better than you. You then save for yourself whatever coordination responsibilities and powers you need to make sure nothing falls through the cracks.

Transfer It

Even though you can manage the risk, even though the exposure is well allocated, if you are a typical architect, you are not rich enough to finance the consequences of an exposure gone bad. Even if you are financially capable of absorbing the consequences of one failed exposure, you probably are managing dozens of exposures. That rich you ain't. This is where insurance comes in. You say, in effect, to your professional liability insurance carrier, "I'll pay you this much in premium and take on this much liability (that is, the deductible), and you take on the risk that something untoward might happen." Through the mechanism of errors and omissions insurance, you thus successfully transfer the risk to one more capable than you of absorbing the financial complications that might result from your negligence.

Indemnification agreements, hold harmless clauses, and "limit your liability" language have the same intent: to transfer a risk from one party to another. Think about that the next time you are asked (or ask anyone) to sign up to absorb the costs of a wayward exposure.

Managing the Seemingly Unmanageable Risk

Dividing up risk into five easy pieces is perhaps too simplistic an answer. The five options are easy to use when the risk is easy to box up, but not all risks are that simple to identify or compartmentalize. What do you do when the risk elements aren't clear-cut?

Some background: A particular insurance company came out with a directive to its insureds telling them to stop designing condominium projects. They were losing too much money paying condo claims. Like many in the profession, I was offended, deeply offended. Don't architects give insurers premiums to have them pay claims? By what right did an insurance company exact a premium and then dictate an architect's practice? Who were they to tell all their architect insureds to stay away from this project type? Could no architect anywhere successfully design a condominium? There had to be a better way to help architects manage their risks than to limit their options so severely. There is, but it only becomes accessible after you develop strong analytical antennae that sense risks and the creativity to devise methods to handle them.

Let's take on condos as an example. What makes many a condo project a claim looking for action? For the purposes of this exercise, here are possible causes:

> ➤ The architect's client is usually a developer who wants to design, build, sell, and get

out—all on a very tight budget. Profit is the developer's muse, not long-term quality.

➤ The architect may design or be responsible for the outer building and surrounding landscaping, while the interiors are completed by numerous other parties of varying levels of accomplishment. The multiple numbers and skill levels increase the likelihood of problems and complicate the determination of liability.

➤ The architect generally has no relationship with the ultimate users of the project and often has completed the design work long before the units are purchased. Therefore, there is little opportunity to discuss or resolve problems with users before they become significant.

➤ The developer usually wants the designs but not the designer. The architect is rarely hired for construction administration.

➤ During construction, the architect's designs are dumbed-down with lesser-quality substitutions being used.

➤ The condo is advertised as "deluxe" to people who can afford to buy, but not maintain, the project. None were involved in the design of the project, so they are not that committed to the building as they find it. They want what they think it should have been.

➤ A single mistake in a design that has been replicated throughout the complex can turn into multiple lawsuits.

➤ Condominiums, in particular, and residential projects, generally, are highly regulated in many jurisdictions, and liability limited or disclaimed in the contract with the developer may nonetheless be imposed on the architect by stringent state and local laws that vary from location to location.

Some of you reading this might be thinking the insurer was wise. Only a foolish architect would walk into this quagmire. Others of you might be thinking each of these causes can be managed through contract language or, better yet, by figuring out ways to maximize architect involvement so as to both help the developer make even more money and minimize the risk of a claim. How you decide and what you decide reflect your business goals and objectives, given your personal risk-o-meter.

Why am I going through all this? After all, this isn't a book about risk management. It's about negotiations. True enough, but let's remind ourselves: one purpose of a contract is to allow the parties to predetermine how they want to manage the risks inherent in doing business together. If you are to become an expert at negotiating contracts, you will need to develop the skill of reframing issues to find common ground. You can't develop elegant options to manage risks if you can't first see how to identify and classify them and then see creative ways to minimize them. With the four key concepts of exposure, capability, responsibility, and power and the five risk management options of take it, leave it, abate it, allocate it, and transfer it readily in mind, beefing up your skills at creative analysis and risk-management design will help you increase your negotiating flexibility.

The importance of developing those antennae and making friends with risk and reward cannot be underscored enough. Architects are living in both a changing practice and a changing business world. If you are doing big commercial projects or international projects of any size, you may find yourself being asked to share your designs on a dedicated Internet web site or project extranet that allows the owner and contractors and consultants to see what you're thinking and to affect your designs.

This is a new world, one that standard contract documents are just beginning to address. Read what one Fellow of the American College of Construction Lawyers, Howard Ashcraft, Esq., wrote in a paper prepared for the Fall 2000 meeting of the American Bar Association's Forum on the Construction Industry:

> The legal issues related to these changes (in the design paradigm) are largely being ignored. There are no efforts to prepare contract documents that reflect the parties' responsibilities in a collaborative, electronic-based environment. There are no efforts to amend professional registration requirements to accommodate the design participation of object designers. Few construction documents discuss the responsibilities for coordinating and maintaining Web-based documentation and none adjust the parties' risk allocation to reflect these new realities. Some construction documents are beginning to address the transfer of electronic files, but few adequately deal with the problems created by three-dimensional, object-oriented design, or Internet collaboration. (*New Paradigms for Design Professionals: New Issues for Construction Lawyers*, p. 8.)

You may be asking yourself, "Is techno-design any different from old-time, highly partnered manual design? Are the rules really changing that much?" No one knows, simply because of the newness of technology and of globalized practice. But one thing is clear: It is the rare architect indeed who will sit around doing nothing until the law catches up with reality. If there were ever a time to develop exposure-sensitive antennae, to learn how to analyze risk and reward probabilities well, to negotiate complex situations reasonably and prudently, yet flexibly, it is now—if only because, ten to one, the changing nature of practice will offer as many opportunities for increased rewards as it does occasions for concern. It is the assertive practitioner who reflects knowledge and know-how to the client with competence, candor, and concern who ultimately provides value. Let that practitioner be you.

Power and Leverage: How to Get It and Keep It

4

There is a story behind this title. After I wrote the chapter on negotiation for the twelfth edition of the AIA *Handbook*, I was invited to teach a session based on it at the next AIA Convention. "Architects don't read," explained my sponsor. "If you want this material to be used, you'll have to teach it face-to-face." So I developed a seminar to teach the chapter face-to-face. Only 30 people showed up. I was devastated. Later, I bemoaned my lack of drawing power to Boyce Appel, a successful training consultant. "Rename it," said he. "Call it 'Power and Leverage: How to Get It and Keep It.' People will come." I scoffed and did as I was told. The next time, 120 architects showed up.

There is a lesson here: *How* you communicate is as important as *what* you communicate. Expert negotiators know this. They use several techniques that make them expert. In this chapter, we will learn first about the process called *principled negotiation* that expert negotiators use. In the next chapter, we will explore their preparation techniques. In Chapter 6, we will discover the communication skills of expert negotiators, and in Chapter 7 we will see how they are used collaboratively. In Chapter 8, we will apply the lessons of all these chapters to actual owner-drafted contract language. But first, principled negotiation.

Negotiation: What Is It?

We now have a conceptual foundation from which we could start negotiating. In Chapter 2, we introduced research on claims prevention data and what it says about putting a successful project together. In Chapter 3, we learned about the law and how to translate those legal constructs into architecture. (We will learn more about how to *use* them in Chapter 8.) But a conceptual foundation alone is not enough. We need to know "Where are the windows?" and "Where are the doors?" and, most important of all, "How do you get in and out of them?" before we can start negotiating. In other words, we need to know the ins and outs of the negotiation process.

There is a massive amount of literature about "how to negotiate." A Google Internet search proved that—4,520,000 hits—more than 100 percent increase in six years. Overwhelming! And that probably doesn't include all the audiotapes you can listen to as you commute to work each day. Some of the material will teach you that negotiation is a verbal sit-down version of war, where the slyest, craftiest, most aggressive party wins. Others will teach you that, if you listen hard and try to make friends with the Other, everything will work out all right.

This chapter teaches you neither. Architecture is not a one-off deal where you will never see the Other again. Buildings take years to complete, so war is not an option. Nor is architecture a love-fest. Even at their best, design and construction are fraught with tension, usually creative, sometimes not. The stakes are too high, the enterprise too complex, the variations in participants' skills and perceptions too wide for it to be any other way. So let's start with the basics and build from there.

If it's not war and it's not a love-in, what is negotiation? At its core, the whole idea of negotiation is to get you and the person with whom you are negotiating from two places that are apart to one place—together. For all of you who are hoping that negotiation means no more confrontation, unfortunately it does not. *There has to be a conflict* for the two parties to need to negotiate. Think about it: If you and the Other agreed about everything, there would be nothing to negotiate. You would both be in the same place at the same time. You would have a deal. On the other hand, *there has to be a need*—some common ground—that creates a desire for accommodation, for the two parties to want to negotiate. If you and the Other had absolutely nothing in common and were in 100 percent disagreement, then you would have nothing to negotiate either.[1]

You have to have something in common to negotiate. Usually that something is a scarce item—an item that

---

[1] Instead, what you are doing is selling. You are trying to persuade the other person that what you have to offer is something that they want to "buy." Depending on the reasons and depth of disagreement, they may or may not buy. Expert sellers know this, so they spend a lot of time asking the prospective buyer questions, looking for buyer needs they can fill, thus creating that "something" in common.

one party has that the Other party wants. Without that scarcity, there would be no incentive to deal. Indeed, the more scarce the item, the more the Other needs that item, the greater the power and leverage its possessor will have in the negotiation.

An example: If you go to a meeting, and there are enough chairs for everyone, you don't have to negotiate who has a chair. But, if the room is several chairs short, then chairs become a scarce resource, and you must negotiate with the others who will sit and who will stand. In architecture, it is the scarcity of talent, expertise, time, money, budget, and more that puts a premium on negotiation and developing negotiation skills.

Power and Leverage: What's the Difference

I want to get these two concepts on the table right away, because architects are always telling me they have no power and leverage in negotiation. I say, bunk. You have power, and you have leverage. You have to distinguish between the two and understand both to appreciate how much of each you really have.

Take the concepts out of architecture. Imagine you're negotiating with children. Who has all the power in the room? You or the children? You do. You are a grownup. Grownups don't usually negotiate with children, and children know that. Who has all the leverage? Well, that depends. If the children are crying hysterically in a public space, you may have all the power in the world, but, I assure you, they have all the leverage.

Power, then, is formal. It is vested in your authority, whether that authority comes from your position or from your contractual or legal status. Leverage, on the other hand, is informal. It stems from within you or from the situation you and the Other are facing. And it gives you an advantage to influence the Other, to get the Other to agree to what you want.

Leverage is a moving target, if only because the Other's perceived needs and your ability to fill them can move also. One architect increased his leverage with a large Japanese prospective client by telling the client during their first meeting that his firm selected its clients carefully and did not work just for a commission. The prospective client did not want to lose face and spent time selling his needs to the architect.

But just as you can increase your leverage if you read the Other right, a misreading of the situation or your influence means you can lose that advantage. One architect obliterated his leverage by insisting owners competitively bid the project, even though he knew the owners didn't believe in competitive bidding and had already decided on the contractor they wanted for the project based on that contractor's qualities. The more the architect insisted competitive bidding was in the owners' interest, the more long-term leverage the architect lost.

So you bring power and leverage into a negotiating relationship, and you can acquire power and leverage through your conduct during the course of a relationship. But power and leverage have to be appreciated, respected, and maintained, else you can lose them on a moment's notice.

What gives most architects their power and leverage—at least in the beginning—is design scarcity. Owners don't have the talent, expertise, and skills architects have, and owners need them to accomplish their goals. The objectively (and subjectively) greater the architect's talent, expertise, and skills, especially the ability to envision and communicate a series of space and place solutions to the owner's business or personal needs, the greater the architect's power and leverage. The more routine the need or the solution, the more interchangeable the architect, and hence, the less power and leverage the architect has and can have.[2]

---

[2] The client's impact on the architect's power and leverage was brought home to me in a book I edited, entitled *Rethinking the Sales Force: Redefining Selling to Create and Capture Customer Value*, Rackham and DeVincentis (McGraw-Hill, 1999). The authors explain that increasingly today's buyers are looking for either transactional or consultative sellers, depending on their own needs and proclivities. Transactional sellers are often fungible and are valued for their ability to provide

So remember: Whether the Other is your client, a contractor, or your spouse, you have something the Other party doesn't, but wants, otherwise the person wouldn't be negotiating with you in the first place. The need for that something is the start of your common ground and the basis of your initial power and leverage. *Don't underestimate the power and leverage you have.* It is real. Don't throw it away.

Why Architects Fear Negotiation

Let's be honest: Lots of people fear negotiations, not just architects. And there are real reasons to feel anxious before you negotiate. There are usually stakes in negotiation, sometimes big ones. One management consultant to architects is known to say, "There's more money to be made or lost in the negotiating stage than at any other point in the entire process of getting and keeping a contract." How's that for anxiety-inducing?

My experience is that's not usually the case. First, it puts too much weight on negotiation, and the negotiation process is too fragile to support it. Second, I have been persuaded that *more is lost through the sales process than through the negotiation process.* You give away your power and leverage with the hope of getting the commission, and then you use the

---

commodity services fast and cheap. Consultative sellers, on the other hand, are valued for their ability to provide creative, dovetailed, strategic solutions to complex seller needs. While the conventional wisdom of the profession is that architects always provide consultative services, many owners don't have a need for those services. They have transactional needs and want the architect to perform and be paid accordingly—thus the angst of many architects today who only want or know how to provide consultative services.

negotiation process to try to regain the ground you gave up.

One large national architecture firm known for its negotiating expertise and high customer satisfaction did just that. Its principals wanted the project so much that their proposal implied they could deliver a multisite project using design-build, with them serving as prime. They had not *intended* their proposal to be interpreted that way, but they were selected, in part, because the client read it precisely that way. Negotiations struggled around the scope of their construction contract administration services. They didn't want to serve as prime and could not have done so even if they had wanted to. They didn't have the skills or the stomach to take on the risk, especially with that client. The client was very annoyed and ultimately chose to hire a CM to provide the services the client thought the architect had promised to deliver. Although a contract was finally eked out, with the firm doing limited construction administration services, the project was marked by hostility from then on.

From the architect's perspective, negotiation after a give-away-the-store, we-can-do-whatever-you-want sales process is asking for too much, too late. And it doesn't matter who makes the promise, if you end up being the negotiator. Because negotiating is such a visible process, because you have to go back to someone and say, "I made a deal" or "I lost," *your ego* is on the line. So the stakes to you are high: Failure cannot be hidden.

Also, researchers found that many architects are introverts, and many owners are extroverts. Couple that with the discomfort and fear of announcing that you lost the negotiation, and it is easy to understand

why many architects would rather sit out the negotiations dance. Introverts need and want time and
space to think before speaking. Extroverts rarely give
it to them, jumping in with a new thought whenever the thought hits their heads. No wonder some
architects loathe negotiating.

There may be yet another reason some architects
fear negotiations. It is a reason that first inched its
way into my brain in 1992, at the Summer Design-
Practice-Education Institute in Santa Fe, sponsored
by the AIA and the Association of Collegiate Schools
of Architecture (ACSA). There the dean of St. John's
College asked us to read Aristotle's *Nicomachean
Ethics* on the virtuous, the ethical man. We learned
that Aristotle differentiated among the idea, the act,
and the result, requiring all three to be separately
ethical for the man as a whole to be ethical. As in-
triguing as that was to the group, even more intrigu-
ing to me was the group's application of Aristotle to
architecture. Not one of the architects in the seminar could separate architecture into the three components. For them, their ideas, the design processes
they implemented, and the resulting buildings they
created were one thing: a reflection of themselves,
their essence. If that is the case for you, then negotiations may prove particularly daunting. Negotiations
require you to be able to separate people from problems, and ideas from acts and results. Learning to do
that may be your challenge.

But all these reasons are negative ways of looking at negotiation, and assertive practitioners strive
to take positive stances. So here is a positive way
to think about negotiations: *Negotiations give you the
time and the opportunity to forge realistic and shared expectations with the Other so that both of you can work*

effectively together. Let's keep that thought uppermost through the rest of this chapter.

Two Ways to Negotiate: Hard and Soft

The conventional wisdom is that there are two ways to negotiate—hard and soft. And there are people out there who are making a lot of money teaching you how to do it one way or the other way. In fact, one tape a friend gave me had the instructor explaining with pride how he knocked the price off used golf balls from $5 to $3, during an intense negotiation with an eight-year-old kid who had worked all day long retrieving them from the golf course. He was that hard a bargainer. Given that people still use those hard/soft terms and teach those hard/soft techniques, I am going to review them with you. Then I am going to give you an alternative tested by research and proven to work for those hoping to maintain strong, long-term working relations—the very kind to which most architects aspire.

Soft Negotiators

Soft negotiators negotiate as if both parties were linked together in friendship during the entire negotiating process. They are intent on maintaining that friendship while coming to agreement. Indeed, all their conduct is colored by these twin goals—friendship and agreement. How does the soft negotiator respond to the Other's demand for a concession? Viewing the request through the prism of friendship, and wanting to craft an agreement more than anything, the soft negotiator tries to find ways to accept the demanded concession. After all, the soft negotiator reasons, the Other is a friend, and friends don't make requests for concessions unless the request is truly important to them. Besides, friends don't hurt each other, so though the concession at first blush seems difficult or hurtful, I'll nevertheless try to accommodate it, as a friend is asking it of me.

This unending trust can backfire because it can hurt the project and, sometimes, the soft negotiator. Owners need the architect to share their expertise during negotiations. Without a substantive compass, soft negotiators can accede when the owner wants them to, even though the project needs them to stand firm. They may end up feeling liked, but they may lose the respect of the Other and their own self-respect in the process.

My favorite example of a soft negotiator came in a phone call I received when I was counsel to the AIA. The architect, who was from Tennessee, needed help negotiating a contract. "Here's my problem," he explained. "The school board I'm working for wants me to program the building, design it, do the CDs, get the permits, put it out for bid, and manage the bid negotiation process. Once they get the lowest bid, they then want to go for a bond for that amount of money. If the bond passes, *then* the school board wants to retain me to do the building. Until then, they want me to provide them free services. Can you think of any way I can ask for some payment for those services, just in case they don't get the bond?" I asked him what was stopping him from just asking outright that he be paid. "They'll ask somebody else to do the project," he explained. "And I really, really, *really* want the project." I pointed out he was not going to get paid unless if, if, if, if, if, and if all came true. "Why would you put yourself in that position?" He answered, "These are my friends." I said, "That's wonderful, sir, but if these are your friends, who are your enemies?"

So here we have a soft negotiator, a person who views the Other as friend and has as his primary goal coming to agreement so he can "do the project" for his friend. In the process, this architect deprived the school board of the reality of project formation, allowing them to have what they thought they wanted without making the financial and psychic commitments necessary to effect solid decision making. Can you imagine the problems the school board (and hence the architect) would face when reality hit them, assuming the bond ultimately passed?

You Don't Want Just to Do the Project

If there is one easy way to fritter away the power and leverage you have, it is to enter negotiations with one goal: getting the project. *Know your interests.* Even in a recession, you are not that desperate. You want more than just to do the project. What that "more" might be will differ by architect, but I venture to say most architects I know want a project that is good business, a project where they:

➤ Provide the client valued and valuable services

➤ End up with a happy client and a solid reference

➤ Do good design

➤ Manage the tensions of design and construction well

➤ Make money or at least break even (or bring in new business as a result of the consciously taken loss-leader project)

➤ Have a claims-free experience

➤ Feel ethical about the entire experience

In other words, if you are like the architects I know, you are not a Johnny-one-note. You enter negotiations with many interests and the hope that you will achieve most, if not all, of them.

Hard Negotiators

Hard negotiators enter into negotiations very differently. They look at the participants as adversaries. In their world-view, if one side wins, the other side loses, and they intend to be the winner. For them, the goal is not an agreement. Friendship is not the issue. Winning the war is. They want to win, even if the cost of winning is an unworkable agreement or no agreement at all. Accordingly, while soft negotiators make concessions in order to win the Other's friendship and keep the project, hard negotiators demand concessions as part of getting an agreement. The more easily they get concessions, the more they want. In fact, the hard negotiator will take a position, regardless of its value, and stick to it in order to win. Many hard negotiators will use guile or threats to make things go their way. ("There are 10 architects willing to sign this agreement, and, if you aren't willing, I'll go to one of them."[3]) Hard negotiators project their own conduct onto others, so they have a tendency not to trust the Other, even when they should. As a result of their winner-take-all-approach, hard negotiators get reputations for being difficult.

To summarize: A soft negotiator is soft on the Other and even soft on the project. "Look, all I want to do is the project. Just tell me what you want me to do, and I'll try to find a way to agree to it." The hard negotiator is hard on the Other and often hard on the project. "Ah, forget the project. All I want to do is win. It's my way or no way." Yet, if you think about it, both have one thing in

---

[3] How many times have you heard that? It could be a dirty trick to make you accede when you shouldn't, but it could be the truth. Figuring out which is one of the challenges of the negotiation dance.

common: Their approach makes no dent, or the wrong dent, on the negotiation problem that is the focus of their attention. And that is to produce a quality and affordable project that meets client needs. Put them up against each other in light of what we learned about front-end alignment in Chapter 2, and we have a catastrophe in the making.

Another Way of Negotiating: Principled

There has to be a better way. There is. It's called *principled negotiation*, and it was developed way back in the late 1970s by the Harvard Negotiation Project, based on its own research and that of others. Principled negotiation says that there is a better way of negotiating. You don't have to be a hard negotiator. You don't have to be a soft negotiator. You can be a principled negotiator. You can negotiate on the *merits*.

How does it work? At its core, principled negotiation views the Other not as a friend nor as an adversary, but as a joint problem solver. Often called *interest-based negotiation*, principled negotiation asks both parties to set aside their positions and explore their interests, developing together elegant options for mutual gain. Because positions do not rule—interests do—principled negotiation urges the parties to seek and use objective standards whenever they get stuck.[4] It exhorts the parties to keep their

---

[4] Of course, if both sides are given a choice between two conflicting yet objective standards, each side will pick the set that best meets their interests and try to show how their standards are more appropriate for the situation. Why not?

eyes on the problem while they are negotiating and address issues on the merits, so that any resolution that does occur will solve the problem, meet the interests of both parties, and last. It also urges the parties to develop, outside of the negotiation, a Best Alternative To a Negotiated Agreement (BATNA) so each party will have freedom to choose to agree in the negotiation.

With this approach, you can take your personality, with all its strengths and weaknesses, off the negotiation table and focus on the problem. As you learn to do it well, you should find that, when you and the Other stop looking at each other as friends or as adversaries and start looking at each other as co–problem solvers, *both* of you will want to work together to solve the problem—and the problem will be solved.

If you're neither friends nor enemies, how do you relate to the Other? Do you have to trust the Other for principled negotiation to work? The research on negotiation suggests no, although appropriate trusting and being trusted make the negotiation process a lot less contentious, and even fun. I say, "appropriate trusting" because trusting is a question of choice, and sometimes we all make bad choices.

Trust Is a Double-Edged Sword

While we'll learn more about how expert negotiators gain and give trust in Chapter 5, some discussion of trust is necessary here to understand its role in principled negotiation.

One of the key attributes of principled negotiation is that you do *not* have to trust the Other. Please don't misunderstand me. Trust—that kind of unquestioning reliance and understanding that comes from closely working well together for a shared goal and objective—is critical for having an effective project. For everyone involved in the project, trust makes the project fun. It makes it easier. It makes it faster. It makes the project cheaper. But you can work effectively through principled negotiation with persons who do not trust you and persons you do not trust.

Let me share a brief story: I once worked for an organization where there was one person nobody trusted because that person always looked out for himself first and foremost. I wondered aloud, "How can you *not* trust him? You know he's going to look out for himself first and foremost. So you can *always* trust him—always." Think about it.

Remember, trust is a question of choice. You choose to trust people. They choose to trust you. You can build trust. You can destroy trust. And you can give the Other opportunities to prove to you they are worthy of your trust.

The easiest way to build trust is by being trustworthy. Research conducted by Huthwaite, Inc., a negotiation and sales performance consulting firm, found that, the more professionals proved themselves to be *concerned*, *candid*, and *competent*, the more the client judged them to be trustworthy. You can use those three components as guides for building trust.

➤ *You can build trust in little ways.* You say you're going to be there at 9:00 o'clock in the morning? Be there at 9:00 o'clock in the morning.

➤ *You can build trust in big ways.* As soon as you know something's going to go against client expectations, you can call and tell your client about the changed situation.

➤ *You can build trust in bigger ways.* If the client is concerned about something, you can be concerned about that something, too.

In other words, choose to build trust as much as you choose to trust and expect to be trusted. Let your clients see you working to address their concerns. Give them a reason, before and after you get the commission, to build on the common ground that is there for you both. In this way, the two of you can come to rely on each other's judgment—and rightly so.

That's a very different way of thinking. Not hard. Not soft. Principled. *On the merits.* And for anyone who is an architect, that is a great way of thinking. What were you trained to do in school? Solve problems. And how does the profession define itself? Architects are problem solvers. So principled negotiation is your cup of tea. *The key skill a negotiator needs is the willingness and the capacity to solve problems,* and *that's what you do every day.* So your goal doesn't have to be agreement or victory. Instead, your goal is to work with the Other to solve the problem.

The wisdom of this approach was brought home to me at a gathering in the mid-1990s attended by Itamar Rabinovich, then Israel's ambassador to the United States and chief negotiator with Syria on a prospective peace accord. "Can you win an agreement with Syria for peace?" he was asked. The ambassador answered, "You know, winning is not my goal. My goal is to develop an agreement that will solve the problems between our two countries, produce a lasting peace, and still be in the interests of my country and its people." If the Israeli ambassador could define a successful agreement that way, when the stakes were World War III, then certainly, I thought to myself, architects and their lawyers can define success that way when just a project or a contract is involved. *And isn't that what we are seeking when we negotiate—a wise outcome, efficiently produced, and effective between and for the parties?* That is the goal—an outcome that will resolve the problem and will stick.

The differences between these three types of negotiation are summarized in Table 4.1.

How Principled Negotiation Works

Every negotiation is different. Each has its own cadence, its own pace, depending on the needs of and demands on the parties. So I cannot tell you, no one can, that first you always do this, and then you always do that. There is, however, research on negotiating that you can use to prepare for, and be effective at, a negotiating session.

Table 4.1

Three Types of Negotiation

Soft	Hard	Principled
Participants are friends.	Participants are adversaries.	Participants are problem solvers.
The goal is agreement.	The goal is victory.	The goal is a wise outcome reached efficiently and amicably.
Make concessions to cultivate relationship.	Demand concessions as the price of relationship.	Separate people from the problem.
Be soft on the people and on the problem.	Be hard on the people and on the problem.	Be soft on the people, hard on the problem.
Trust others.	Distrust others.	Proceed independent of trust.
Change your position readily; make offers.	Dig in to your position; make threats.	Focus on interests, not on positions.
Accept one-sided losses to reach agreement.	Demand one-sided gains as the price of agreement.	Create options for mutual gain.
Insist on agreement; yield to get it.	Insist on your position; apply pressure to get it.	Insist on using objective criteria; yield only to principle.
Disclose your bottom line.	Mislead about your bottom line.	Avoid having a bottom line.

Now if you have read a good deal on negotiation, you know that the advice usually given starts with "Focus on the problem," and that is very good advice. But I have been around architects a very long time, and many of them have a few discrete weaknesses in negotiation that other professionals do not share quite as vividly. As this book is for architects, the advice has been fine-tuned for architects. So before we discuss how to engage in principled negotiation, there are some "presteps" you may want to take, if only because, by and large, the architects I have worked with wish they had.

Prestep I: Know Your Interests

You can learn to be an effective negotiator on the merits, but you have to master the difference between interests and positions first. To begin, let's take it out of architecture completely. You are the head of your family, which consists of you, your spouse, and three children. You have one inviolate rule in your family, one that you set yourself: On Sunday at noon the family sits down together for a weekly, family-only lunch. It is a rule that no one questions. Everyone enjoys the family hour, even the children. It all works perfectly until your eldest is 14 years old. She now has a life of her own, and, for the very first time, that life doesn't involve you on a certain Sunday at noon. She has some important peer event to go to with her friends, and she is bent on getting there. It is an event you would normally support, but at noon on Sunday? Not a chance.

So ask yourself the following questions and use the gray spaces for your answers.

What is your position?

Sunday lunch on Sunday @ noon = rule + she knows this.

What is her position?

Happens every week, growing up — hanging w/ friends instead

If you answered that your position is that she has to join you at family lunch, and her position is that she has to be with her friends at that time, you got it right. And if the two of you negotiate from there, assuming your daughter is a typical teenager, you may still be negotiating a week later (or fighting or not talking to each other—you know the drill). If one side wins, by definition, the other side loses.

Principled negotiation says, *Don't argue over positions*. Go behind each other's position and *explore your respective interests*. Then you can develop enticing options to meet the critical interests of you both. Sound easy? It may or may not be easy, depending on the circumstances. Try it out on our teenager.

What are your interests, as a parent?

Spending time as family, communication, not having kid hate me, traditions

---

What are her interests?

Making friends/social life

Did you have trouble trying to discern the daughter's interests? You might very well have, not only because interests and positions may be new concepts for you, but because you don't have a real person in front of you whom you can question. You had to guess to answer the question. To do that, you may have found yourself projecting your teenage experience onto what you think a girl teenager would be thinking, feeling, wanting, needing that might affect her negotiating stance. As smart as you may be now, as insightful, as empathetic, as experienced, whatever, you probably realized that you can project wrong. *You are not the Other.*

This point is not an aside. I want you to remember this exercise, because you are no better at imagining what motivates your client than you are at trying to figure out what's driving your teenager—no matter how insightful or experienced you may be. You may have pretty good instincts about this stuff, but you have to ask—openly. You have to listen—actively. And then, you have to deal with what was actually said, rather than ignoring it or wishing that it was something different or hoping that it will change over time.

Now back to the exercise. These are the interests that I came up with.

Your Interests

- You want family time.
- You want your daughter to respect your authority.
- You want her to enjoy being a part of the family.
- You want her to want to be a part of the family.
- You want her to learn how to exercise judgment, set priorities, make trade-offs.
- You want to have her, and help her, grow up to be a person both you and she are proud of.
- You want her to be happy.

Her Interests

- Your daughter wants to be accepted by her peers as one of them.

- She wants to be independent of the family.
- She wants to be part of the family.
- She wants you to accept her as an independent, nearly grown-up woman worthy of pride and admiration.
- She wants you to accept her authority over her own life.
- She wants you to set appropriate boundaries that allow her freedom and security.
- She wants to be happy.

Do you see how much more complicated *and* easy the negotiation dance becomes when you focus on interests? Complicated, because people are complicated. They are inconsistent, driven, ambivalent, and ambiguous as to their true motivation. They may not know where their interests truly lie. The architect in Tennessee who wouldn't confront his school board friends certainly didn't. Getting the project and inviting bankruptcy was no great deal, yet he wanted to figure out how he could swing it.

But do you see how knowing each other's interests also makes negotiations easy? Look how much the parent and daughter have in common. Both want to maintain the family and their respected and respective positions in it. Both want the daughter to feel loved. Both want her to be happy. Both want her to act in such a way that everyone is proud of her. Do the parent and daughter have to hold to their respective positions to accomplish these shared interests? No; in fact, *they may even have to let go of their positions to achieve those interests.* A 5:00 P.M. Sunday family dinner might be just the elegant option that will permit everyone to win.

And that is where the fun of negotiations begins—and the challenge. Once you understand your interests and those of the Other better, you can then work together to solve the problem that brought you to the negotiating table in the first place.

Prestep II: Understand the Nature of the Owner's Problem as the Owner Is Experiencing It

In architecture school, you learn how to search out an owner's design needs and design to them. You learn about place and parti, theory and practice, and how to go about integrating them into an aesthetically pleasing whole full of commodity, firmness, and delight. When you leave school, your client is your employer, who demands of you what your teachers did, but at a higher level and a faster pace—for money. After three years of internship, you have your skills down pat. When you start your own firm, you are ready to design for your client just as you were taught and so carefully learned.

But that's not what today's owner wants. What you learned in school is just the bare minimum that the owner expects—and rightfully so—from anyone who is licensed to practice architecture. Today's owner wants more, much more, and your second negotiation prestep is finding out what that "more" is.

When owners call you to design them a building, the owners do not think for one minute they are asking you to solve just a design problem for them. On the contrary, they are calling you because they have a personal or business problem they think a building will help them solve. If you address their self-stated building issues as a design challenge, you will find yourself missing the mark. This came home to me big time during a partnering meeting on a commercial building my husband needed designed for his company. The contractor asked him this series of questions: "What business problem led you to decide you needed a new building? Who do you want it to please most—yourself? Your employees? Your clients?" My husband tussled with that one and finally decided: his clients. The contractor continued, "Tell me about your clients. What type of people are they? What kind of facility will they find most comfortable? Would it help your bottom line if the building also gave you a measurable marketing advantage?" These questions warmed us to the contractor immediately. They should have been asked by the architect, who clearly did not know to ask them.

Your Deductible vs. Their Bottom Line: Where Do Your Interests Really Lie?

It has always amazed me that architects allow insurance companies—and, for that matter, lawyers—to have so much power over their thinking. For lawyers and brokers, because of all their learning, architects suddenly suspend judgment.

I remember way back in the '80s when Limits of Liability was being pushed on architects. I never got it. Why buy a $1 million insurance policy with a $50,000 deductible, pay the premium for a $1 million insurance policy with a $50,000 deductible, and limit your liability to $50,000? Whom are you protecting? Certainly not yourself. Under the insurance policy, your firm's maximum exposure most probably is only $50,000, assuming that that is your deductible. (I know, firms worry about being sued for monies in excess of their policy limits, and it can happen. But it is so rare for anyone to bother suing for excess monies that insurers of architects and engineers can count the cases on their hands.) For some of your clients, that $50,000 ceiling will be your floor. Extracting from them a limit of liability arguably guarantees up front that they'll find a reason for you to cough up your deductible. So, aren't you really just protecting the insurance carrier and the

(*continues*)

(continued)

$950,000 worth of limits they sold you—and the premium you gave them—hoping you will cap their exposure at $50,000? Am I missing something? Carriers get rich. Where does that leave you?

And look what limiting liability has done to your practice, your reputations your fees. "Architects only look out for themselves." "Architects don't take risks." "I'm a construction manager [you fill in the blank—interior designer, design-builder—it doesn't matter]. I'll take care of you better than any architect will." The number of insurance companies jumping into the A/E market has grown. The architect's world has gotten smaller—all for just a 10 percent credit savings in premium. And that doesn't take into account all the goodwill you lose with some clients when you argue for the insurer's language. *Clients want you to be concerned about them—not about you,* and when you ask a client to limit your liability, you are advertising: I care only about me. Nor does it take into account the egregious indemnification agreements owners have responded with, to counter Limits of Liability language.

If your next-door neighbors ask you to "just run by and check out the house" that their son Johnny wants to buy, sure, limit your liability. Risk and reward are too disproportionate, and, unless you have x-ray vision and can see through wallboard, there is no way to make the "run by" otherwise. When you are asked to design a nuclear power plant, feel free. For most architects, there are just too many unknowns to make the risk reasonable. But for anything else in between, ask yourself: Where do my interests truly lie?

To help you prepare for the next time you have a client call, list the business and personal questions you need to ask, to be certain that you understand the nature of the client's personal or business dilemmas as the client is experiencing them. Clients will appreciate your asking, but more important, they will need to hear you focus your questions on *their* problems and *their* needs, confirming to them that they selected the right architect. And when you hear the answers, don't translate them on the spot into design challenges. You can do that later in the quiet of your studio. Deal with them as if they were *your* business or personal problems. Ask your client enough well-targeted and thought-out questions so that both of you understand their implications for your client and where the greatest payoff can be had. Preparing these questions is hard work. You cannot wing it, but the owner will be grateful that you know enough and care enough to ask and listen.[5] And in that process, you will prove yourself to be the candid, competent, concerned professional the client is right to trust.

Prestep III: Develop Your BATNA

I once was offered a job and asked a good friend whether I should take it. "What are your options?" he asked. I said I had none. "Without an alternative, a choice, a fallback position, I don't know what to advise you. You need to build yourself a BATNA." Thus, I was introduced to the concept of a "**B**est **A**lternative **T**o a **N**egotiated **A**greement."

Have you ever walked into a negotiation thinking that if you don't win this one, you'll lose everything? If you have, you probably entered into the negotiation without having a BATNA, too. A BATNA is a well-reasoned, acceptable, alternative course of action *with someone else*, should you fail to achieve a negotiated agreement with the Other. Having an enticing BATNA gives you a reason not to settle for just any deal. It also gives you the leverage you need to negotiate freely. In other words, without a strong BATNA backing you—a BATNA that

---

[5] *SPIN®Selling* by Neil Rackham (New York: McGraw-Hill, Inc., 1998) will walk you through the process step by step, teaching you about *Situation Questions, Problem Questions, Implication Questions*, and *Need-Payoff Questions* and how to make them work for both you and your clients, raising your value in your clients' eyes in the process.

you would willingly accept instead of a negotiated bad deal—you give yourself no options. Without a BATNA, at best you slide into being a soft negotiator, thus reducing the flexibility you need to keep your eye on the problem. At worst you hand over what leverage you have to the Other, depriving yourself of the freedom to walk comfortably away from a bad deal.

Why deprive yourself of leverage when you could deprive the Other of it by having a strong BATNA? All you need is *one solid alternative* to have the freedom to walk away from a bad deal or push for a good one. Now, what your BATNA should be is up to you and will vary depending on your personal practice and business goals. If it is to serve you as a true alternative to a negotiated agreement, you will have to spend substantial amounts of energy designing one. Indeed, you may find yourself opting out of a negotiation not because you are losing, but because your BATNA is winning.

When You Feel You Really Have No Choice

If you entered practice in the 1990s, you have never experienced a widespread construction recession, though you may be starting to feel one now. Historically, they have been a fact of design life. During recessions, designing solid BATNAs is even more important and will require you to plumb the depths of your creativity. Remember, even when you think you have no options, you do have choice. Here's a story:

A pair of engineers was in Europe to negotiate a contract with a major international company. Unfortunately for their firm and for the two engineers, the engineers knew that, if they did not get the contract, the firm was going to go under. The pressure on those engineers to get that contract was enormous. They were doing all the preparation they could think of, but they were still beside themselves with anxiety because they knew they had to win. The afternoon before the negotiation, they were still reviewing their presentation just one more time. The CEO of the company came into the conference room to announce, "Guys, go home. We just got another contract. Whatever happens tomorrow is neither here nor there. We're going to be alive, even if you don't end up with an agreement. You go do your best. It would be great to have two projects, but we're going to do fine." So they went home. They went to sleep, rested, woke up the next morning, did a bang-up job of negotiating, and they got a great contract—much to the relief of the CEO, who knew that if they didn't get that contract, the company was going to go under.

The point of the story is this: In their minds, those engineers finally had a BATNA. And that BATNA, and that BATNA alone, freed them to concentrate solely on the negotiation problem. So what you have to do for yourself is be your own CEO and say, "You know, if you don't get this project, that's okay. Life is still going to go on. Work for an agreement if you can get one, but keep your interests foremost in your mind, as well as the interests of the Other, and you'll have a better chance of coming to agreement."

Now on to principled negotiations.

How to Negotiate on the Merits

Just to build common ground, let us remember together the goal of principled negotiation: a wise outcome, efficiently produced and effective between and for the parties. That is the goal: an outcome that will resolve the problem and will stick. How do you get there? *Focus on the problem and how to solve it.*

It can't be said enough: If principled negotiation is at its essence creative problem solving, *you have to focus your eyes on the problem—not on the win.* As information is power, the person with the deepest understanding of the problem and the widest gamut of possible solutions will be the one potentially to hold the most sway at the table. Usually, that's the owner. You may know more about architecture, but owners know more about why they need an architect, what they hope to get out of the building after you are long gone, and what challenges are limiting their goals and aspirations. Unless you learn what they know, you may be marshaling your expertise to focus on the wrong problem. If you've done your homework well, you know what your interests are before you walk into the room. If you have done your homework superbly well, you know a good deal about the owner's problems and interests, and long-range goals for the project. If you don't, relax. Ask, and concentrate your energies on understanding the problem as the owner is experiencing it.

This focus on the problem logically and inevitably will change the nature of your negotiations. No longer will you look at the person facing you as the *barrier*. Instead you will steer yourself to start thinking of the Other as the joint *carrier* of the possible solution.

Separate the People from the Problem

If my earlier observation about some architects being unable to separate themselves from the idea, the act, and the results of design applies to you, you may also have difficulty separating yourself (and the Other) from the negotiation process. That's a challenge many architects face. But because taking yourself out of the process takes you out of the hot seat, learning how to separate is important. You want to keep yourself independent of the negotiation process, for with that separateness comes freedom. You will find yourself freer to listen, to think, and to decide how and when you want to react. Just as important, by your conduct you create an atmosphere that frees the Other to act similarly.

Now, no one can control the conduct and thoughts of another. You are in charge only of yourself, which is why it's so important to separate yourself from the negotiation process. How do you do that? By keeping yourself unerringly focused on the negotiation problem. That will save you from personalizing everything. Instead of responding defensively or aggressively from your personal perspective, you will find yourself asking, "How does this solve the problem?" By evaluating the Other's statements in the light of the problem, you will no longer have to feel personally attacked. Nor should you feel the need to attack. Instead, you need only to refocus the Other on the problem at hand. So when the client says, "This proposal is way too expensive," you don't get into arm-wrestling about whether you are worth your fees. You don't argue value in any way. Instead, the issue becomes the nature, depth, and urgency of the owner's problem, the resulting project scope, budget, staffing, timing, quality—all problems to be rationally discussed and mutually resolved.

To keep your problem orientation, it may help to remind yourself that the goal is not to win over the Other, *but to win the Other over*. This gives you and the Other permission to cease looking at each other as either adversaries or friends, but instead as two people, albeit with disparate interests, who are in it together.

Do not bargain over positions. Focus on meeting each other's interests instead. Negotiating over positions usually ends a negotiation before it begins. The owner wants one thing; you, another. If you both stick to your guns, both of you get shot. If you both give in just to avoid the confrontation, more likely than not, you end up fighting about something else in its stead, down the road. Either way, you both miss the opportunity to build the relationship and the common ground you will need to get you through the project successfully.

Once you get the hang of interest-based negotiations, don't be surprised if you no longer change your position easily or quickly or demand that the Other change theirs. Expect instead that you will focus on the problem and on building common ground even as you look out for your interests and the Other looks out for theirs.

Knowing your interests alone will make a big difference. It will help even more to remember that, if you and the Other each fight for your own position, neither of you has any place to go. Working together to solve the problem, while achieving the interests that are most important to you both, will give everyone a greater chance of a negotiated success.

Luckily, one thing that is in your interests is usually in the interests of everybody else. Everyone on the construction site—the owner, the architect, the engineers, and the contractor—wants a project that is on time, on budget, profitable, and without claims. So you have something in common with the Other every time you enter a negotiation—no matter who the "Other" is.

How do you focus on interests? We'll learn more in the next chapters, but for now let this suffice: Suppose someone comes up with an idea that may or may not make sense to you. Instead of saying "no" to the other person, you ask, "How does that meet your interests? How does that help the project? How does that solve the problem?" And you listen hard to the answer. In turn, you ask yourself that, too: "Is their idea in my interests? How is it going to help solve the problem that we're facing?" With your analysis done and shared, you both have somewhere new to go.

If You Put Your Feet in Concrete, All You Can Do Is Break

I teach negotiation for lawyers with the American Law Institute-American Bar Association. One day, the general counsel of a very large engineering firm asked to talk to me privately. He was at odds with a new client over

---

insurance. The client wanted $5 million dedicated insurance to cover his project. The firm wanted to cap its exposure by inserting the words "up to." The argument had been going on for weeks. I asked, "If I remember your firm correctly, don't you have at least $10 million of coverage?" "More," he said. "We just don't want our client to feel the coverage is his. That's why we are insisting on the words 'up to.' That way, if we have paid a $1 million claim to someone else, this client will have access only to the remaining $4 mil."

Can't you hear the concrete cracking? Wouldn't it have been easier and savvier to say to the client, "My broker is so good he can help us buy a dedicated project insurance policy just for your project. Let me have him call you." That way, one position-based argument could have been utterly avoided. As important, the engineering firm, by offering an empowering solution to the client's need, could have proved its concern and commitment to serve—regardless of whether the owner chose to buy the project policy or not. So, instead of seizing the opportunity as one to build trust, the firm whittled trust away. Sad, isn't it?

Make Your Own Interests Known

A lawyer friend of mine represented a major American museum intent on building a new signature building. The architect they retained was as talented as he was famous. The lawyer came to me with a problem. The architect designed a moving roof that undulated with the sun, the light, the wind, and the time of day. He was afraid it would collapse. He wanted to buy insurance that would cover the museum in the case of catastrophe, and wondered where he could buy it at an affordable cost. As much as he had looked, he couldn't find any. "Why would you jump to an insurance solution?" I asked. "Wouldn't it be easier to tell the architect your fears, your interests, and have the architect address them?" "Oh, no," he said. "This architect is so special, we would lose him if we confronted him. And the museum has made clear that I would lose it as a client if the architect bolted."

Ah, said I to myself. Even good lawyers confuse interests and positions. Even good lawyers fail to recognize that *for empathy to succeed, you need a balanced amount of assertiveness.* Looking out for the feelings of the architect without looking out for the interests of his client would condemn whatever agreement resulted from the negotiation to a high risk of failure.

Had the lawyer been comfortable with the two concepts of empathy and assertiveness and the need for a balanced use of them both, he would have seized the problem as an opportunity to explore with his client and the architect lots of ways to highlight the museum other than some future headline of gloom. Is there a lesson here? Even good lawyers box themselves into the corner and miss the opportunity negotiation provides to deliver unique services that endear them to their clients.

What can architects learn from this vignette? Knowing the attorney, I can tell you that here the lawyer had confused being assertive with being aggressive and had therefore cornered himself into silence. He just could not see himself projecting an idea or raising an issue with the client and the architect quietly and solidly and in such a way that they both would see the *issue* as the issue, and not see the lawyer's concern as the issue. He expected to be blown out of the water the second he suggested that there might be a problem needing attention.

What a terrible position he put himself and his client in, all by thinking that "good service" required only his empathy and the unthinking accomplishment of the client's goal. Assertive practice for all professionals requires you to know and communicate what you need to be effective, as much as it requires you to have the empathy to hear and appreciate what the Other needs to be effective.

If knowing your own interests is the first step to increasing your power and leverage at the negotiation table, and communicating them is the second,[6] why then do people keep their interests secret? There are at least three reasons. First, many people, like my lawyer friend, fail to realize that effective negotiations require the parties to be as assertive as they are empathetic. The Other cannot read your mind any more than you can read the Other's. Whether through questions or statements, if you do not make your interests clear, they cannot be addressed. Empathy and assertive practice go hand in hand. Only together can negotiations, effective design, and solid practice succeed.

Second, many people keep their interests secret because they get interests and positions confused, and thus they fail to see alternative ways to get what they want. Too often for them, the position that started out as a goal becomes an obstacle-course wall that no one can clear. Had they understood how their interests related to their positions—if indeed they did—they could have conveyed their positions with enough information about their interests to help the Other understand where they were coming

---

[6] You will learn in Chapter 6 that how you convey that information is just as important as the information you convey. Suffice it to say, for the time being, that your asking questions often can bring you and the Other greater understanding than your merely giving answers, because questions allow the Other to noodle through the problem and own the conclusion.

from and figure out how to meet them, given the Other's own interests.[7]

Finally, sometimes people keep their interests secret because they are afraid the Other may use the information against them. In so doing, they deprive themselves of the chance of having their interests met, as no one has the capacity or the incentive to meet an unknown need. Better, had they conveyed the fact of the interest to the Other, keeping the intensity of the interest and the priority of the interest to themselves, there would at least be some chance their needs would be met.

When Stuck, Look Outside for Objective Criteria

Principled negotiation teaches this: Concentrate on the merits of the proposal, not the mettle of the parties. Be open to reason but closed to threats. The easiest way to do this is to look outside the argument to objective criteria that are mutually respected and independent of each party's will.

Feel free to insist on this. While each of you will probably seek out objective criteria most supportive of your interests, the very process of searching out objective criteria and discussing them will free you both to rethink the problem. Does this criterion really apply to our situation? What does it tell us

---

[7] This confusing positions and interests makes it harder to listen to alternatives and to develop them. Even if a party can hear the ideas of the Other as a possibility, they may not be able to decide how to react, if they have no "interest meter" against which to evaluate new information. Accordingly, they may be too quick to set aside good ideas that differ from their position, rejecting them out of hand because it seems the safest thing to do at the time. Thus, they deprive themselves of the resiliency that comes from having figured out their own interests first and the chance to build common ground.

about the nature of the problem facing us? Possible solutions? How can we use them to advance both our interests?

The Air Outside Is Always Cleaner

I had a client who had commissioned a building that included deep-well geothermal heating. The general contractor believed that the probable cost would be about 20 percent higher than the price of conventional heating. The client said okay, and they broke ground. When the subcontractor sent him a bill charging 45 percent more than the cost of a conventional heating system, the client came to me ready to sue for extortion. I set up a meeting instead. Fortunately for all, the subcontractor came armed with actual cost figures not only for the client's site but also for two similar installations nearby that had been put in by a second contractor. He also brought a series of articles, some from the popular press, some from the trade press, on the cost and benefit of geothermal systems. These objective facts prevented an acrimonious argument and one unnecessary lawsuit.

Insisting on using nonpartisan objective criteria also helps when you get stuck. You do that routinely when you compare owner-generated contract language to the AIA standard agreements. You do that when you compare owner and contractor conduct to the general conditions that govern the project. In both these cases, the use of outside objective criteria allows the parties to depersonalize their arguments and maintain a focus on merit interests, and the good of the project.

Develop Options for Mutual Gain

The premise of principled negotiation is that, when facing a problem of consequence to two parties, two heads are bigger and better than one. The challenge of figuring out how to meet your interests *and* their interests requires both players to hunker down, stay the adversarial games, and create options together so enticing that they meet the interests of two disparate parties in special and appropriate ways. In that way, everybody gains. After all, why argue about the size of a slice of pie when you can make the pie bigger?

Developing enticing options is no mean trick. You have to know more about the Other and the Other's problem than you might suspect, or you risk developing options that have no resonance for the Other, just for you. One way to acquire working knowledge of the Other is brainstorming. You both toss out options that you think might work. You then collaborate, building on each other's options until the best ones belong to you both. Selecting the very best of the options becomes an easier task because, in the process of brainstorming, you also have been building understanding and consensus.

Designing an Elegant Option

My husband and I rarely disagree on design, but there is one fundamental issue on which we are far apart. He loves L-shaped buildings and also very long, what I call barracks, buildings. (What can I say? He was born British.) I don't. We had commissioned two very talented architects, Elizabeth Reader, AIA, and Charles Swartz, AIA, to renovate and extend a late 1800s farmhouse on our property. Their preliminary sketches included an L-shaped building, which, naturally, my husband loved and I (rightly so) did not. My solution of offshoots felt too boxy for my husband's tastes. The two architects had to face two owners with radically different ideas of taste.

When the four of us worked together to generate more enticing options, Beth and Chuck came up with a design we all loved: a building canted at a 20-degree angle, telescoping from the original building so that the designed building looked as if it had grown naturally out of the ground. As a result, we had two happy owners who were delighted with their architects.

There You Have It: Principled Negotiation

With a solid understanding of your interests and the client's problem, entering into negotiations should not be difficult, but if you still have trepidations, let me alleviate them for you. Let's reiterate our definition of principled negotiation: *Principled negotiation is the design of enticing options that meet critical interests of disparate parties in special and appropriate ways.* Would you buy that definition? Most probably you would, because its essence is problem solving, its process is collaborative, and its result is positive for both parties.

But I submit there is another reason principled negotiation will work for you. Read the definition again. Isn't it also the definition of good design? And isn't the only real difference between the two processes the fact that design communicates through images, and negotiation through words? Now, I tease that, for some architects, English is a second language, but if you think about it, if you can communicate to the Other in the design world, certainly you can do it in the practice world. So why fear negotiation? There's no reason to. Negotiation at its essence is just another form of creative design. Go for it.

Preparation Tips

5

We now have a negotiation process under our belt, but that is still not enough. We next need a method to help us prepare so we can make maximum use of that process. Fortunately, we are not in the dark on this one. The way expert negotiators function has been studied by Huthwaite Research Group.[1]

Let me share with you what Huthwaite meant by "expert negotiators." (By the way, I use the terms "expert" and "skilled" interchangeably throughout this chapter, when describing the exemplary negotiators studied by Huthwaite.) To be classified as "expert," negotiators had to share three characteristics:

- ➤ They had to have a track record of reaching agreements.

- ➤ They had to have a track record of their agreements being implemented successfully.

---

[1] For access to the published data, read *The Behavior of Successful Negotiators* by Neil Rackham (Huthwaite Research Group: England, 1975).

➤ They had to have a track record of the Other being willing to negotiate with them again.

In other words, Huthwaite was looking for people who, time after time, successfully resolved their principals' long-term and short-term problems through negotiation and in such a way that the Other was willing to work with them again.

That is a very high bar that Huthwaite set for the expert negotiator. An "average" negotiator, by contrast, shared two out of these three characteristics. In other words, in measuring the performance of negotiators, Huthwaite was comparing the experts to people most outside observers would label as reasonably good negotiators. No bad negotiator's performance was studied. No one-off negotiator was evaluated—that is, a person who will never have to deal with the Other again after the negotiation. Rather, Huthwaite focused on evaluating negotiators who, like architects, are retained to solve problems and maintain, if not foster, ongoing relationships in professional settings.

In this chapter, we are going to learn how expert negotiators prepare for negotiation. In Chapter 6 we will learn how they communicate during the negotiation, and in Chapter 7 we will learn how they collaborate with other team members. After that, we will be in a better position in Chapter 8 to negotiate owner-drafted contract language.

Who Prepares More?

Let's start at the very beginning. Who do you think spends more time preparing for a negotiation, the expert negotiator or the average negotiator? Would you be surprised if I told you they both spend a considerable amount of time and the *same overall amount* of time preparing? There is a difference, though: They spend their time differently.

Average negotiators spend their time fretting and worrying, mistakenly thinking that they are preparing. They try to figure out what they will say to the Other when the Other raises a difficult issue with them. They worry about their own weaknesses. About what could embarrass them. About what they could lose. About how they could lose. In other words, average negotiators think, not so much about the problem that brings them to the negotiation table in the first place, but about themselves, their own personal success or failure, and how others will view them both during and after the negotiating process. In a way, they spend their preparation time concentrating on their own weakest elements, negotiating away their confidence in the process. Until finally, for them, anxiety trumps preparation.

Expert negotiators spend their preparation time focusing on the issues. In contrast to average negotiators, expert negotiators plan and strategize various ways of solving problems and resolving issues. They try to ferret out the Other's interests and solidify their understanding of their own. They look for common ground, and they look for options to build on that common ground. They research objective, fair standards, both in support of and in opposition to the positions they expect to take, as well as the ones they expect the Other to take. They build their BATNA. All this, they do with only one goal in mind: to arrive at the negotiation table free to listen and work with the Other as joint problem solvers committed to developing one elegant and implementable option that entices everyone and stands the test of time.

So, fretters of the architecture world unite. Let's see how expert negotiators prepare, so we can prepare better from now on ourselves. After all, research shows that it is preparation that tips the negotiation in one's favor. Let's prepare ourselves for success.

Where Should You Focus First?

If you accept the fact that in a negotiation everything is negotiable, where do you think an expert negotiator focuses first, on differences or on common ground? Differences, because if you can identify and bridge differences, you can come to "yes" more quickly? Or areas of agreement, because the more you have in common, the more likely you will be able to bridge differences?

That's a tough choice, and the correct answer is counterintuitive. *Expert negotiators concentrate more of their preparation time on finding and building common ground.* During negotiations, fully four times as many of their comments focus on areas where there is agreement, not disagreement, compared to those of the average negotiator. An example: One expert A/E negotiator was brought in at the last moment by his colleagues to save a faltering negotiation. The staff had readied a presentation on the deadlock to prepare him for what they feared would be the final session. He read everything—the areas where there was no dispute, the areas where they had hammered out compromises, and the one clause that was tearing them apart. But while the rest of the team focused their planning attention on how they would handle the show-stopping clause, his focus was on what had *already been agreed to,* which puzzled his colleagues greatly. "Why is he wasting his time on things we've already settled, when it's clear that this one critical clause will sink the whole negotiation?" they asked. The next day, as the team sat at the negotiating table, the evidence suggested that the team's fears were justified. Looking across at the Others, they could see that everyone's draft contract had been opened to the controversial page, and their copies of the contract either had the clause struck or had angry-looking scrawls surrounding it.

The expert negotiator was unruffled. He sat through the negotiation, listening patiently as everyone pored over the contract language in dispute. When it was finally time for him to speak, he said, "I see you all struggling hard with the language, but I am wondering why you are struggling so. The reason I wonder is because you all have already solved many more difficult issues together, so I am surprised this one clause is causing this much trouble. I mean, look at how much you all have accomplished. You wanted a certain delivery approach, and we gave on that. We wanted more control over time, and you gave on that. We collaborated late into the night to pin down a workable scope, and all of you worked together to create a money package acceptable to all sides. Now indemnification language is giving you pause. I suspect you're all just a bit tired. Take a break. Go around the corner and have a cup of coffee on me. Then come back and sit down together and talk about what safeguards are really important.

Any group that has worked this hard and this effectively to solve the complicated issues you already have solved will certainly crack this last issue. I have total faith in all of you." Later that evening, they had not only a signed contract but also the goodwill necessary to implement it successfully. So expert negotiators build on common ground. Query: If the expert negotiator hadn't spent most of his prep time thinking about how to build up common ground, rather than concentrating on contention, would he have been able to build on that common ground in the negotiation itself? Probably not.

Other Than What

This vignette of the expert negotiator who helped the team break the deadlock over one clause in the contract encapsulates why, throughout this entire book, I refer to the "Other" and not the "other side" when talking about the people with whom you negotiate. "Other side" implies the people are *opponents* of yours. "Other" implies they are *just not you*. It is hard to build common ground with opponents, but a bit exciting, invariably challenging, and sometimes even fun to build common ground with people who, although they want a solution to a shared problem as much as you do, view that problem differently because they have different sets of eyes and experiences. A small change in mindset, but it's an important and useful one to use and remember. Not a friend. Not an enemy. Just an Other.

Why does focusing on common ground work more effectively in fostering agreement than focusing on differences does? Remember in Chapter 4, I talked about the need to have some area of agreement for someone to *want* to negotiate, and some area of disagreement for someone to *have* to negotiate? *If you focus on the areas of disagreement before you secure the areas of agreement, you have to negotiate the tough, possibly contentious issues without either the Other or you being certain that both of you are totally committed to the negotiation's success.* With either's desire for getting to "yes" somewhat shaky, either or both of you may hedge where you should be forthright or be definitive where you should retire. Negotiations under those circumstances become sticky and difficult. Since research shows that people like to work with people who are easy to work with, starting out on the road of disagreement only makes it easy for you to put your worst foot forward.

Conversely, if you start out focusing on common ground and begin building from there, the entire negotiation process becomes easier. Commitment to finding a solution quickens, ability to serve as joint problem solvers deepens, and, when you finally come to the tough issues, each of you will have the goodwill necessary to talk openly about your interests and then address the differences intelligently and sensitively. As important, both of you will have sunk enough costs, whether in time, money, or ego, that you both will be more likely to want to go the distance and get an agreement.[2]

That's good news for architects because when you sit down to negotiate with the owner, the engineer, and the contractor—the three biggest players in the design and construction enterprise—there is more common ground than anything else to build on. Each party wants a successful project—that is, an

---

[2] The old 1997 B141 could have worked to build common ground if scope, and not general conditions, had been printed and then discussed first. Unfortunately, the way it was published, differences got the first nod. Remember this when you use the new B101-2007. See if focusing and fusing scope first doesn't make negotiating terms easier.

on-time, on-budget, claims-free project. Each wants to make a profit. And each wants to accomplish all of the above with a minimum of headaches and strife. Those differences that exist most probably revolve around strategy, but there are only so many ways to produce a building, so once the strategy issues are resolved, including the strategy for dealing with unplanned events, the project should come together nicely.

I can hear you thinking, "Famous first words." I know the preceding paragraph assumes knowledgeable people, honorable people, working together for shared success. And I know that's not always the case, but my experience is that generally parties have more in common in terms of goals, needs, and outcomes than they have differences, and the claims data bear me out. *Success is more often the case in the building enterprise than not.* Most projects succeed because most of the parties in the building enterprise work hard and in good faith to make the projects succeed. We will discuss in Chapter 9 what to do when that is not the case, but for now let's take a tip from expert negotiators: *Focus on building common ground.*

Sunk Costs

Building common ground with words, however, is a quite different matter than building common ground with actions. The former costs time, and therefore, money, but the latter can cost ever so much more. The difference is easy to overlook in your excitement to get work and serve.

For example, architects often start designing without a contract, possibly thinking they are building common ground; and, in a way, they can be.

One architect asked my help when he was at loggerheads with the owner's attorney over contract language. I asked whether he had started design. "Started?" he said. "We are two months from substantial completion." "Are you being paid?" I asked gingerly. "Absolutely, and on time—every bill," was the response. Given that, I advised the architect to keep on negotiating, if he thought his owner wanted him to, until the owner took possession, but not to sign a thing. "Contracts are prospective," I counseled. "The building is already done, and you and the owner may or may not have adhered to the contract the lawyer is drafting. Don't place either one of you in breach if you can help it. Just keep your eye on the project and your ear to your owner so you can make sure your owner is happy with your services."

But what happened to that architect—no contract, no disputes, and on time, every time payment—is not always the case. Sometimes architects design away, and owners are not there for them. Whether intended or not, this can set the architect up for a fall. In fact, there are some hard negotiators who use the tactic of sunk costs to gain bargaining leverage over the Other. The more they can get the Other to sink real time, money, or energy into the project, the more likely they can force the Other into settling for less in order to get the contract.

Expert negotiators don't fall for this game, and you don't have to either. They make sure that they and their Other invest equally in the negotiation process. You can, too. You can say to your client, "We don't start work until we have a front-end aligned contract with our clients, as that is the best way we know to look out for them." You can sign a letter agreement, which is a contract—albeit a form of a contract with a friendlier name—to work on one part of the project, say scope development (for a fee, of course), until you both are in a position to sign a contract for full services. You can start work, but, if the first invoice is not promptly paid, stop work until you and your client are reading off the same page. You can ask the owner to invest, say, by conducting surveys on intended building use before you continue to design, so that the owner, too, has something at stake. *Whatever you choose, just remember that one dollar sunk by you is lost forever. A second sunk dollar won't bring the first one back.*

Issue Planning

Back to planning. First question: When thinking about addressing an issue, do expert negotiators choose the one best option and then plan an in-depth way to address it, or do they plan a wide range of options for dealing with the issue? This question is easier to answer if you think about what design has in common with negotiation. As we discussed in the last chapter, both negotiation and design focus on the flexible creation of problem-solving options. Both are deemed successful when they efficiently and effectively develop one implementable option that meets the disparate interests of different parties in special and appropriate ways.

So how would you answer the question if it were a design-only question? Based on 20 years of watching architects, I'm guessing you wouldn't go to your owner during schematics with only one design, and a complete one, to boot. It's too early in the relationship for you to know enough about the Other's interests and needs to form the perfect solution. Even if you thought you did, you wouldn't risk the relationship on one design. Can you imagine what would happen if you came with just one design, and the client didn't like it? Would you be trusted enough to be given a second chance? Even if your client liked the first design in the overall scheme of things, the one-shot approach to schematics wouldn't work. The client would think the solution too easy and would question its and your value. The project is not your project; it's their project, and, if you give them only one solution, *the project and every problem that ever happens with it become yours,* too. You want the Other to play a part in the design's creation so it becomes theirs in every sense of the word. As important as all of those reasons may be, you want to develop several options so when you sit down to discuss schematics, your ego rests in none of the options. Then you are free to hear whatever your client has to say about each of those options so you can help them to a solution they can live with.

Expert negotiators are just like you. They don't want to enter a negotiation with only one in-depth answer to an issue. They want to use options to learn about the Other and what makes them tick. They want to use option development to maintain their flexibility and leverage and to build trust, understanding, and commitment to overall success. They want to get shared commitment to any solution that gets developed. They want this so much that *skilled negotiators entertain at least five options per negotiable issue, average negotiators half as many.*

Second question: Do expert negotiators concentrate their planning on long-term issues, say two to four years out, or on short-term issues, say within-the-year issues? If you are answering from the perspective of an architect, this may be a toughie, especially if you do projects that can be finished in less than a year. Would it surprise you to learn that, regardless of the duration of project implementation, *expert negotiators focus more on the long-term, focusing twice as many comments (or questions) on long-term considerations as average negotiators do?* Why?

Remember the definition of "expert negotiator." These people succeed not only in reaching an agreement, but also in securing an implementable agreement that, in and of itself, succeeds for all parties. They want an agreement that will stand the test of the market as well as the test of time. And, if the agreement is to fall apart, they want it to disintegrate in front of them at the negotiation table and not later, behind their backs, in a courtroom. So they prod, and they push, and they ask, "Will this work for you? For me? In the short term? Over the long run?" Every reasonably foreseeable potentiality is managed visibly for all parties to explore in the safety of the negotiation room. So, while average negotiators think as far as getting the contract, expert negotiators think beyond the contract to the long-term success of the parties.

Focusing on the long term may be smart for negotiators, but it also has special benefits for architects and their clients. Buildings may take only one year to design, but they can last forever if they are well maintained. When you take into account the claims data that show that some 60 percent of the claims are filed within three years of substantial completion and 80 percent within six years of substantial completion, you realize that 20 percent of the claims will still be hanging out there after six years.[3] Now, those claims may have more to do with bad maintenance than bad design; nonetheless, thinking long term is just plain smart for both the architect and the client.

Back to planning. If you're like me, when you're running a meeting that covers several topics, you probably plan an agenda that puts these topics into a logical sequence. You begin with topic A, and, when that's resolved, you move on to topic B, and so on, until you've run through the whole sequence of items that made up your agenda. That's how we normally plan, whether we're planning a meeting or a project. We put events into a timeline—first this, then that, then the other. This type of planning is called *sequence planning*, and it's generally what we use to develop any plan—from complex, critical-path project plans to humble back-of-the-envelope meeting plans.

Do expert negotiators plan for the negotiation the same way? Do they craft an agenda in their brain, thinking sequentially, "First, we'll resolve this issue, then we'll resolve that issue, then we'll resolve this issue over here"? Or do they just think through each issue independently of every other issue, so that when any issue comes up, they are prepared to address it? The latter. Why?

To answer that question, think what would happen if you planned sequentially, only to discover that

---

[3] This is based on the experience of architects and engineers insured under the CNA/Schinnerer program.

the Other wanted to address the issues in a different order. You probably would be in the same position as a young person I knew who had planned for a negotiation with a very important CEO of a large A/E firm. He had his sequence down pat, and he walked me through it as we sat on a plane. He was confident and assured and ready to go. Only problem was, the very important CEO of a large A/E firm had his own agenda, and he didn't want to listen to anyone else's. "Let's not talk about premiums or underwriting or loss prevention. Let's talk about claims," said he. In one moment, the young'un was struck silent. That's the problem with sequence planning. *If your goal is flexible listening and effective problem solving—which are the crux of negotiation—sequential planning just doesn't work.*

If you're still not convinced, think about design. Do you decide one issue, then another, and then a third? Or do you think about myriad issues when you sit down to design? And when the owner says, "I want more light," do you respond, "Let's talk about heat loss first"? No, you go with the flow. Issue planning facilitates that flexibility, which is why expert negotiators rely on it when preparing to negotiate.

To summarize: Expert negotiators don't spend more time preparing for negotiating than average negotiators; they just spend their prep time better. They explore more options than average negotiators, seeking always to find more avenues to build common ground. They give more thought to long-term issues than average negotiators do, and, when they think issues, they analyze them independently of each other so they have maximum leeway to listen and to use new information to create elegant solutions at the negotiation table.

Negotiating Fees

Okay, all you good readers who looked in the Index and came straight here. If you think there is a magic bullet that guarantees you'll get your fees, may I be the one to tell you there isn't. In fact, if there is such a thing as a fee guarantee, it's this: *If you start your negotiation thinking first about your fees, you won't get them.* If that doesn't make sense to you, do yourself a favor: Read the earlier chapters, and then come back here and we'll talk about money.

Architects and engineers have me crisscrossing the nation teaching negotiation, and I love doing it. (For a fee, of course.) There is a knowledge gap out there, and it needs to be filled. But it doesn't take but five minutes into the session before someone asks about negotiating fees. Most typical is this question: "How do I negotiate with a client who says, 'I will pay you 5 percent' when I want 8?" I always want to respond, "That's not the issue. That's the end of a series of issues, each of which, if managed differently, would mean you wouldn't be asking me that question." But I usually respond that the issue is too complex for this session. That may be, but it is not too complex for this book, so let's parse the issues behind fee negotiation and see where they take us.

First, let's understand what your "fee" means to a client and what it means to you. There is a tremendous difference between the two, and bridging that chasm is part of your challenge. Architects typically view fee as the money that enables the client to have an architect design the project and see it through to completion, though architects do make some money in the process. Clients see your fee as money they have to spend to get what they want. Depending on the actual value of your services from the client's perspective alone, as well as the client's orientation to the value of any professional service, they may or may not see much value in what you do. If they see value, they will pay you readily. If they don't, in time, they will view you and your invoice as an impediment to their accomplishing their more important goals. Don't believe me? Think about how you feel when you receive your lawyer's bill.

There's another difference, too. Architects tend to view their fees and the costs of construction as two separate phenomena. Clients tend to see both as costs of construction. Being told the two are different makes the client wonder whether the architect understands building economics, no matter the cost concerns of the client. Don't believe me? Think about how you feel when your lawyer explains to you that their legal fee saved you from paying a claim and shouldn't be viewed as a cost of litigation. After all, you won, didn't you? No cigar.

Does that mean you and the client are doomed to be at loggerheads over your fee? No, but it does mean that you have to be savvy in setting your fees. Fortunately, we have an operational theory and Huthwaite research to help us in the fee development process. But before we get to them, ask yourself: Is your fee really the issue?

Is Your Fee Really the Issue?

Whatever the profession, people complain about fees when they do not receive value for their money. That's a given. But people also complain about fees (a) when fees do not relate to activity they can see and measure, (b) when fees seem uncontrollable, and (c) when fees are unpredictable. Clients may complain, "Your fees are out of sight." The cure, though, is not to change your fees but the way you manage your client's perception of both your fees and how you arrive at them.

It is always a good idea to talk money and cost control before you spend a penny of your client's money. It's a conversation you can avoid. You can say to your client, "Trust me," as one architect tried to say to me, but if you're an assertive practitioner committed to no-surprise design, you will learn to welcome the conversation. An all-cards-on-the-table, show-me-the-money conversation is the best protection you and your clients can buy if the client wants services, and you want your bills paid on time. At the end of that meeting, both of you should have a good understanding of what the client will owe, even if just a range, and when, why, and what the client will be getting according to that schedule. Trust will be had because trust will have been earned.

At first blush you may be thinking that is asking a lot of you. The design process is not that clear-cut or predictable. Maybe so, but your clients know they will be asking even more than that from the contractor. Why not glean some cost parameters from you, if not early in the process, then sometime after schematics and the pinning down of scope? It will make their lives easier from the get-go. It will make your life easier later, especially when you start invoicing your clients. You can then tie your bills to a shared understanding of effort. Your clients can then review them, knowing where you are coming from and where you will be going together.

Then you can start viewing your invoices as the marketing pieces they are. You can begin using them, not only to keep the project on track, but also to let your clients see that you are working for them—hard. "Two hours of design services," says nothing about what you've done, so a client can analyze the invoice and conclude you did nothing. Have you written anything to stop them from reaching that conclusion? "Two hours of meetings and coordination with mechanical engineers to review preliminary mechanical layout and explore impact on overall design and short- and long-term operational costs" says that you and your consultants are working on (and off) your client's agenda. In other words, if your client understands that making measurable progress and controlling design and operational costs in the process are as much a value to you as they are to your client, they will be substantially less likely to question your fee and its basis. If they can also see the value in your services, and like what they see, the battle over invoices is one less war you will have to fight. So fees may not be the issue. How you arrived at them and control them may be what's open for debate.

Fees as Grease: An Operational Theory

In Chapter 3, we discussed contract theory and a way for architects to redesign that theory out of law and into architecture, so that the theory can be readily and easily applied by architects in support of architecture and the clients they serve. Specifically, we discussed four key concepts: *capability*, *authority/power*, *responsibility*, and *exposure* (CARE). We noted that the best contracts had all four concepts aligned so that the most competent people to manage an exposure were assigned full responsibility for managing it. We then discussed the need for the client to give those people all the power they required, including both authority and fee, to effectively manage the assigned responsibility and to minimize the chances of anything untoward happening. In this way, we protected both the project and the client. Remember those four concepts and how they interlocked? Well, now you get a chance to use them again.

When you ask for your fees, you are not asking daddy for an allowance. You are asking your client to supply you with the "grease" necessary to get their project done frictionlessly. You are telling the owner that, in your professional opinion, you need those monies to manage effectively the exposures and consequent responsibilities they are assigning you to handle on their behalf. They think your fees are too high? You should be able to explain how you arrived at them, of course. But once you've explained the basis, you can set further fee discussion aside and concentrate solely on building in project success. Use those four same concepts to help you. "It would be okay with me to reduce my fees. How do you want to decrease scope? You don't? All right then, what exposures and responsibilities currently assigned to me do you want to reassign to someone else? Is that other party the most competent to manage the reassigned exposure? If not, will they have to charge you more to manage the risk, as it's not their expertise?" "As it is not their expertise, are you worried about increasing your risks?"

Do you see where I am going? Take yourself out of the fee negotiation. Keep your eyes focused solely on helping your client get the project your client wants, in the most cost-efficient and claims-avoidant manner. A reduction in fee—that is, *authority/ power*—requires either a reduction in scope—that is, *exposure*—or a reduction in duties—that is, *responsibility*. Or else, a client has a claim looking for a place to happen. That's why you and your client, after reading Chapter 2 together, worked so hard to front-end align the project. That's why you need fee—to effectively manage the responsibilities the client needs you to do. You owe your client this discussion, as the competent, candid, concerned professional you are. Don't be afraid of it, and certainly don't shy from it.

What Research Has to Teach Us about Setting Fees

You may have noticed I wrote that you should be able to explain to your client how you arrived at your fees. This entire chapter assumes you know how much it costs to deliver services and that you plan for and incorporate profit in your fees; else you will have a hard time having that discussion with your client. Even if you can hold your own in the course of that discussion, you still may feel under the gun. For example, if, during the sales process, you gave away the store, you can't expect to regain store ownership during fee negotiations. It ain't going to happen. And you don't need research to tell you that. You know it from experience all too well.

But assume you haven't oversold your capacity to do wonders with minimal fee, how do you go about deciding what to charge? Do you enter the negotiation with a fixed objective in mind? "I want

$140,000" (or 8 percent, or $225 an hour, or whatever). Or do you enter a negotiation with a range in your head? "I want somewhere between $120,000 and $150,000 to do the project" (or 7 to 10 percent, or $215 to $240 an hour, or whatever). Is there any research to help us out here? Absolutely.

Expert negotiators develop and use ranges in their fee negotiations. Experts are not dumb. They don't communicate the range, because that would guarantee they got the worst end of it. But they create ranges to maintain their flexibility throughout the conversation, progressively narrowing that range as they understand more about the scope of services to be required of them, as well as more about their client's match points. In that way, they avoid being too expensive and losing the commission, or leaving money on the table.

What do I mean by *client match points?* Just as in no-surprise design, you don't want to blindside your client with some new idea or concept or insult them with an approach that proves you weren't listening to them, so too in fee negotiations, you want your client to be comfortable with you and your thinking. You want your fee to match your client's expectations. Whether it does or does not stems in no small part from how you and your client define your value. If your definitions differ, your fee may be too high or too low.

Defining Your Value

Let's define value: *Value equals the benefits you bring the client minus your cost to the client*—costs and benefits as your client defines them, not you. I know architecture books and management consultants to architects rarely define value that way. But that's how your clients define value, and as long as they, and only they, pay your bills, their definition of value is the sole definition that controls. Therefore, if you want your fees to meet your client's match point, you'll want to attract clients who value you as you want to be valued.

When I said this at a continuing education seminar for AIA, one of the architects looked at me as if I came from another planet. "I don't know whom you have been negotiating with or whom you have been negotiating for. All I know is, my clients phone, ask me how much it will cost for me to design a spec building, and, if my price is right, I get the job. If my price is wrong, they keep on telephoning architects until they find someone whose price is right. There's no negotiating fees as far as I can see."

He was right—for his clients. He had them pegged correctly. Profit was their motivator and price, their architect delineator. But what he was describing was a certain kind of client, what Rackham and DeVincentis in their book, *Rethinking the Sales Force*, call the *transactional client*. Transactional clients want their services delivered fast and cheap. For them, most designers are fungible. High design is not a value. Fast construction is. They need a building, and they need it now. You can make money serving this type of client, but delivering design services cheaply and at the speed of light is an art, and not all architects can do it well.

Most architects are geared to helping the *consultative client*. Consultative clients value the architect's ability to provide a customized solution to their business or personal problems. The more strategically important their problem is to them, the more they will value and hence be willing to pay the architect–problem solver. The more innovative and expert the architect is in solving the strategically important problem, the even greater the fee the architect will be able to muster. Sounds good, eh? Not really. Most clients do not have highly strategic problems. They would like a new office, but, unless the architect can design an office that will increase their profits measurably (or design a house they can afford), how the office (home) looks is interesting, even important, but rarely does it rise to the level of "strategic." With respect to those clients, if they can't afford the offering, they can live without. For these lower-end consultative clients, the architect (or the project) also can all too easily become fungible.

With this insight into client thinking in mind, you can start thinking ranges. Is your client a high-end consultative client with a truly strategic problem that you and only you can solve due to your special expertise? Go for the gold. They need you, and no other architect can take your place. Is your client a lower-end, albeit still consultative, client? Set your high range at as high a level as you think possible, but only after you have a very good sense of your client's match point.

How high a high range do you set? One of the exercises I do in continuing education courses sponsored by the American Law Institute and the American Bar Association involves lawyers setting ranges in groups. Invariably, there are groups who set their expectations high and ones that set their expectations low. The ranges they arrive at reflect their expectations and, even more interestingly, predict their negotiation results. Those who thought they could get little, got little. Those who expected more, got more. So where do you set your high range? Start by thinking, "Assuming I have to make no concessions, in the best of all possible worlds, what should I realistically expect to be paid, given the services to be exacted of me?" Put that number down.

Now, you can turn to your low range. Here again, be realistic. How low can you go to still deliver on the project? Is there any chance the project will attract bigger, or at least better, business? Is it worth it to you to discount your present fee some for that business? Can you still make a profit at this figure? At least break even? Does the figure include monies for contingencies? Is this the lowest fee that you—and your partners—can put up with? That's the figure below which you need to walk away—in negotiation lingo, your reservation number.

Your work isn't done, though. You have set these ranges thinking only of yourself, your needs, and what you bring to and require of the project. Now you need to refine them both, tuning in to the needs, values, and expectations of your client, the nature of the project, its own building economics, and the reality of the market. Given all those factors, you need to review your high and low ranges and ask yourself, "What is the most I realistically can get at the high end and the least I realistically need to give up at the low end and still get the project?" You have to be realistic here because there are penalties if you aren't:

> ➤ If your upper range is too high, you risk either losing clients to the competition or, if

you should get the project, being nickel-and-dimed by your clients every time their projects require an additional service.

➤ If your lower range is too low, you risk making clients more demanding, because clients may interpret a too-low fee as a mark of desperation.

➤ If your range is so far off at either end, you risk either having to drop your fee substantially to get the project or creating a credibility gap if the client concludes that you don't understand them or their projects.

Developing Your Fees

This is tough work because, not only do you have to be realistic, you have to be reasonably optimistic in your analysis. As research shows, the more reasonably optimistic negotiators are about their expectations, the more likely they are to see them met. (Interestingly, negotiators from towns and rural areas tend to set tighter and smaller ranges than negotiators in cities, because everyone knows one another and knows the local market.)

To summarize: Set a realistic but optimistic range for your fees, making sure that the entire range is high enough to give you latitude but low enough not to violate the client's expectations and sense of you, your value, and the project's needs. It is within this range that you will negotiate.

Where do you start? Expert negotiators start near or at the top of their range. After all, they have been realistic and practiced no-surprise design. That is, they worked closely with the client, listened hard, and listened well, understanding the client and the project accurately. As a result, that fee should come as no surprise to the client. Regardless, wherever they start, expert negotiators have a reason for their fee, a logic behind it, so that if the client asks how they arrived at the fee, they can explain it convincingly and well.

What do you do if the client wants to pay you less? Expert negotiators make concessions if required. But they give a reason for them and make their concessions in small increments, responding appropriately so as not to insult the Other, but signaling their bottom line by making smaller and smaller concessions. And expert negotiators make their concessions reciprocal, as they know that for every *quid* there is a *quo*. Hence, expert negotiators demand things in return from the Other for each decrease in fee that the Other is exacting from them. And these fee reductions get progressively smaller. In this way, the Other gets a clear signal that expert negotiators have reached their bottom line.

Making the Pie Bigger

Sometimes the process I described is relatively cut and dried. The architects have their BATNA and the clients have their BATNA, which each party has incorporated into its thinking.[4] The two parties gradually work their way to common ground and come to "yes."

---

[4] It is always smart to probe for the Other's BATNA, as it will give you greater understanding and, therefore, leverage during the negotiation process. It is less smart to convey your BATNA.

Sometimes it is easy. An example: The client has you in front of them. If the two of you don't settle on a fee, they will have to start again. If your client is a high-end consultative client who has searched hard for an architect before selecting you, their BATNA is to go to their second choice—a person they have rejected in favor of you. While that gives you leverage, it doesn't give you rights, and you know that. So you make the fee negotiation process easy for them. Easy does not mean you lower your fees. It means being thoughtful, reasonable, and concerned about your clients and their needs. And it means listening hard so that you react appropriately to what they are and are not saying.

Sometimes reaching agreement is hard because neither party has much latitude within the existing rules, and the parties are some way apart on fees. When this happens, the only way to bring the parties to "yes" is to change the rules.[5] That way, no one is talking about the pie on the table, where for you to get a bigger piece of that pie means the Other's piece is going to be smaller.

For example, you can make the project pie smaller. You can reduce the cost of providing your piece of the pie without suffering financial loss by rebalancing scope to be in line with a lower fee. You can encompass this lesser fee by using the CARE package introduced in Chapter 3, trading off

---

[5] This entire section has been written from the perspective of an architect who is negotiating from scratch with the owner. There are different rules when the architect is responding to a request for a proposal. For more on what to do when your owner/buyer is at a different stage of the buying cycle, read Chapter One, "How Customers Make Decisions," in *Major Account Sales Strategy* by Neil Rackham. (McGraw-Hill, 1989).

authority/power, responsibility, and exposure for a lesser fee, making clear to the client the impact of these trade-offs on the project.

A more attractive alternative, however, is to change the rules so that both of you end up getting more out of the deal. I threw this challenge out to a continuing education seminar at an AIA convention: How can an architect change the rules so that all parties benefit? This is what they came up with. When your client has issues with your fee, you can:

➤ Take a percent of the project's profits in lieu of fee.

➤ Provide a menu of services and costs for the owner to choose.

➤ Phase the design and construction process so the project is more affordable for the owner.

➤ Establish value-added scales so that if the project produces certain results, the architect gets paid more.

➤ Participate with the owner. Somehow. In a way that's useful to you and to the owner.

➤ Change the calculation of the fee. Instead of providing services on a percentage basis, provide them on an hourly basis (maybe with an upset limit) or on a lump-sum basis, or any other way that will suit both parties' needs.

➤ Swallow a lower fee now in exchange for more later. On a commercial residential development project, you might consider splitting your fee and saying to the developer, "Pay me 'A' now for preconstruction services; and when you get your construction loan, pay me 'B' for construction administration services. And, as you sell each unit, pay me 'C,' say 1 percent of the sales price per unit." That way, the developer pays only when they have money, and both the developer and the architect benefit.

➤ Separate design fees and incentive fees, with the latter to be triggered as the owner accomplishes objectively measurable owner goals made accomplishable by your design.

To summarize: How do you make the pie bigger? You think from the client's perspective and work back to your own.

When "You're Too Expensive"

Ever had a client say you cost too much? How did you react? Did you take it personally and want to hit back? "You have no idea how hard I've worked." "You don't appreciate my value." "If you had to put up with a client like you, you would be charging twice as much." Or maybe you just collapsed under what you perceived as an assault ("Why me?"), and then thought, "If I reduce my fee, will my client like me better?" Maybe you even reduced your fees. But, you had another choice: not to personalize and internalize the statement, but to explore your client's needs directly with them.[6]

---

[6] But do read Chapter 9 on dispute resolution because, if your client is upset about project progress and is using complaints about your costs as a communication mechanism, you will want to know how best to handle that, too.

Clients change over the course of a project. Before they take it on, they question whether the result and the benefits will exceed the cost of the project. The more serious, the more strategic the business or personal problem they hope the building will solve, the more willing they will be to pay for the resolution. This came home to me in one second flat when I wanted to break through a wall to expand the kitchen. "Go to Kitchen Guild," the architect advised, "and ask them to design and cost out two kitchens—one within existing space, the other with expanded space. Then add $50,000 to the cost of the larger kitchen." Right then and there I knew, and the architect knew, I would live with a small kitchen. I would get no increased strategic value out of the increased cost, which made the project "too expensive." Had the architect been able to help me understand that current conditions would interfere with my enjoyment and use of the house, then the cost of mitigating those impacts might have receded, and the strategic benefits of remodeling would have shimmered more brightly. In that case, I might have gone for it. Instead, I thanked him mightily for putting me ahead of the project (and his practice) and promptly sent him two referrals.

Maybe you have been told you were too expensive after the client had already decided to do the project and was now deciding which architect to hire. Again, "you're too expensive" should be heard as code words for something unrelated to your fee. Here, the client is questioning the superiority of your solution compared to those of others under consideration. Here, you need to show how your services and understanding of the problem are measurably better than those of others under consideration, particularly as they relate to the greatest needs your client has expressed. In other words, as value equals benefits minus cost, the client is giving you a choice—increase the benefit of hiring you or decrease your costs. Seize the opportunity to demonstrate your value. Welcome it.

Or maybe your situation is still different. You are now before the client's board of directors, and the client is questioning your fee. Again, "you're too expensive" is code here, for "we have concerns about committing to you." To a client, committing to an architect is scary. Look at it from the client's perspective, and you will easily see why. Clients are buying you, your services, and your solution. Two of those three are utterly intangible. Indeed, from the perspective of clients, in no small part, they are buying a pig in a poke. *You* may have an idea of what you will provide, but clearly, if they are still questioning your fee, *they* don't. You may have shown them pictures, given them references, tried to demonstrate what you will provide, yet they nonetheless have concerns. A client who questions fee now is telling you they need "more." Again, welcome that reticence as an opportunity to raise and resolve concerns. And honor those concerns. Don't pooh-pooh them. Whether you see them or not, whether you share them or not, the concerns are real to the client. Mitigate the client's risks in hiring you by providing the room and the support to work through those concerns. Help them feel safe in giving you their business.

Have you the energy for one more scenario? You are at the top of the short list. You have successfully jumped through every client hoop that has come your way. The contract has been negotiated and is ready for signing, and now you hear "you are too expensive." Inhale slowly and think. If your client has gone through the entire qualification-based selection process, and you are number one on the short list, they want you most. To reopen negotiations with number two is not going to get them what they want—which is you. (It would also be very expensive and delaying for them.) Further, if you have done everything we have discussed in this chapter in setting your fee, your fee is probably market competitive. But get real. This is your client's last best chance to get concessions out of you. Yes, you can hang tough, but you also can play, if you have stored in your pocket one concession of low cost to you and of high benefit to your client. And when you bring it out, bring it out slowly so the client will appreciate it fully.

Ava's Preparation Cheat Sheet

It is one thing to say that preparation tips the table in favor of the one most prepared. It is another thing altogether to transform yourself into the one who *is* the most prepared. Having watched many people, including myself, struggle with where-to-begin, I developed a "cheat sheet" to help my clients and me spend the preparation time fruitfully. I know this book is copyrighted, but the publisher has kindly agreed that the "cheat sheet" that follows is available for your use. It is yours for the taking. Play with it. Amend it. Transform it into a prep sheet that works for you.

Why You Should Negotiate Your Own Contracts

If you think your lawyer should negotiate the contract, may I suggest you reconsider. Sometimes, you may want your lawyer to negotiate for you, but you may not.

Let me tell you a story. I was once asked to join a law firm, and, for a brief while, I considered it. A lawyer friend of mine offered to negotiate my contract for me. I said, "Not a chance. Negotiating is my opportunity to come to 'yes' with the law firm. It is my opportunity to come to a shared understanding with it. To find out if its values are ones I want to live with. To find out its concept of excellence and its commitment to reciprocity. I mean, if they are not what I want in the negotiation stage, they'll never be what I want after I've signed on the bottom line. So why would I want *you* to negotiate *my* contract? You're not going to be the one who has to work with these people. This is my chance to be sure I have the right partners, and it's their chance to be sure they have the right partner. So, no offense, but you're just going to get in the way. I'd be happy to talk with you every night in case I'm uncertain about something, but I want to be part of a legal enterprise that's on my wavelength, and this is my chance of making sure I get what I want." The stakes were high for me, very high, but I stuck to my guns. My lawyer friend served as my counselor. I served as my own advocate.

I feel no different about you and your clients and your contracts. In my opinion, unless you negotiate your contract directly with the owner, both you and the owner will miss the front-end opportunity to align the project. Both you and the owner will miss the chance to decide if you are the right fit for each other.

Now, many lawyers will tell you I am off-base. Before you buy that, understand that not all lawyers know how to be true counselors to their clients. If you want to negotiate your own contracts, you will want to make sure that the lawyers you retain support that and have the skills to be true counselors to you. Do they understand your design aspirations? Your practice goals? Do they know your business? The business of your clients? Can they help you sort out interests and positions? Are they creative enough to help you fashion the law in support of elegant options? Will they help you manage risk, or do they just want you to run from it? Can they set their strengths and limits aside and help you with yours?

(continues)

(continued)

If the answer to all these questions is yes, then you are in the position to use your lawyer as the secret weapon good lawyers can be. With a legal counselor, you can bring your negotiation weaknesses to *their* table and develop strategies to deal with them before you arrive at the negotiating table. You can complete the cheat sheet together. (You'll find it at the end of this chapter.) That way, you can learn how your lawyer approaches problems, and vice versa. That way, you can more easily and effectively brainstorm elegant options together. Then you will have more going for you when you enter into negotiation. More important, you'll have much more going for you when you leave the negotiating table with an agreement.

Also, if you are working in a firm, consider filling out the sheet with others familiar with the issues and the people with whom you will be negotiating. I am a strong believer that magic occurs in groups. I have seen it in trial juries. I have enjoyed it in my work. More heads think bigger and better than any one head can alone. Fill out your cheat sheet with people who want you to succeed as much as you do. If you are a sole practitioner, find yourself a buddy, whether it's another architect, your insurance agent, a lawyer, or your spouse. The preparation time you spend with them will allow you to walk into the negotiation thinking a little bit more expansively than if you'd prepared solo. And remember to use the form iteratively. The more you go over it, the more insights you will have, and the more options you will develop that get you to "yes."

The point is, rehearse—not to pin down one script, but to develop for yourself a gamut of ways the negotiation could go. That way, armed with a well-researched cheat sheet, you'll be better prepared and hence more confident. Then set that cheat sheet aside so you are free to focus when you sit down at the negotiation table, not on yourself and your negotiation anxieties, but on the Other and solving the joint problem you share. Then you can relax and listen—which, we will learn in the next chapter, is one more reason skilled negotiators succeed so often.

Ava's Preparation Cheat Sheet

What are the needs that are bringing you together?

What's your position?

What's their position?

What are your interests?

What are their interests?

Where's common ground?

Where are discrepancies?

What options would resolve the discrepancies?

Any real deal breakers?

What's your target goal?

Why may they say no to your goal?

What would make you walk away—i.e., what is your resistance point?

Any objective standards for you to rely on? For them?

What gives you leverage?

What gives them leverage?

What's your BATNA? What's theirs?

Any elegant options to make the pie bigger?

Any low-cost concessions you can make to close well?

The Communication Behaviors of Expert Negotiators

6

In previous chapters, we laid out a negotiation process and a preparation process. With insights into how expert negotiators communicate, we will soon be ready to work with the Other to build common ground, designing elegant solutions where no common ground yet exists. Negotiating contract language will then fall readily into place.

To understand how experts negotiate, it may be a whole lot easier if you start by thinking about what negotiation has in common with other problem-solving meetings.[1] One commonality, as research shows, is that it relies on the same three classes of communication behaviors that people call on in meetings for their success.

---

[1] This section evolves from the study entitled *Models for Explaining Behavior*, by Neil Rackham (Huthwaite Research Group, England, 1975). Unfortunately, the study is out of print, but the information is as relevant today as it was when written.

The Three Classes of Communication Behaviors

Think of a typical meeting in your firm that you called to resolve a problem. Imagine that an owner wants changes in a project, and you are meeting with the design team to decide how you should move forward. In order to come to decisions, first you need some ideas, some proposals, on what to do and how to do it. Finding those is a class of behavior called *Initiating.* Without the options, possibilities, and ideas generated by Initiating behavior, your meeting won't get very far. But ideas, however good, don't automatically translate into decisions, when you are working with other people. They would, if you were by yourself. If you were sitting alone at your computer and you had a brilliant idea, you could just start designing. But when you're in a group, Initiating an idea is only the first step. Other people have to accept it or reject it. They have to react to it in some way before any decision can be taken. So you also need another class of behavior—*Reacting*—in order to reach decisions.

However, in real life, it's hard for people to react before they fully understand what is being proposed. They will have questions. "What do you mean by that?" "How would this piece work?" They will want to explain how they see things. They'll want understanding, and they'll want clarity. Which brings us to the third class of behavior—*Clarifying.* In any meeting called to resolve problems or make decisions, including a negotiation, *Initiating, Reacting, and Clarifying must all be present and must be balanced in their use.* How people Initiate, React, and Clarify ideas can determine the effectiveness of the meeting or the negotiation, as well as how people feel about themselves and each other during the meeting and afterward.

What do these three classes of behavior have to do with negotiating? Research shows *you need all three behaviors*—Initiating, Reacting, and Clarifying—in a negotiation *for progress to be made.* Two out of three won't cut it. Have you ever been in a client negotiation where you put forward lots of ideas—in other words, where you did a lot of Initiating—but your client did little or no Reacting? More likely than not, you had a meeting where no real progress was made because you were left in the dark as to what your client was thinking or feeling. Any action you took after the meeting, you took at your own peril.

What about a meeting that was high on Initiating, but low on Clarifying? Most likely you and the Other left the meeting with two different ideas of what happened there and what should happen next. Without Clarifying behaviors, even good meeting notes won't resolve such a discrepancy and may even exacerbate it—especially if there is a huge gap between your notes and the Other's experience of the meeting. (Can't you just hear the Other saying, "Geesh! Architects just don't listen.")

Or maybe you've been at a meeting that was too high on Clarifying. More likely than not, it fared no better than the other two types of meetings. At best, you probably found that the attendees tended to focus undue attention on details, given the marked absence of proposals to consider or build on. At worst, attendees felt the meeting was a bore and walked out shaking their heads, thinking, "What a waste of time."

In short, *you need all three classes of behavior to move.* You need all three to build common ground. You need all three behaviors to negotiate.

The Three Classes of Behavior That Move Meetings Forward

For those of you interested in learning more about behavior in negotiation and other meetings, let's look at the three types of communication behaviors more closely.

Initiating

Initiating behaviors put forward ideas, concepts, suggestions, or courses of action. They take two forms—*Proposing* and *Building* on the proposal of another. "I have a suggestion to make. Let's set the house into a hill" is an example of Proposing. "Let's site it into *that* hill, so that users will see the mountain" is an example of Building on the proposal of another. "Let's put it *on top* of the hill instead" is a counterproposal, which is both a second proposal and a rejection of the Other's proposal.

Reacting

Reacting behaviors constitute evaluations of, and reactions to, other people's contributions. Reacting behaviors take three forms—*Supporting*, *Disagreeing*, and *Defending/Attacking*. "Neat idea. Let's do it" is, of course, an example of Supporting. "No, I don't think the owner will buy that idea" is Disagreeing. "I could have joined you this afternoon for the presentation if you had just told me about it earlier," and "Well, I would have told you about it earlier if you had bothered to return my call!" are clearly an example of Defending/Attacking.

Clarifying

Clarifying behaviors exchange information, facts, and opinions, and offer clarification. These behaviors take four forms—*Testing for Understanding, Summarizing, Seeking Information,* and *Giving Information*. "Let me see if I understand you: Are you saying that a house built totally into the hill could feel claustrophobic?" *tests for understanding.* "So you're saying that it is all right to design some of the house into the hill but not all of it for fear users will feel trapped and not nestled" *summarizes* what you heard the Other say. "Did you have a reason for suggesting *that* hill over the other one?" *seeks information.* "I am meeting the owner in the afternoon to go over the concepts we select this morning" *gives information.*

Each of these forms of behavior has its place in a negotiation, except for Defending/Attacking, which has to be used very carefully, or it gets you nowhere fast. The best negotiators are comfortable using any one of them as the behavior of the Other suggests they should.

What Schools Don't Teach That Architects Need to Know

Now, before we apply the three classes of behavior to negotiating, let's think for a moment about how you learned to design in school. During programming and pre-schematics, you were taught to Clarify by seeking information. (Initiating and Reacting behaviors weren't stressed in the exercise.) Students were graded on the depth of their analysis and understanding of the assigned problem. When you designed, you engaged in Initiating behaviors, but there was no need to work on Clarifying and Reacting behaviors, as you probably designed alone. (Only recently have schools broadly encouraged teamwork and putative client involvement.) When you presented your work, your client, so to speak, was your professor or the jury. Depending on the quality of that experience, you were called upon to Clarify your work, explaining why you did what you did, or you were pushed into Reacting. More likely than not, once you presented your work, all further Initiating was done by the professor or the jury. Whether and how much you learned and grew was dependent on how balanced the session was between Initiating, Clarifying, and Reacting, assuming it was balanced at all.

In other words, unless your school was extraordinary, rarely were you called upon to develop all three classes of behavior and use them consciously in a balanced manner in the same exercise. If that rings true for you, then you, like many architects, face a special challenge: learning how to balance a meeting. Without that, without enough Initiating, Reacting, and Clarifying underway, it is tough to achieve maximum progress in a no-surprise design way. And it's hard to ensure that all parties, you included, leave the meeting knowing what the next steps are and feeling comfortable with them.

How to Put the Three Behaviors to Work for You

While most architects have proposing down pat, many are uncomfortable with building on the ideas of another. Others are low on Clarifying behaviors when the need for clarification is paramount, and low on Reacting behaviors when Reacting is necessary. Hence, the owner and architect are deprived of the chance of enjoying no-surprise design. Conversations are left without a joining of the minds, and no one is 100 percent certain about what happens next.

Here are a few examples of how Initiating, Reacting, and Clarifying can help the owner and you come to a true "yes." And though this book discusses the law and also contract negotiation, please note that each of the examples here involves design negotiation, not the negotiation of words. This is intentional. Negotiation is an integral part of the design process. After all, aren't you negotiating with some Other—either a colleague in your office, a consultant or contractor, or your client—whenever you design?

Research shows the best Initiating comes from building on the client's ideas. During the design process, most clients give their architects possibilities and concepts to consider. The client expects that some, if not all, of these ideas will be incorporated in the architect's final design. If you reject the client's ideas outright, they will feel you don't respect or understand them. (One architect told us one of our ideas was "dumb." It may have been, but we don't work with that architect anymore.) But if you accept the client's "bad" input in silence—that is, without Reacting—the client will be thinking you concur with their suggestion. (Alternatively, and just as likely but more immediately harmful: If, the next time you get together, your design doesn't incorporate the client's idea, they will think that you didn't listen to them.)

What to do? First, try using Clarifying behaviors, and then initiate through building. Respond with questions, seeking information and summarizing client input. At minimum, clients will at least feel they have been heard. If your questions lead them to understand the adverse implications of their suggestion for their problem or the building design, they themselves might conclude on their own that their idea was a bad one. Even better, you might find out more about your clients and their problem than you had known originally. Then you can build on their idea with designs that incorporate the essence of the best of whatever your clients brought forward.

If words fail you, use your design skills to Clarify, then build. Most clients are not imagers; they cannot see what you see. They do not think in three dimensions or see the whole. If they did, they probably would have chosen to be architects. Between Building Information Modeling (BIM), doodles on napkins, and everything in between, you can help them "see" the "reality" of their design ideas as well as your own concepts. They will love you for it because they will be in a better position to understand and appreciate the reality of what is being proposed.[2]

---

[2] No matter how long I have been around architects and architecture, I remain an incurable nonvisualizer. For me, the best clarifications have been the solid models our architects have created to show me what the structures would look like. One architect talked me out of a model, saying it was "too expensive" given that the building was "just a farm building." The savings proved expensive and led to a series of change orders.

The best Clarifying involves complex, have-to-plan-for questions. During schematics and design development, architects use some Clarifying behaviors to advance their understanding of client needs, desires, and expectations. They seek information, and they give information—two important Clarifying behaviors—but, if my experience is typical, they do not test for understanding or summarize all that much. Furthermore, they do not ask questions that correlate highly with consultant success—questions that explore the implications of explicit problems identified in conversations with the client and questions which explore the benefits of various approaches to those problems. Rather, they focus on the client's situation and the problems that situation is causing the client. "How many rooms do you want?" "Is overcrowding a problem?" "How do you work?" "What do you require to work better?" Because these latter questions attach directly to the task of design and often are easier to think of and less intrusive to ask, architects stop their Clarifying behaviors with them.

But for owners to truly understand the relevance of the design to their personal and business problems, as well as to see the value the architect is bringing to their resolution, architects need to delve more deeply into the issues facing the client. They need to ask the more important questions that relate to the business or personal problems that forced the client to seek an architect in the first place. And they need to explore the implications of those problems for the client—not just for the design issue facing the architect. "You say staff turnover is a problem that costs you money and client unhappiness with the quality of your services. Have you thought about our exploring whether adding a gym or day care center to the design would decrease staff turnover?" "How much will you save in interest and gain in sales if we add enough staff to finish the construction documents a month earlier?" These kinds of complex, have-to-plan-for questions correlate highly with customer satisfaction and project success. They demonstrate consultant competence and concern. They build trust. Only a knowing consultant who is deeply sensitive to the problems facing the client and cares about solving them would be witting enough to ask them. More important, they bring value to the client by raising issues and suggesting new solutions the client has not previously considered.[3]

The whole purpose of Reacting is to get and give feedback. Lots of people, not just architects, have problems Reacting. There's the person who says no to everything. There's the person who says one thing today and another tomorrow. There's the person who loves it, just loves it, and then gets cold feet . . . and so on and so on.

For architects, though, there is a special danger due, in part, to *The Fountainhead*'s Howard Roark stereotype. There is a slim line between confidence and arrogance, respect and obedience, and architects who do not react well can be seen by their clients as crossing the line. The blustery response of some architects to compensate for professional reticence can be all too easily misinterpreted as inappropriate egotism. The I-know-more-than-you response fares no

---

[3] *SPIN®Selling* is dedicated to exploring the question process and its impact on buyers of high-ticket items and services, such as architecture.

better, no matter how accurate that assessment may be. Silence, as we just discussed, makes the whole situation worse. What are architects to do?

As each client and each architect is unique, no one answer could possibly be correct. I do have a hypothesis, though. Could it be that architects set themselves up for this predicament by their communication behaviors? Take, for example, those architects who, during the early design stages, are high on seeking design information, but low on seeking client information. If these architects are even lower still on testing for understanding and building on the ideas of the Other, they may be shocked to discover, when they finally show their designs to their client, that the client doesn't like them. Here the failure quite possibly is not a design failure; it's a communication failure. By not getting their clients to react enough, these architects denied themselves the chance to enjoy adequate client feedback. As a result, their design ideas drifted away from their client's personal and business needs.

Or consider those architects who are high on Initiating and high on Clarifying, but themselves low on Reacting, always greeting their clients' ideas with "uh huh" or silence. If that's the case, those architects may find, when they finally do react to their clients by showing them their designs, their clients may be nonplussed. And, if these architects are expecting applause, even gratitude, after all their very hard work, and receive none or, worse, are met by questions (which they may take as second guessing), confusion will reign and communications worsen. Their clients didn't intend to hurt the architect's feelings, but the architect wants to fire the client. If this hypothesis about communication behaviors has any merit, then increased testing for understanding, summarizing, and building throughout the entire design process would be the answer, *as the design would have no surprises in it*, save for commodity, wonder, and delight.

Two Successful Persuasion Styles: Push and Pull

Let's go back to the three classes of communication behaviors and the art and science of negotiating.

When Huthwaite Research Group investigated the persuasion styles of expert negotiators, they found two successful, albeit different, styles at work. One involved strong arguments from the persuader, well presented, where the energy came from the persuader. "I have a proposal to make. We should do A, then B, then C. Here is the data that show why we should do it this way." This style was forceful and strongly argued, giving the Other little chance to have a say. The alternative style involved good questions from the persuader, skillfully asked, but where the energy came from the persuadee. "What do you think is important here? What kind of evidence would it take to convince you to take one approach over another?" For ease in use, we will use the Huthwaite labels. They used the term *Pushing* for those communication behaviors, such as proposing and giving information, where the energy comes from the persuader, while *Pulling* denoted those communication behaviors, such as seeking information, building on the idea of another, and testing for understanding, where the energy comes from the persuadee.

Unbuilt Buildings: What Really May Be Going On

Have you more unbuilt buildings in your portfolio than built ones? Do owners walk away, saying they loved your design but just couldn't afford it? Research shows that, in big-ticket purchases, money is usually just a pretext for walking away. In studies of buyers in other fields, researchers found that people state money concerns as their primary reason for backing out of a contract when, some 64 percent of the time, money is not the issue.[4] Instead, the customers' real reason for not going forward usually has to do with their belief that it is more risky to go on than to stop right there. In aborted-sale post interviews, buyers attached their reluctance to going forward to potential risks, implementation hassles, and other fears emanating from their lack of confidence in the seller or in the product. Money was the excuse they gave because it was a socially acceptable and impersonal way of achieving distance from the seller and the sale.

[4] Neil Rackham's *Major Account Sales Strategy* (New York: McGraw-Hill, Inc., 1989) discusses why, for most buyers, "price is a smoke screen for consequence issues."

Now, both the Pushing and Pulling styles of persuasion work, but not equally well in all circumstances. Pushing works best in tight time constraints, Pulling when there is adequate time for discussion. Think about it. Can you imagine the captain of a sinking ship asking each of his crew members, "What do you think is the best way to save our lives?" Not a chance. Time is of the essence. A quick decision is called for. Fast communication is necessary. Pushing is what's needed—"This is what we're going to do"—and everyone is persuaded to act accordingly.

Pushing also works best with small decisions; Pulling works well regardless of the size or the gravity of the decision. "I want to go to the movies" can be just as effective as "Do you want to go to the movies tonight?" But when the stakes are high, Pulling works better. Have you ever tried to talk a client into going substantially over budget by

Pushing? "I urge you to go over the budget by a substantial amount now to accommodate growth for the following five reasons." Did it work? Wouldn't you have had a better chance if you had Pulled instead? "Yesterday you mentioned the need to expand your operations substantially over the next 12 months if you are going to beat your number one competitor. Would you rather expand the design for the building to accommodate that growth while it is still in the design stage, even though it will put you over budget now, or do you want to wait until you grow and expand the building later, even though it will cost you substantially more? Why?"

Pushing works best when the persuader has power either because of their position or expertise. People are willing to be persuaded by someone's arguments when that someone knows more than they do or has the power, resulting from position, to support or enforce their argument. But just as Pulling works well independent of the size of the decision, so, too, does it work well regardless of whether the person has position powers or expertise. Indeed, it works best for people who are short on both. Maybe that's the reason behind linguists' discovery that women historically persuade by asking questions rather than by making statements.[5] After all, women historically have been short on position powers, and their expertise underestimated.[6]

---

[5] Deborah Tannen in her book *Talking from 9 to 5: Women and Men in the Workplace: Language, Sex, and Power* (Avon, 1995) explains this phenomenon in detail.

[6] A great book on negotiation for people who don't speak up for themselves, male or female, is *Women Don't Ask: Negotiation and the Gender Divide*, by Linda Babcock and Sara Laschever (Princeton University Press, 2003).

Pushing works well in one-off negotiations, that is, where the persuader will never have to negotiate with the persuadee again. That's why it is often the style of choice of salespeople of commodity goods. "With the deal I'm offering you today, you really should take me up on it and not quibble about the price. In fact, if I were you, I would buy it right now." Pulling works well where the persuader expects to have to negotiate with the Other on numerous occasions. "Help me understand why that is important to you, so that I can take your interests into account in my thinking. Maybe then we'll both be in a better position to think of elegant options that will work and please us both." In particular, Pulling works best where commitment of the persuadee is crucial to the successful resolution and implementation of the negotiated issue.

Now ask yourself, which approach works better for architects? Pushing, when the parties are facing time constraints or a small decision, and the persuader has position or expertise power and will never see the persuadee again? Or Pulling, when there is adequate time for discussion, decisions of various sizes, and consequences to be made, people of unequal or just differing power, and a longish working relationship where mutual commitment to the negotiated agreement is critical to both parties' success?

While either Pushing or Pulling can serve the architect, Pulling does seem the better approach given the long-term, high-stakes commitment being exacted of the client. But there is another reason why Pulling works so well for architects: It is the same technique architects use every day in design. Moreover, to the extent that many architects are introverts and their clients extroverts, Pulling lets the parties enjoy their preferred mode of communicating: Clients give information, and architects build on it, Clarifying and Reacting along the way.

How Pushing and Pulling Work in Negotiation

No person is a Pusher or a Puller all the time. People aren't that simple. Moreover, no one faces the same circumstances in every case, so to be one thing day in and day out, regardless, doesn't make much sense. Sometimes circumstances demand you push; sometimes they suggest you pull.

Whether you *inherently* tend to be a Pusher or a Puller is part training, part personal preference, and part proclivity. Most lawyers, for example, are trained to be Pushers. "Ladies and gentlemen of the jury, I stand before you today to represent Mrs. C. Mrs. C has been grievously hurt by the defendant and should be compensated mightily. Here are the reasons why." Most architects, on the other hand, are trained to be Pullers. "When you say you want heavy design development documents, what exactly do you mean?"[7]

Do Pullers have a chance when they are up against Pushers? You bet they do. Let's look at three scenarios with three different pairs of negotiators: two Pushers, two Pullers, and a Pusher and a Puller.

Imagine a Pusher with a three-point negotiating agenda—A, B, and C in highest to lowest priority order—meeting up with another Pusher with a three-point negotiating agenda—E, D,

---

[7] This is a gross generalization and absolutely not a true and fast rule. I am a lawyer, but by preference a Puller. I know a goodly number of architects who are Pushers.

and C, again in highest to lowest priority order (see Figure 6.1).

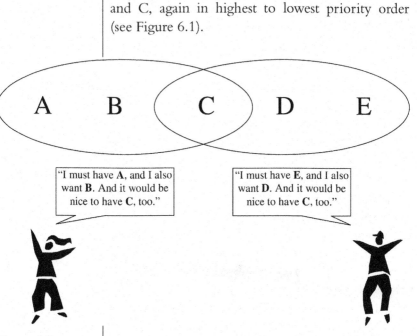

Figure 6.1

More likely than not, the first Pusher, uninterested in the Other, will quickly tell the second Pusher his highest priority. "I want A." The second Pusher, just as uninterested in what the Other wants, will tell the first Pusher what she wants. "I want E." The two will try to persuade each other of the rightness of their positions (and why the Other should accede to it), using the tools of the Pusher's trade—strong arguments that are well presented. If they keep at it and enter into logical give and take, assuming they don't deadlock altogether, they predictably will agree—after a fight—to trade off two of the first Pusher's priorities (A and B) for two of the second Pusher's (D and E). They will probably both give up and give out without reaching and discussing C.

Two Pullers would negotiate differently. Using their tools—good questions skillfully asked—they would quickly discover that both of them wanted C. They would then build on that common ground to see whether they could develop elegant options that would deliver on the interests represented by each of their other priorities. The results would vary depending on their problem-solving capabilities and creativity. It might be that they could agree only on C. It might be that everyone would get everything they wanted.

A Pusher and a Puller would negotiate differently still. The Puller would first find out what the Pusher wants, and the Pusher would be quick to tell him. If the Puller were particularly skillful, she would zero in on the fact that both parties want C and use that to her advantage. "Oh, you want C?" she would say to the Pusher. "I could agree to C, if you could agree to my getting D." If they entered into logical give and take, the Pusher would agree to the Puller's D and then ask for A. The Puller would accede to that if the Pusher would accede to E. At that point, the Puller, without having asked for everything, would have gotten everything, *simply by building on common ground without identifying it as such.*

Is this fair? Ethical? The ethics of negotiation is a big field, and much has been written on it. I happen to believe the only thing of value that I own is my name, so I strive for maintaining my personal integrity in all that I do. Consequently, I do not see outright lying as an ethical move. But passive bluffing is okay with me, as long as the bluff is not hurtful. Here the Puller, by maintaining her silence, was passively bluffing, allowing the Other to believe that his priority, C, was a matter of contention, when it was, instead, common ground.

But don't listen to me about ethics. Ethics is a personal matter, so decide your ethics for yourself. The following thought from the director of the Wharton Executive Negotiation Workshop, G. Richard Shell, and his book *Bargaining for Advantage* (Viking, 1999) may help your thinking:

> Negotiators who value "personal integrity" can be counted on to negotiate consistently, using a thoughtful set of personal values that they could, if necessary, explain and defend to others. . . . Your personal beliefs about ethics also come with a price tag: The stricter your ethical standards, the higher the cost you must be willing to pay to uphold them in any transaction. The lower your ethical standards, the higher the price may be in terms of your reputation. And the lower the standards of those with whom you must deal, the more time, energy, and prudence are required to defend yourself and your interests.

A word of warning before we go on to something else: Don't confuse Pushing with being competitive and Pulling with being passive. A Puller can be competitive—he just uses questions in his quest to win the Other over. A Pusher can be Passive—she just uses statements to persuade. You can be a Pusher and practice principled negotiation. You can also be a Puller and practice principled negotiation. We are talking about persuasion *styles* here, nothing more, nothing less.

Whom Do You Trust? Who Trusts You?

We talked in the last chapter about the fact that principled negotiation works independently of trust, but we know from our own experience how valuable trust is in the design and construction world. Does the choice in communication behaviors and styles make a difference in trust building? Research shows it does, and so probably does your own experience. Think back to the last time you negotiated with clients you had known for years about a new project. There may have been some issues to work out, but weren't you, on the whole, comfortable? Didn't it help that, without much trouble, you felt you could predict how they would react to your ideas? Wasn't it easier because you knew more or less where they were coming from? In short, wasn't it advantageous to be able not to worry continuously about the Other and focus instead on working with the Other to solve the problem? Now think about negotiating with potential clients you don't know. Wouldn't you wish to know how to transform a negotiation with someone you don't know into an experience as comfortable and effective as negotiating with someone you do know?

Highly skilled negotiators work at creating just that kind of environment of comfort and trust for both themselves and the Other. They rely on the three communication behaviors to make themselves seem accessible and trustworthy to the Other, and they focus just as much energy on learning about the Other. They ask questions, they disclose information about themselves, and they practice the "three Cs" introduced in Chapter 3—*competence, candor,* and *concern.*

Asking Questions

Research shows that 20 percent of the expert negotiator's behavior revolves around using questions; they seek information from the Other nearly *three times more often* than the average negotiator. Ten percent of their behavior has them testing for understanding—*more than twice as often* as the average negotiator. That means at least fully a third of their behaviors involve Pulling. When they do make statements, some 8 percent of their behavior involves summarizing what they heard the Other say. And they use summarizing, a Clarifying technique, nearly twice as often as the average negotiator. Putting those percentages all together, we find that some 40 percent of expert negotiators' behavior involves Clarifying the Other's thinking—twice as much as the average negotiators' behavior.[8]

Why do expert negotiators rely so heavily on questions and other Clarifying behaviors? For many reasons. Perhaps the most compelling is that, *questions help you persuade the Other.* This comes home to me daily, most recently when a client asked me whether he should buy a certain piece of real estate with a small business already on it. I thought the deal might ultimately prove dreadful, but I knew, if I told him that, he always would feel cheated of the great opportunity that would have let him retire for life. So instead of telling him my gut reaction, I suggested that neither of us knew enough to answer his

---

[8] Interestingly, though, when you add in the data on giving information, which, as you remember, is a form of Clarifying behavior, Pushers end up "Clarifying" more than Pullers. They spend that *much more time than expert negotiators giving information* about the rightness of their negotiating stance.

question. I listed 15 things I needed to know before I could comfortably answer. My questions triggered five more in him. He called back the next week with answers to all of them. He walked me through what he found out and his analysis of the data. By the end of our conversation, he had persuaded himself to abandon the deal. Nothing I could ever have said would have been as persuasive.

Questions expose problems in your own thinking. As useful as questions are in persuading the Other of the weaknesses in their thinking, questions are great for discovering the weaknesses in your own thinking. And because all you're doing is asking a question—and not telling your idea—nobody needs to know how shoddy your thinking is. I know this one, too, from experience. When I first arrived in Virginia, I was introduced to John Stowers. John was the contractor of the farm we then owned. Irascible, crafty, clever by yards, wiser than I will ever hope to be, with just a bit of curmudgeon woven in, John is a craftsman of the old school, then unused to dealing with us City Women. I approached him with caution and respect, knowing full well he was taking my measure every step of the way. I watched as he started to sand a stair clearly below code. I wanted to tell him he was wasting our time and money: No inspector would approve that stair. But few people tell John Stowers how to build, and I wasn't going to be one of them. Instead, I asked about the stair: When did he think it was originally built, what wood was used, how did they plane it, and how would an inspector view such a stair today? He gave me a 15-minute, in-depth insight into wood building in the early 1800s, during which he also explained that Virginia code had special exceptions for historic properties. Asking questions has the benefit of keeping your own thinking—and naïveté—a secret. I ask questions a lot.

Questions reveal the Other's needs, values, and priorities. It cannot be said enough: Even if you know the Other, you can't read people's minds. Their heart and soul are a secret. Their problems and fears are their own. You have to ask questions to delve into what's making people tick. You have to ask questions to ferret out people's interests, to find out what is driving their positions, what is driving them. You cannot project from your experience. You cannot guess. We learned this together from our teenager in Chapter 4. We relearn it with others every day.

What's more, if you ask the right questions, you may discover the strategic information that helps you clinch the deal. I helped settle one A/E claim just that way. During a coffee break, the owner mused, "Oh, if I could only make this case disappear!" "Disappear?" I asked. He explained in great detail how sick he was of the entire matter. He "would drop it in an instant just to get on with life." There was only one more question to ask. "If I could get my client to drop his counterclaim, would you drop your claim?" The parties filed jointly for case dismissal with prejudice that afternoon.

Questions help with elegant option development. Even the best of negotiators gets stuck from time to time, and a game of "What if. . . ?" can prove just the strategy for bridging an impasse. Here the players, using questions, bounce ideas against the wall and explore their implications without tying themselves to any one of the ideas. I used this once to mediate a copyright infringement claim. All the parties were deeply mired in mud, and no one wanted to take the first step to solid ground, for fear of losing his footing further. By asking a series of "what if" questions, testing for understanding, summarizing when necessary to secure agreements (and disagreements), and encouraging everyone to build on the best ideas of all the parties, we figured out not only a way to settle their dispute but also a system whereby the two architects could work together profitably in the future.

Questions are a solid alternative to saying no. There is one reality in all negotiations: Anyone can ask for anything at any time, and they often do. Sometimes askers may be unwise to press for something because, had they been practicing no-surprise design, they should have known the Other wouldn't agree. Timing may be inopportune. Agreeing may not be in the Other's interest. Whatever. And, with a wrongly made request, goodwill may be lost. But people will ask for anything nonetheless.

Sometimes it is necessary to say no to win the trust and respect of the Other. More often, however, saying no ends the negotiation prematurely or at least derails it for a while. This is unfortunate and usually unnecessary, especially when a well-thought-out question often can readily take the place of no.

A question like "Why is that important to you?" shows, for example, that you are intent on understanding the Others' needs. "How do you see that working?" clearly signals you want to know how they are viewing the situation and are open to their ideas. If it becomes clear to all of you, as they explain their idea, that it will or won't work, so much the better. Had you said no and their approach was better than your own, both of you would have been cheated. Had you said no and their approach would not have worked, you would have deprived them of the opportunity of discovering that for themselves through your artfully posed questions.

In any event, asking questions buys you time to consider and develop more workable responses. Which brings us to this point:

Questions let you control the negotiation. If you are asking questions, the Other is talking. That alone gives you more time to think (and even regroup mentally) than the Other has. When you couple this advantage with all the others we have just explored, it is no wonder that skilled negotiators rely on questions to the extent they do to win people over.[9]

All that said, asking questions can be turned into a dirty trick, if one person does all the asking. But just as we learned in kindergarten, you can say, "I answered five questions. Now it's your turn to answer some questions of mine." We're all brought up on your turn–my turn. It invariably works.

Questions help you build trust. We know that, the more competence, candor, and concern the client perceives, the more the client trusts the Other. As you can't buy or beg trust, what better way is there to build it than by asking targeted questions that cause the Other to think, "Wow. He gets it"? And, if the Other has any doubt as to your trustworthiness, a thoughtful use of the information the Other has just given you proves without you saying that you listened and understood the Other. Good questions well used, then, are a key building block of trust,

---

[9] *Difficult Conversations*, by Douglas Stone, Bruce Patton, and Sheila Heen (Viking Penguin, 1999), is a wonderful book that was brought to my attention after I finished this chapter. It brings home the effectiveness of using Clarifying behaviors in tough situations.

allowing you to demonstrate your competence and concern without your becoming a talking brochure.

Disclosing Information

Skilled negotiators also use "your turn—my turn" when disclosing information. The art of reciprocal disclosure helps negotiators increase the Other's comfort as well as their own. It also tests whether the Other is worthy of trust. If you open up and get no response, it signals you to be wary.

Research on developing trust also centers on how people disclose information, particularly about themselves, to the Other. Some people communicate *external information;* that is, when they disclose personal information, they translate it into statements about the objective, observable world. ("It's 5:00 o'clock. Let's explore your proposal tomorrow.") Others rely on *internal information* when they communicate, making statements about their own feelings, motives, and concerns. ("I want to be fresh when I focus on your proposal, but as it is past 5:00 o'clock, I'm too tired to be fresh. Let's explore your proposal tomorrow.") Still others *put internal information in an external form.* Instead of saying, "I feel uneasy about your proposal," these people would say, "Your proposal won't work." Research shows that expert negotiators, who are more adept at developing trust, tend to give internal information quite often. In fact, 12 percent of their behavior involves giving internal information, one and a half times as often as average negotiators. *By talking more about their inner feelings and perceptions, expert negotiators encourage and facilitate reciprocal disclosure by the Other.*

Deal Breakers

Though it's a good idea to look for alternatives to saying no, there are times when no is the only answer available to you—when it's a deal breaker. At that time, it's best to say, "I'm sorry; that's a deal-breaking issue for me. I'm going to have to say no." Why mess around when "no" is absolutely "no"? Just make sure you have thought through the issue, and it is truly a deal breaker for you.

Trust me on this one. The Other will be grateful for your candor. This fact came home to me when once I had to negotiate a construction loan for the farm, which we operated as a separate business from our other work. We didn't mix cattle and consulting (although some would say they have bull in common). The bank, however, wanted to cross-collateralize the loan for the farm with my husband's consulting business—a complete deal breaker for us. But the bank kept saying it wanted to work with me on the issue. Ten days later, I finally realized the bank was never going to budge on the issue. So I had to hustle and find another bank. I fumed—so much time wasted. Why couldn't the loan officer have been candid with me?

Expert negotiators also do something else to induce trust: *They label their behavior.* "I have a proposal to make." "I have a question." "I need to call my office at noon and will need to ask for a 10-minute break then." Why do they do this? Just as contracts make commercial life predictable and thus more comfortable, expert negotiators signal their behavior before they act, to make themselves and the negotiations more predictable, hence more comfortable for everyone. In this way, they induce trust.

There is one exception to this "rule." Expert negotiators rarely give advance warning of disagreeing behavior, and, when they do disagree, they make their point and then retreat quickly into their old predictable, getting-to-yes mode. We'll talk more about this when we get to strategies for disagreeing and counterproposals later in this chapter.

Practicing the Three Cs

In Chapter 3, we learned about Huthwaite research on trust: Clients look for competence, candor, and concern in the professionals they retain. *The more the client sees the consultant being competent, candid, and concerned about the client, the more the client tends to trust the consultant.* It is easy to say, "Be candid, concerned, and competent," but it is not always easy to do and even harder to prove that you are being candid, concerned, and competent. Try proving you are trustworthy by saying to someone, "Candidly. . . ." Saying that invariably puts the Other on guard. Additionally, it raises an issue where none existed: Were you not being candid before? When will you deceive again?

There are clearly ways to prove you are Other-focused. Asking questions, as we have just learned, helps prove to the Other that what they say, think, and feel is important to you. Disclosure of internal information helps, too, particularly when it makes your motivations and perceptions transparent. But is there something more you can do?

In one of the best books on earning and deserving trust, *The Trusted Advisor*, David H. Maister and his colleagues, Charles H. Green and Robert M. Galford, take earlier findings one step further, developing what they call the *trust equation:*

$$\text{TRUST} = \frac{\text{Credibility} + \text{Reliability} + \text{Intimacy}}{\text{Self-Orientation}}$$

In other words, the more credible, reliable, and intimate (in our parlance, we would use the word "concerned") you are with and about the Other *and* the less self-oriented you are, the more you will be trusted by the Other. How do you communicate that you are *not* being self-oriented? You don't. You *demonstrate* it by your conduct, including:

➤ Not relating your clients' stories to yourself

➤ Not reciting your qualifications

➤ Not having the need to appear clever, bright, or witty

➤ Not being afraid to say you don't know

➤ Not dropping the names of your other clients

➤ Not going on about buildings you have designed

➤ Not answering questions too quickly

➤ Not putting forth hypotheses or problem statements before hearing the client's hypotheses and problem statements

➤ Not watching and listening to the client as just a source of data for your design solution

Does that list come as a surprise to you? It certainly did to me. After all, every lecture geared to architects, every article, and even my much-loved twelfth edition of the AIA *Handbook* tells architects that every behavior on that list attracts clients, sells projects, and persuades the Other of their value.

I learned the truth of this empirically when my husband and I interviewed more than a dozen architects for a complex historic preservation project we were considering. To a person, the architects told us about their past projects and clients and why they would be great for the job. One architect took everything we said and related it to a building the architect had seen or designed. Another refused to tell us what he was thinking about the project, as if we were asking for free services. Except for a few questions they needed us to answer to begin their design thinking, no one asked about us much. We hired none of them, as we knew they were all great architects but had absolutely no clue as to whether they would be good architects for us.

So what can an architect do to demonstrate competence, candor, and concern? Your options are as plentiful as your creativity, but here are a few to start you off:

➤ You can prove you are credible by asking insightful questions about the issues facing your client, their situation, their industry.

➤ You can prove you are reliable by arriving on time, following up as promised, and being honest about what will happen next—both good and bad.

➤ You can prove that you are concerned by being willing to recognize and explore the real risks the Other is facing, should you work together on the project.

➤ You can prove you are not self-oriented by never discussing your liability and by focusing only on managing the Other's risk.

Strategies for Disagreeing

I mentioned that expert negotiators label their behaviors. They do—with one exception: *Expert negotiators do not signal disagreement before they disagree.* How then do they disagree?

First, they actively listen, using questions to seek information and test for understanding. And often, they summarize what they have heard. They do this for several reasons: to ensure both themselves and the

Other that they have heard correctly, to confirm that everyone is on the same page, and to demonstrate their concern by proving to the Other that they have listened. And, of course, their questioning may lead the Other to discover flaws in their own thinking, thus making disagreement unnecessary.

But expert negotiators do this extensive testing and summarizing for a self-oriented reason, too: *They would rather a negotiation fall apart in front of them at the negotiation table, where they can pick up the pieces, brush them off, and put them back together, than later in the marketplace, or worse, in a courtroom.* And what better strategy is there to discover disagreement than by summarizing the view of the Other?

Before I understood this, I used to say, "Yes, I've heard exactly what you've said, and you're wrong." But people would not give up on their points because they did not think they had been heard, else why would I think they were wrong? And, as we all now know, until people believe they have been heard, they cannot get off the dime, wherever their

Active Listening

It does no good to ask questions unless you listen, and expert negotiators are great at listening and conveying to speakers that they have been heard. That is because they know that "active listening" has little to do with the listener and everything to do with the speaker. In other words, *you have not listened until the speaker signals that they have been correctly heard.* This reality provides yet another reason why expert negotiators do so much testing for understanding and summarizing. In addition to wanting to suss out the Other's positions and interests, they want to demonstrate concern, to make it eminently clear to the Other that what the Other has to say is important to them *and that it has been heard.* So, if you really want to build trust, ask away and make sure you listen actively.

dime is located. Once I understood what expert negotiators know, I changed my ways. Now I stop and gain agreement from the speaker that I have correctly heard the point being made. Only then do I disagree. For example:

> "Let me see if I understand you correctly? You're saying this and this and this and this and this? Do I have that right?"
>
> "Yes."
>
> "And the reason you're saying that is because you're concerned about the liability issues?"
>
> "Exactly, that's right."
>
> "I can see why you'd be concerned, but here's why I think your concern is misplaced. . . ."

That person has been listened to. And again, as we know, once people feel they have been heard, they feel freer to extricate themselves from their positions and reconnect with you as a joint problem solver.

But expert negotiators do more than summarize and then disagree. We know that expert negotiators, as a rule, do not announce when they are going to say no. They don't say, "Excuse me, sir, I'm going to say no and tell you why you're wrong." They don't do that because then nobody listens. People who are going to be told they are wrong immediately begin to muster information to tell you why you're wrong. The conversation just stops. They will never hear your reasoning. They are just too busy thinking about how they are going to respond to you. So how do expert negotiators disagree? They put their reasoning first and their disagreement last. They say, "Because of A, because of B, and because of C, I'm going to have to disagree with you." That way the

Other has to deal with their reasoning, not just their disagreement. An example:

> "Let me see if I heard what you're saying. You're saying that if we work an 18-hour day and produce for you construction documents (CDs) that the contractor can use unstintingly and without change orders, and we do it on a shorter schedule than either of us imagined when you retained us to design the building, you will be able to recoup twice the profit you had anticipated and would cover all the overtime costs our staff and our consultant's staff engendered? Do I have it right?"

> "Yes."

> "I hear you, and I can see why the idea is so attractive. It's hard to resist doubling your profit. And your idea could work if we could guarantee perfect CDs that didn't need any change orders. But I've never seen perfect CDs in real life, and I'm concerned that 18-hour days could introduce errors that would end up cutting your profit rather than doubling it. Because of that, I can't accept your proposal."

To summarize: Expert negotiators tend to be Pullers, relying heavily on certain communication behaviors—building on the proposals of another, seeking information, testing for understanding, summarizing, and supporting. In addition, to build trust and create a comfortable negotiation environment, they ask questions, label their behavior, disclose internal information about themselves, and foster reciprocal disclosure. As important, they seek out opportunities to demonstrate by their conduct that they are competent, candid, and more concerned about the Other than about themselves.

That's not the end of it. As important as what expert negotiators do is what they don't do: They don't use common negotiating behaviors that most of us do use. (*Quel surprise!*)

What Expert Negotiators Don't Do

There are four things that expert negotiators do not do:

- ➤ They do not counter the Other's proposal with one of their own.
- ➤ They do not give a string of reasons in support of their proposals.
- ➤ They avoid defend/attack spirals.
- ➤ They assiduously avoid "irritators," words that neither persuade nor break deals but serve only to annoy the Other.

Given everything you've learned about how expert negotiators communicate, you may be able to figure out for yourself why expert negotiators avoid these strategies, but let's think them through together, one by one.

Counterproposals

When a person has laid a proposal on the table and you counter that proposal with one of your own, what, in fact, is going on? Aren't you really saying to the Other, "No, I don't want to do it *your* way. I want you to do it *my* way"? Even if that is not your intent when you put forward a counterproposal, could you blame the Other for hearing it that way?

Now, we know that expert negotiators disagree by giving their reasons first and their nonacceptance second, so, on that basis alone, we wouldn't expect them to use counterproposals in negotiation. But are there other reasons to avoid giving counterproposals? One is quite obvious: *People are least capable of hearing a new idea when one of their own is being rejected*. No matter how good the idea, when one person's idea is pending, that person is the least receptive to hearing the idea of another. So wrap a good idea in a counterproposal, and odds are you will watch it be shot down before it is even considered.

But there is an even better reason why expert negotiators avoid using counterproposals (as if that one were not good enough). To figure out what that reason is, you have to think through how counterproposals work in a negotiation. Let's take a "typical" situation. Your client wants you to speed up your design services to complete CDs in two weeks. If you work your tail off, you can get them done in eight weeks. You counter their two weeks with eight. The client counters that with three, and so on and so on until you split the baby and settle on four weeks. But will the client be happy? No, not if they really needed the documents in two weeks. And will you really be able to produce them in four weeks? No, not if you really needed eight to do a passable job. So why do expert negotiators avoid counterproposals? *Because the game of bargaining and compromise that counterproposals engender ends up with no one's interests being met.* The counterproposal strategy just does not work.

So how do you react to proposals you do not want to accept? With questions, most certainly. What better way to get others to recognize the weaknesses in their proposals from your perspective than by helping them expose those weaknesses themselves? You could follow "We had eight weeks scheduled to do the CDs, and that required 10-hour days to do them well" with questions like these:

- Which is more important to you: getting the CDs fast or getting them right?

- Cutting corners means taking risks. How much risk are *you* ready to assume in order to get the CDs faster?

- A rush job inevitably means that we'll have to put whoever is available onto the project. Does it worry you that the least-experienced team members will be managing this very compressed schedule?

- Would it help you if we got the demolition and foundation CDs to you in two weeks so you can start construction? We could then get the rest of them to you later.

Argument Dilution

In our litigious society, we know that you will win a court case if the *weight of the evidence* cuts your way. Even outside the courtroom, we use "weight" images when we talk of persuasion. We say "the argument hangs in the balance," or you "tip the argument" in your favor, if your reasoning is more compelling than the Other's. But does research bear out that the argument-listing negotiator with the heaviest accumulation of toys wins? It does not. On the contrary, it shows that expert negotiators give fewer reasons in support of their positions than average negotiators do—nearly one-third fewer. Why? *Because the more reasons you give, the greater the risk that you will give a weak reason that dilutes the impact of the strong ones.*

Now this may come as news to you, but it shouldn't. As little kids, we already knew this. When our parents asked us why we didn't do something, we gave them one reason and only one: "I don't want to." As teenagers we also knew this. When our parents asked us why they should agree to whatever we wanted to do, we said, "Mary's parents (or Joe's) are letting her (or him) do it." Only after we over-educated ourselves, did we start compiling lists as to why we should get our way. Research suggests we work too hard. One compelling reason, or possibly two, should suffice.

As interesting as this research finding may be, there is a dirty trick hidden therein. You can ask the Other for their reasons, and, after the strong ones come out, you can ask, "Any other reason?" And you can keep on soliciting reasons until the weaker ones come out. Then, you can say, "Is that why? Well, if that's your reason, I have to say 'no.'" Am I suggesting you use this dirty trick? On the contrary. I am describing it solely so you can recognize it and not get ambushed by it.

Defend/Attack Spirals

Defend/Attack spirals are as human as wishful thinking. They start with someone tossing a small stone at the Other, and the Other tossing a slightly bigger stone back. Before you know it, both sides are attacking each other with boulders. Finally, someone tosses a grenade, and both sides walk out in a huff. You know the drill. There is no reason to describe it.

Expert negotiators, by and large, don't get sucked into Defend/Attack spirals, although average negotiators do—nearly three times as often as expert negotiators.[10] Expert negotiators attack rarely but—on the few occasions they decide to attack—they attack without warning. They fire off their strongest point of disagreement up front, straight between the Other's eyes. In other words, they don't telegraph their unhappiness about how the negotiation is going. They don't let their emotions leak out. If they are really upset, they tell the Other once, and so strongly that the Other can make no mistake about what they are saying.

This may go contrary to the way you were brought up, especially if you were told to be nice to the Other. Being nice in a negotiation about something critical to your interests does all parties a disservice. "I'm not entirely happy with the idea that. . . ." allows the Other to think you are partly happy with the idea. Being gentle with your disagreement allows the Other to discount it. So, if you really disagree, don't soften it. Give no preliminaries. Do it once. Do it unambivalently. Do it unequivocally. Make your disagreement clear.

I learned this the hard way. I did not like an architect's design, but I wanted to be nice, so I said, "I am not completely comfortable with some aspects

---

[10] Note: Expert negotiators did get caught up in the Defend/Attack spiral, but not often. The fact that they did, though, means one thing: There is hope for all of us.

of the design." As a result, I was not heard. I may have thought I was putting it gently, but in reality I was being unfair, frustrating, and expensive both to me and to the architect.

Irritators

Average negotiators use *irritators*—those words or phrases that add nothing to persuasiveness but irritate the Other—five times more often than skilled negotiators do. Which words exactly are they? "Fair" is one. "Reasonable" is another. And "generous" is right up there in the top three. Why do these trigger words irritate so? Because when you say to the Other that you are being fair or reasonable or generous, you are, by definition, implying that the Other is being unfair or unreasonable or mean. People don't like that.

This is a real problem for architects who have been brought up saying that the AIA standard documents are written to be fair. To those architects, any deviation from the standard documents is probably "unfair." This attitude puts off any owner who uses their own form and causes those architects no end of negotiating trouble.

I warned an architect of this once and agreed to help him negotiate an owner-drafted contract—but only if he promised not to use the word "unfair" at any time throughout the negotiation. He sat on his mouth throughout the negotiation as we won point after point. Finally, we came to agreement. The owner said, "Well, I think we have a good contract, and I am eager to start work." This, even though the architect had won 98 percent of what he wanted. The architect could not stand it any longer.

"I just wanted a fair agreement," said he. It took us another 15 minutes to peel the owner off the ceiling. The contract was signed, but I have always wondered how it worked out. So avoid the word "fair." Try "workable" instead, and isn't that what you and your client are striving for—a solution that works for you both?

So, where are we? We have the principled negotiation process pinned down; we are prepared to execute it, with the skills of expert negotiators supporting us. Now it is time to learn how to work in groups.

Collaboration and Team Building

7

With the economy tightening and clients calling for increased focus on cost control and speeded construction, many in the profession are responding with increased use of IPD supported by BIM technology. For those to work, there will be a new premium on solid negotiation skills. Chapters 4, 5, and 6 will get you only partly there. You will also have to know how to apply those negotiation skills in groups. That's why I've added this new chapter "Collaboration and Team Building."

Now, you may ask, "What's the difference between negotiation and collaboration?" In the olden days, the answer was easy. Negotiation was outcome-oriented haggling, and collaboration was working together to create something. Today the answer is tougher. In both principled negotiation and in collaboration, you work to build common ground. Both require you to treat the Other—and the Other to treat you—as a joint problem solver with interests and needs, knowledge and perspective, and complexities to be shared and understood for the problem to be solved. And both require you to be an assertive practitioner, as we have defined that in the previous six chapters. Indeed, today interest-based negotiation calls on so many of the same skills as collaboration that many refer to it as collaborative negotiation.[1]

Perhaps the difference stems from nuance: In negotiation, you're exploring whether or not you will work together; in collaboration, you have already agreed to work together. Perhaps the difference revolves around substance: In negotiation, the focus revolves more around people and positions; in collaboration, more around issues and ideas. Perhaps the difference is timing: negotiation helps you to arrive at an agreed-upon plan, and collaboration takes that negotiated agreement and implements it in a way that satisfies everyone involved. Wherever the demarcation, any negotiator will tell you that, if a negotiation goes well, they lose the sense of "sidedness," so closely are they communing with the Other. And any collaborator will tell you that when issues get sticky, they put on their negotiation hat and hope that, together, the collaborators can rebuild common ground.

And collaborations have their own tensions, which is why so many of us don't jump at the chance to collaborate. As much as collaboration means "to work together, especially in a joint intellectual

---

[1] Yes, there is such a thing as competitive negotiation. It is outcome-oriented and usually involves one-off players, people who believe they will not be negotiating with the Other again in the future. It is marked by high assertiveness and low empathy. As architecture would crumble under that motif, we will relegate competitive negotiation to this footnote.

effort," and as much as that definition reminds us of what we enjoyed most about school and the design studio, collaboration also means "to cooperate treasonably, as with an enemy occupation force in one's country."[2] If you collaborate with the wrong people, or with the right people but in the wrong way, you may come to regret it. And that is precisely how we may have felt after Johnnie got an A when we did all the work—or worse, after we got all the blame when we followed Susie down her forcefully argued, seemingly beautiful, ultimately thorn-ridden primrose path. And, if you think of yourself as the best designer at the table, sharing control is not much fun. Worse, collaboration can be dangerous when what you say can be used against you in a court of law, as any architect who has been sued over a throwaway idea conveyed in the middle of an intense meeting and acted on without more examination can tell you.

In other words, collaboration is risky. It involves putting your ideas on the line to be evaluated by others who may not share your values and sensibilities. It involves the risk of having your ideas rejected, as well as the risk of having them accepted. It requires you to be open to the ideas of others, even though at first blush neither the idea nor its progenitor may make sense. It requires you to work with everything you have to pursue a path with no road map and possibly no discernible endpoint. It is scary. It is exhausting. When collaboration works well, the process is exhilarating. When it works poorly,

---

[2] I used the definitions in the *American Heritage Dictionary of the English Language*, fourth edition (NY: Houghton Mifflin Company, 2000).

debilitating. And yet, if you believe, as I do, that the magic of great endeavors only springs from the minds of many, collaboration is an opportunity for greatness that you can't pass up.

Oh, yeah? How many brainstorming sessions have *you* been to, Ms. Ava, where everybody works in groups and then presents their group's ideas to a larger group, and nothing, but nothing, comes out of it? Yes, we may all leave happy. It was a great way to spend the day, but geesh! To what end? If that's what you mean by "collaboration," spare me! And it doesn't seem to make a difference even when the group-think is managed by a professional facilitator, with minutes kept by a professional illustrator. Nothing comes of it, except maybe a printed collection of the illustrations mailed six weeks after the meeting. If that's collaboration, I have better ways to waste my time.

Rest assured, I've been there, too—but let's look at those meetings and, in fact, all sessions where people are called on to collaborate, in light of the communication behaviors we explored in Chapter 6.

Types of Meetings

A bit of administrivia first: There is a lot written on collaboration, how to run a meeting, how to facilitate group endeavors, and the like. To help you access those books, I have highlighted a few of my favorites in the Appendix. This chapter is not intended to replace them, but to give a design and a communications tilt to those issues, building on the principles and communication behaviors that you have acquired so far through this book. Whenever possible, design or fee issues will be used as examples, to grab your attention and make counterintuitive research more easily accessible. First, though, let's look at types of meetings, because different communication behaviors you have acquired will be called on, depending on the type of meeting.[3]

The Filtering Meeting

Have you ever gone to a meeting with an idea in your head? Excited as can be, you propose your idea. So does another fellow and another. The team leader takes the second idea, and the meeting proceeds from there. You and the third person feel a bit downhearted, so you sit through the meeting, contributing some, but with your hearts and minds elsewhere. The two of you later enjoy coffee together and grouse about the team leader. "She has her favorites. My ideas never get picked. They don't even get a fair airing." But you have missed the point. This team leader wasn't looking to brainstorm and come up with new ideas. This team leader had a decision to make, and the way she decided to reach it was through a *filtering meeting.*

Filtering meetings are used to reduce alternatives on the table to a manageable number—often to one. They are high on proposing and low on building on the ideas of others. If they work well, participants may find the clash of opposing ideas stimulating. The team leader may leave thrilled that a decision was reached. If they work badly, those whose ideas were

---

[3] The idea of Filter and Amplifier meetings was first proposed by Neil Rackham in 1975 in a paper written in England entitled "Models for Explaining Behavior." The description of the two meetings and their management comes from that paper. The application of his research is all mine.

rejected may leave with hard feelings, a reluctance to risk, and no commitment to the path chosen. (Especially if their ideas were not even heard.) The team leader may feel that getting to yes is like pulling teeth. Next time she needs to reach a decision, she may decide to call on different players.

Filtering meetings don't necessarily put a high value on collaboration. They may be called after a set of choices emerges, and the time has come to select among them. Or they may occur in an emergency or when a deadline is pending—for instance, when the marketing department has to decide which stories and pictures to run on the front of a new brochure. In those situations, filtering meetings can be effective, efficient, and valuable.

However, filtering meetings may be less effective if the team leader already has made a decision and is just going through the motions, and the team members know it. To them, that kind of filtering meeting may seem like a manipulative effort at consensus building, rather than a decision-making event. Indeed, filtering meetings may be used, not because of the nature of the management need—i.e., a decision—but because of the nature of the manager's need. Managers who are comfortable only when they control a group situation will choose filtering meetings because they work well for the manager. But don't get too caught up in lay analyzing the team leader who uses filtering meetings routinely. Many use filtering meeting techniques simply because they have been taught that this is the way to run a meeting. Armed with an agenda with decision or action goals and tight discussion times allotted for each agenda item, they think this is the way to ensure meeting efficiency.

Collaboration and Team Building

What is the impact of a filtering meeting? On the upside, as we just mentioned, decisions get made. But if filtering meetings are the *only* meeting method an organization uses, those decisions may not be the best ones. If there hasn't been collaboration in advance, those decisions are not always optimal. Alternatives that could have worked, been built on, or even merged into the idea adopted may be discarded out of hand. Regardless of the timbre of the decisions made, under endless filtering meetings, morale can suffer. People whose ideas are glossed over may feel as discarded as their ideas. If that's the case, "politics" may infest the organization and its decision-making process, creating wasted time in the process.

Let's play this one out. You work for an organization that only has filtering meetings. You decide to outplay the team leader. The next time she calls a meeting, you try a new tactic. You meet with your closest collaborator in the group before the meeting and discuss the agenda and your ideas. You come up with a joint proposal and decide how each will lobby for it before the meeting and who will present it. You divide the decision makers between you, each lobbying those who like you the best. Everyone listens and responds nicely enough, but you enter the meeting uncertain that you have the votes.

When the item comes up for discussion, you jump in with your idea. Your chum says, "Neat idea. How would that work?" You grab her preplanned question as a second chance to present your idea, explaining more fully your proposal and how it will work. Your buddy supports the idea every step of the way, even offering her own idea, building on your proposal. None of the people you lobbied speaks up in support, though one or two nod approvingly. The team leader listens perfunctorily, allows a question or two, and moves on. At the end, you realize you've been dismissed again. You decide next time you have better things to do with your energy than amassing seeming support for a new idea. You hunker down.

The Amplifying Meeting

Back to you and your colleagues. You are now in a firm where the team leader calls a meeting whenever she has an issue or issues to resolve. She picks the people with the expertise she thinks the problems demand, but, other than that, there is no agenda, save for resolving the problems that necessitated the meeting. She enters the meeting with ideas but nothing carved in concrete, describes the problem as she sees it, and asks the group whether she has missed anything. People identify and fill in her blanks. She then asks the group for possible solutions. People jump in with ideas. Up they go on the wall for discussion. She then asks each idea's progenitor, in turn, to explain the idea in more depth.

Your idea comes up first. She asks you to expound on it. You do. She then invites others to build on your proposal. They get caught up in the spirit of the meeting and contribute their own suggestions for strengthening your idea, even though they have ideas of their own on the wall, too. People with concerns voice them, and everybody chips in about how to cure them. In the process, a different idea surfaces from somebody else. Everyone steps forward to strengthen that idea, just as they did with yours. Even you jump into the mix. Soon there are two good ideas on the table, and everybody feels both are worth pursuing. The two ideas have become everyone's ideas. The group deals with the third and fourth ideas, again with everyone building on their strengths and curing the ideas' weaknesses. The group is now faced with five good choices, some stronger in some areas than others, but all worth implementing. The leader asks the group which they should pursue. The group struggles more and finally decides which proposal to try first. At the end, maybe your proposal was bought, maybe not, but you leave the meeting feeling great. A decision was made, and you contributed to it. And your colleagues leave just as exhilarated, as progress has been made, and they believe, like you, that they were essential contributors. You can't wait to do your part to help the group's chosen route succeed.

This is the crux of an *Amplifying Meeting*—low on proposing, and high on building on the proposals of others. *Unlike the filtering meeting, which eliminates choices, the amplifying meeting extends or develops them.* And unlike a filtering meeting, where so much "work," both political and substantive, is done before the meeting, all the work at the amplifying meeting is done at the table.

What is the impact of an amplifying meeting? Increased number of creative ideas, increased group commitment to the ideas as well as to their successful implementation, and measurably better results. Participants are also happier as they see their contributions at work. For an architecture firm, amplifying meetings, like the one just described, ring bells. First, they are comfortable, reminding you of the best group design experiences you have had. Second, they are normal: You are constantly working in groups, whether it is in your design studio, an owner's boardroom, your consultant's office, with a government review team, or on the construction site. Getting the best ideas on the table is the mainstay of practice, and you love being part of that process. Besides, that is where the owner gets to see what a smart choice it was to retain you.

Is there no downside to amplifying meetings? Everything has a downside, and, with amplifying meetings, the problems are time and structure. Amplifying meetings take time, and, if not well run, too much time. And amplifying meetings can easily segue into the drawings-on-the-wall meeting we described earlier, where ultimately nothing gets done.

How to Make Meetings Work

How do you do it? Is it a question of playing nice together? If so, how do you "play nice" in architecture, where the stakes are high and the reality of time and money so often suck the oxygen out of the air? And how on earth do you play nice and still be effective, when everybody is certain that their ideas are the best, and not one idea is spot on.

First, if you know anything about my thinking by now, you know I no more value "being nice" for the sake of being nice than I do being "fair" for the sake of being fair. If those approaches hurt the client and the project, most probably they'll hurt everyone at the table, including you—if not at that moment, in a matter of time. Remember, though, as in negotiations, the best negotiators are not easy, just easy to work with, so too in collaboration, the best collaborators are not easy, just easy to work with. And you already know how to be easy to work with: You use unstintingly the communication behaviors of expert negotiators that we explored in Chapter 6. You actively listen, you get sign-off that you have indeed heard, you Clarify, and you build on the proposals of others, supporting ideas when appropriate, and explaining your reasons first when you can't, so that others can struggle along with you to solve the issues at hand. You stay what the Harvard Negotiation Project calls "unconditionally constructive"—ever willing to meld expertise and perspectives to get a solution everyone can live with that stands the test of time.

Let's go back to that brainstorming meeting described in the beginning of this chapter. That was an amplifying meeting, wasn't it? Lots of ideas came out, scores of options, but nothing was achieved. Why would we want to use amplifying meetings, given that? Okay. Let's analyze that meeting and see what worked, what didn't, and what could have been done differently and better, given everything we now know about communication behaviors and meetings.

Using Brainstorming Well

Brainstorming—the promulgation of ideas without judgment—plays a key role in generating creativity and in amplifying meetings. Collaborators who run amplifying meetings cherish brainstorming as a tool, especially as it also plays a key role in getting people unstuck. What better way to think out of the box than to upend it? But brainstorming, without more, is not collaboration, as we mean it here. Brainstorming, at its essence, is a form of what we called *Initiating*. Without *Clarifying* behaviors that allow focused exploration, any one idea at a meeting of five people may really be five ideas. And without *Reacting* behaviors, everyone may leave the table without knowing which idea was the one idea agreed to by all. *Collaboration, like negotiation, requires all three behaviors to be present—Initiating, Clarifying, and Reacting—if a group is to accomplish anything.*

What does that mean to you as the architect? If you want to serve a leadership role in a group, whether you are the designated leader or not, one of the best ways is to help deliberations along by filling the communication behavior vacuums that so easily arise. At an amplifying meeting of four participants, with lots of Initiating and Reacting but no Clarifying, and with voices beginning to rise as to whose approach the client will like best, you can help by inviting Clarifying behaviors. "We have four good ideas on the table, and each of us, in describing our idea, has said it met the client's 'most compelling needs.' This client, as we all know, has a lot of needs—some of them contradictory. Which needs do each of us think are the 'most compelling'? What has the client said that leads you to think that way? Do any needs require immediate attention for other needs to be met?" With that information pinned down and shared, you can invite Reacting. "Does everyone agree on our list? On the suggested ranking? Anyone disagree?" In this way, you can help the group refocus the conversation (and its energies) from whose design is best to which of your shared client's needs are so "compelling" they should inform the design first. Once consensus is reached, the group should be in a better position to explore and evaluate the various design routes under consideration.

Now, let's apply the communication behaviors to a filtering meeting. Can a team leader use them to increase collaboration in a filtering setting where the players are unused to collaborating? Certainly, but the team leader has to understand how difficult it will be on the players, if collaboration is to succeed. Think back to the premeeting preparatory planning sessions the players in a filtering-meeting-only-organization go through. All of them have formed coalitions and have thought through the problem, their solution, the problems with their solution, and the solutions to those problems. Utterly prepared, they have no intention of losing. Accordingly, at the table, they don't listen to understand, but to gather ammunition to support their idea and torpedo yours. Mired in cement, too used to in-house politics, they have lost the facility to collaborate. You are going to have to help them.

Here the team leader can use the communication behaviors to provide a bona fide service by helping the attendees unstick themselves without feeling challenged in the process. Faced with Initiating, Reacting, and bad-faith questioning, the team leader can call on her Clarifying skills to invite the group to build on each others' proposals. In other words, to collaborate. "Pete, you have a problem with Samantha's proposal. Can you think of any way that problem can be cured?" "Mary, your idea seems compatible with Jimmy's. When we take a break, can the two of you see where meshing the two ideas takes you?" "Bill, if Al could provide your team backup, could you see a way to resolve the conflict between your two approaches?" By remaining unconditionally constructive and by filling the communications vacuum with the missing behaviors, the team leader, even though surrounded by naysayers, can create a safe playing field where collaboration can occur.

Facilitate Process

To create this safe playing field, effective team builders put a premium on facilitating process. They know that results will only be bought if the participants believe the contents were well sold. That means they will want to create a meeting process by which:

> ➤ All participants feel they had the opportunity to speak, and they were heard and understood.

> ➤ Good ideas were explored and made better, and concerns were raised and addressed.

> ➤ The results of the meeting directly flowed from the group's deliberations, notwithstanding whose idea prevailed.

Creating and cultivating process is no mean trick, but facilitating is more accessible if you keep the communication behaviors explored in the last chapter at the forefront, particularly *Pushing* and *Pulling*. Remember how we said that both Pushing and Pulling can be persuasive negotiating styles, but that Pulling works best where, as in architecture, long-term commitment is necessary for the agreed upon goal's success and for adequate time to build it. And do you remember why Pulling works so well? Because with Pulling the energy comes from the persuadee, often your client, who needs time to work through the problem and acquire ownership of the resolution. In truly collaborative meetings, everyone is a persuadee, and thus everyone can benefit from the power of Pulling.

While facilitating collaborative meetings requires you to call on your Pulling skills—seeking information, testing for understanding, and finding that little kernel of *je ne sais quoi* in someone else's idea that you can support and build on, it also requires you to pick up two new process behaviors—*Bringing In* and *Shutting Out.* It is these behaviors that will help you keep a meeting on track. Let's take them one by one.

Bringing in invites an attendee to contribute to the conversation. "Martha, we haven't heard from you in a while. Can you help us out here?" "We seem to need Clarifying. David, what did you mean by 'intensity'?" "Let's hear from Andrew." Used strategically, bringing in can give the reticent permission to speak, the idea generator the floor, and the backstabber the chance to disagree in the open. It is particularly useful when the team leader is awesomely talented or otherwise powerful. It is a simple and considerate way to encourage Initiating and Reacting behaviors among people who feel they are "lesser." And it can change an outcome. Let me tell you a story.

I was at a partnering meeting for a project still in CDs, and the contractor was already on board. The architect and the structural engineer were explaining a complicated part of the terracing design, made even more intricate by the demands of the site. The owner had plenty of questions, especially as the cost was going to be high. Finally, after 30 minutes of intense work, everybody seemed pleased, except me. The contractor had not said a word, and his eyes seemed scrunched, so I brought him in. "Abe, I may be reading you wrong, but you look worried. Are we missing something?" Abe took a deep breath and explained his constructibility challenge. Another 30 minutes or so, we had a new terrace design, constructible, as it turned out, more cheaply, and even more compelling, according to the architect who had designed both options. Every face was beaming, and the owner was thrilled.

Simply put, people like meetings where the level of bringing in is high. They see them as participative, considerate, and interesting, and they especially like team leaders who use that behavior, rating them and their meetings as productive and successful—unless the meetings get out of control. Effective team leaders avoid that happening by making judicious use of shutting out behaviors.

Shutting out reduces an attendee's participation, even to the point of cutting them off or out completely. People routinely do it without thinking by interrupting a speaker, hence, shutting them out. But team leaders shut out consciously in order to facilitate process and keep the meeting progressing. "You've spoken twice. Let's hear what someone else has to say." And it is not uncommon for them to shut out indirectly by using the Chapter 6 communication behaviors more directly. "I have a proposal to make." "I know you feel strongly about that, but the owner doesn't want us going in that direction, so I have to disagree." "Let me give you some more information." In these ways, off-base ideas, lost causes, floor holders, narcissists, and panderers are kept under control.

But watch yourselves. Not every repeater is an obstructer. I was on a board where one member was as smart and as ineloquent as a person could be. Fellow board members had a hard time listening and shut him out constantly. That only served to make him repeat himself more loudly, as he knew he wasn't being heard. I wasn't the board president, but that didn't stop me. "Wait," I would say to the group. "Harvey has said the same thing three times to us, and that means to me that what he is saying is important to him, and we are missing it. Harvey, did you just tell us 'A, B, and C'?" On hearing what I had heard, Harvey would try to make himself clearer. "Thank you, Harvey. I knew what you were saying was important, and I wasn't getting it. Are you saying 'A, C, E, and J'?" This process would continue—oh, usually once or twice more—until Harvey's idea was clear and on the table. And, wouldn't you know, some of his ideas were brilliant! Before we knew it, everyone was listening, eager to support Harvey getting his ideas across.

Shutting out, again if used judiciously, keeps meetings humming and on time. That is why some level of shutting out exists in most meetings. If used excessively, however, shutting out shuts a meeting down. People rate those latter meetings as disorganized and inconsiderate. Learning when and how to shut out is one of the team leader's many challenges.

Encourage Substance

When you're participating in a meeting, you probably get wrapped up in its substance, as well you should. No one invited you to the meeting to watch you inhale and exhale. But when you're the team leader, you're in a tight spot. If you focus solely on process, others at the meeting may feel suspicious—or worse, manipulated—because they know you have something substantive to offer and are choosing not to. If you get too heavily involved in substance, though, others may hesitate to speak up for fear of alienating you. As bad, the more you involve yourself in the content of the meeting, the more likely it is that running the meeting will suffer. How can you balance these two seemingly competing and possibly conflicting demands? Let's look to the research for the answer.

Rackham studied two types of group leaders. In his words, there were "Chairpeople," neutral about content and concerned solely with process—that is, the efficient and fair conduct of the meeting. The second type, "Meeting Managers," used the meeting to achieve objectives but also monitored process by the use of controls. Both used the communication behaviors to keep the meetings productive, but differently, as neutrality was a higher value to the chairperson than to the meeting manager.

For example, as you would expect when neutrality is the goal, Initiating proposals were more often about process than content. "Let's turn our attention next to item six." "I think if we break into smaller groups to discuss the problem, we will make more progress." When chairpeople did put forward content-laden ideas, their proposals usually integrated and built on the proposals already under consideration by the group. "Is there any way we could mesh Michelle's and Ernie's ideas? They don't seem incompatible." And, as you would expect from a process-oriented neutral, chairpeople were great clarifiers, using three of the four Clarifying behaviors—seeking information, testing for understanding, and summarizing. What Clarifying behavior were they low on? Giving information, of course. Were chairpeople so neutral they were non-reactors? Not necessarily, although they were low on disagreeing. And what Reacting behaviors chairpeople did use focused more on supporting people than ideas. "Kate was right to point out that concern." "Thank you, Arthur, for helping us think outside of the box."

Don't think for a minute, though, that chairpeople were utterly neutral. Though the best were perceived as unbiased, chairpeople were not immune from using bringing in behaviors to help the group inch towards ideas they believed important. Faced with a speaker with whom they disagreed, for example, they would scan attendees, trying to assess

The Difficult Person

So easy to recognize, so challenging to deal with, difficult people—not just angry people,[4] but truly difficult people—have merited scores of books. In fact, Google has 1,620,000 sites to help you on this one. From William Ury's *Getting Past No* to Rick Brinkman and Rick Kirschner's *Dealing with Difficult People* and beyond,[5] difficult people act difficult because at some time in their lives those tactics worked for them. And they are easy to recognize. Just a day before I wrote this, I chaired a meeting called to review bylaws that I had disseminated four weeks before, eliciting everyone's input and receiving hardly any. One participant showed up with a copy heavily marked up in Microsoft red. "I emailed you yours just before I came. Oh, you didn't get it? Hmm. Well, my copy has incorporated all the changes that *they* (unnamed) want." Did I know I was in a heap of trouble? You bet! Why am I telling you this? To underscore one thing: *Assertive practitioners know that the only participant in the room that they can control is themselves*, so that is where they focus first. They calm themselves, even extract themselves physically from the situation, so that, when they decide to deal with the situation, they can and do, using all the communication behaviors that usually work so well to build common ground.

---

[4] We explore handling anger in Chapter 9.
[5] I chose these two books from my bookcase just to start you on your way.

reaction. When the disagreeing speaker finished, they would then bring in the most articulate attendee who they believed supported their view. Shutting out, however, was used as a last resort, as people react so adversely to being excluded and oft view shutting out as evidence of bias.

Meeting managers do not have to work so hard to seem neutral. No one expects it of them. While they monitor participation and participation quality, they don't work exclusively on keeping the communication behaviors at the meeting in balance and proceeding efficiently. To ensure sufficient Clarifying and to help move in a wanted direction, they may put a proposal on the table themselves, seeking information in the process. "What do you think of this idea?" They can then call on people who support the idea for reaction. Disagree-ers can be asked for "cures." "What needs to be done to address that problem?" Low reactors can be brought in gently. "Ted, you've seen this situation before. Have you any good counsel for us?" High reactors can be held off, to allow them more thinking time before they speak. "Syl, I'm going to call on Lee and Bill first and then come back to you and get the benefit of your thinking." And the droner who takes 10 minutes to give information when he needs only two can have his remarks summarized by the meeting manager, who, with the droner's concurrence, can then respond, "Thank you. We got it. Let's keep in mind what you've said and move on." Meeting managers often call on the group for help, assigning summarizing to a participant, explaining that they will call on that participant from time to time to report back what the group has been saying, and asking another to keep track of the "parking lot" to ensure that no idea parked there for later consideration ends up being ignored.

And they do more. They take the substantive skills of expert negotiators and apply them rigorously to ensure the building of common ground.

Diffuse Anchoring

Anchoring is one of those substantive skills. Anchoring is one of the most potent subliminal tools available to a negotiator. It occurs daily, and most of us fall victim to it even when we know that it's going on. It is that powerful. *Anchoring is the process of affecting someone's thinking by dropping something—a number, language, an idea—as a reference point.* Owners do this to architects all the time, even when there is no basis for the number. "I'll pay you $25,000 for these services," and immediately you start thinking, "Can I do it for that? Can I talk him into $26,000?" And you don't even know how the owner arrived at that number or what it has to do with the price of beans. Nonetheless, that number is anchoring your thinking, or, to be more precise, you are letting that number anchor your thinking, even your negotiation strategy and expectations.

Don't be upset. You can be an assertive practitioner and still be suckered by anchoring. So powerful is anchoring that James Sebenius, a professor who teaches negotiation at Harvard, split his class in two to test it out. Half the class had to work on strategies for a "Winning on Wall Street" auction. The other half worked on an identical auction, but with a different name—"Community Value Game." And wouldn't you know, the group with the Wall Street mindset came in with a winning price substantially higher than the group thinking Community Value, and only the name of the game was different.

In Chapter 5, when we discussed fees, we also explored how research teaches us that expectations have an impact on results. (If you think high, you'll probably get high. If you think low, you'll probably get that, too.) But in anchoring, it is not *your* initial thinking that stalls the boat; it is a word, a number dropped by the Other. Collaborators make sure that word or number is considered, evaluated, and somehow taken into account, but they refuse to let the Other alone define their strategy.[6] Instead, they enter each collaboration, just as an expert negotiator does, with a range in mind and realistically rooted optimistic expectations in hand.

Use Reframing

Another substantive skill, reframing is the art of saying what you want to say so it can be heard and understood. In some way, it is the flip side of speaking in code, like the owner in Chapter 5 who said, "You're too expensive," and required you to figure out what was meant by those words. Let this story related to me by Robert C. Bordone of the Harvard Negotiation Project bring reframing home, because once you get the concept, you will never want to let it go.

---

[6] As a mediator, I often ask party counsel what they think of the Other's demand. Usually they say "Nothing. It's just a number." Maybe, but when the settlement is close to that number, you have to wonder whether the lawyer was suffering from anchoring or assertively making an independent judgment.

An acolyte asked his Monsignor, "May I smoke while I'm praying?" "Get out!" screamed the Monsignor. "When you pray, all you should do is pray. Anything else is blasphemy." The acolyte left properly chastised and utterly dismayed. He bumped into a fellow acolyte and relayed what had happened. "It's your fault. You don't know how to ask. Stay here and listen." And he did. The second acolyte approached the Monsignor. "Father, a question. May I pray while I am smoking?" The Monsignor smiled broadly. "Of course, my son. Prayer is always good."

Reframing is particularly powerful in architecture, where expertise and language so often unnecessarily separate the parties. Much of the research on reframing comes as much from sales as it does from negotiation.[7] It brings home that *how you say what you say is as important as the message you want to convey.*

Let's bring it into architecture. What do you do with the client who says to you that cost is crucial and aesthetics don't count? I know what you don't do. You don't argue. After all, the essence of assertive practice is, it is your client's project, not yours. And, if your client wants a cheap and ugly building, that is their decision. All it means to you is that you have a decision to make, too.

But don't go there. Typically a client isn't saying, "Design me something ugly." A client is asking you to discuss with them aesthetics and cost and how to manage them both. Welcome the conversation. It is what they retained you to do.

As a first step, you will want to acknowledge the legitimate importance of their criteria. Here,

---

[7] Here I tap into both sets of insights, but particularly those contained in *Major Account Sales Strategy*, cited earlier in Chapter 5.

there is only one—cost. Cost *is* important to them, and, as you are their design agent, it is important to you. It has to be, and your client needs to know that. Then, you can collaborate, using any of four reframing choices to help your client understand the implications of their criterion and perhaps influence it in the process. As the sidebar shows, you can:

> Redefine the criterion, altering its definition
> Overtake it by building up the importance of other criteria
> Trade the criterion off by balancing it with other factors
> Create alternative solutions by developing creative ways to meet the client's criterion

Each helps the Other understand more completely what they are asking and what it means for the project. Each moves you closer to finding common ground.

Reframing

Here is how you can use reframing to build common ground where an owner asserts more concern with costs than anything else, including aesthetics.

Redefine

Cost is very important to you, and so it is very important to me. Presumably "cost" covers the final costs of the finished building, including its aesthetics. Well, there are many ways to control final costs. For example, construction data show that for every $1 spent on preplanning, owners save $4 on implementation.

Overtake

Aesthetics are not important to you, but renting the building quickly is. So while the building doesn't have to win design awards, it is crucial that the building be differentiated in some tenant-valued way from the 30 other buildings available for rent today. Let's talk about how we could use design to differentiate your building so it rents out quickly.

Trade Off

The only way anyone can give you the quality you want at the cost you want is for you to give on either cost or quality, as your proposed budget won't support that definition of quality. Which one is the more important to you—quality or budget?

Create Alternative Solutions

You know, one way we can help you control costs is to have you bring the contractor on board as soon as we pin down the design. We could even do this project design-build, if that would help, with me as prime. Better yet, may I tell you about Integrated Project Delivery and Building Information Modeling?

Build on Differences

Expert collaborators, like expert negotiators, do not pretend that common ground exists when there isn't any, and they don't hide a show-stopper when there is one. They recognize there are indeed times where one issue is a deal breaker, and it makes limited sense to spend hours building common ground only to have that deal breaker destroy the effort in the last moments. But they also know that bona fide deal breakers are not the norm. Rather, the reality is that the parties have real differences between them and those differences compel them to argue, but they can be worked out.

Experts use differences to build common ground, and, for that reason, they welcome them. In fact, they use them to trade, as Robert H. Mnookin, Scott R. Peppet, and Andrew S. Tulumello, in their definitive book *Beyond Winning: Negotiating to Create Value in Deals and Disputes*, explain. It is the old story of "I want the inside of the orange to make juice" and "You want the outside of the orange to make chocolate orange peel" that excites their imagination, for finding the differences that meet critical, albeit diverse, interests unleashes the expert negotiator's ability to create value and the expert collaborator's ability to forge a lasting solution.

For architects, especially those who practice globally or in an IPD setting, building on differences is a substantive skill to be mastered. In one real way, in architecture, it is easy. No one is competing. All contribute to excellence, though differently. Tapping into what Mnookin calls these "non-competitive similarities" works splendidly for architects. "Wait. Let's calm down. We all want a project we're proud of brought in on time, on budget, and claims-free. We just differ right this second on how to achieve that. Let's listen to each other's proposals and. . . ." By now, you can finish that sentence without me. So let's move on to the world of owner-drafted contracts.

How to Say Yes, How to Say No

8

There's a story behind this chapter's title, too. It came from architects who called me when I was at Schinnerer, asking for help negotiating owner-drafted contracts. "How do I say no to my client without losing the commission?" I couldn't answer because between "yes" and "no" lay a myriad of options. Instead, I asked them to send me the contract so we could develop a comprehensive strategy and not get lost in a word war. Additionally, I asked them to send me the *entire* contract, because I was (and they had better be) just as interested in their client's design and business objectives as in the insurability of the contract. (Also, there are some lawyers out there who insert obviously objectionable language under miscellaneous provisions where it is more likely to be overlooked. Can you believe that?)

I then made the following deal: I would analyze the contract for them and with them, and help them devise negotiation strategies. But for future negotiations, they had to do the analysis and take a stab at strategy formation before sending the draft contract to me. I would then comment only on any problem language they had missed and coach them on strategy. We would do this, contract after contract, until they had the skills and confidence to analyze and negotiate their contracts alone. As I explained, *my goal was to empower them, not to facilitate dependency.* In that way, they would learn for themselves how to say yes and how to say no.

This chapter has the same goal. In order for both of us to achieve it, where I quote contract language, I've left space for you to jot down your analysis. Annotate it freely. The book is yours to mark up. To achieve maximum benefit from the book, you will want to do so. But let me stress: If you have read the earlier chapters, you know that *contract negotiation, when done well, is merely a memorialization of a problem-solving process, not a tug of war over words.* To the extent discrepancies in words signify anything, they signal differences in understanding and expectations. Therefore, they should be welcomed as an opportunity for you and the client to build common ground.

This chapter is not, nor could it be, a comprehensive review of owner-drafted language. Nor could it be a comprehensive review of construction contract language. If it were either of those, this book wouldn't be able to address the broader issues of negotiation that you need to master to be a crackerjack contract negotiator. But you are not the poorer for the focus. There are *scores* of comprehensive contract books around. A/E insurers publish them routinely. What this chapter does is take some of the most commonly found, hard-to-deal-with owner-drafted language and empower you to handle it effectively the next time you see it. The chapter also gives you a way to approach, analyze, and negotiate difficult language that is yet to be created, so you can recognize and deal with it when it comes your way.

You should know I didn't make up one word of the contract language that follows. I collect bad owner-drafted language. I do it as a hobby. In fact, the more "owner-ous" the language, the more I enjoy storing it.[1] It takes a lot of work, a tad of creativity, and often big-time legal fees to draft *really* bad contract language. It also takes lawyers who are either new to design and construction or who think their primary job is to protect their clients from real and imagined slights, rather than to assist them in achieving their overall long-term business objectives. This is not a "diss" of my profession. Lawyers who write this stuff may be reading their clients' desires correctly.

Now, how do I define bad contract language? Being an assertive practitioner myself, I look on the bright side of things whenever possible, so let's define good contract language instead. You know from Chapter 2 that I like language that supports project success, because if the project succeeds—that is, if the project is finished on time, on budget, claims-free, and profitably for all parties,[2] and (and this is

---

[1] Feel free to email me your worst, but only your worst. I have enough merely bad contract language in my files already. You can reach me at AvaEsq@aol.com.

[2] I believe in profit for all, else people will not do their best work. I just want to make sure that no one makes a killing at my or anyone's expense. Not all owners have this as a policy. For that matter, not all architects and contractors have it as a policy, which is why owner and party selection is so important. Sophisticated parties recognize that, just as payment is an incentive to do well, insufficient compensation results in behaviors detrimental to the project, such as cutting corners, shoddy workmanship, cheaper materials, minimal effort, and finding fault in others.

pure Ava) the owner, the architect, and the contractor are proud of the result—then the language served the parties well. And, if you have read Chapter 3, you know that the easiest way to achieve that success is to assign each exposure to the party most capable of managing it, and then give that party all the responsibility and the power—*both authority and fee*—they need to manage that exposure well. Once those assignments are made, it is then up to the owner to make sure that those responsibilities and powers are coordinated among the parties, both on paper and in reality.[3] From Chapter 5, you know that "fairness" alone is not a value to me. The word "fairness" too often serves solely to irritate the Other. Moreover, language that is fair to both sides, in and of itself, may or may not be good for the project and ultimately the parties. Rather the focus should be: Does this language work to support the parties and the project? Please keep each of these premises in mind when you read what follows.[4]

One more thing: In this chapter, we are analyzing contract language paragraph by paragraph. Contracts have to be read as a whole, analyzed as a whole, and signed as a whole. They also have to be understood as a whole and implemented as a whole. So, if as a whole the contract is riddled with grave problems, you may find it in your interests *not* to negotiate it line by line, paragraph by paragraph, lest you run

---

[3] Standard documents that are issued in families, like those issued by the AIA, intend to do this for the owner.

[4] This definition of good contract language is clearly mine, but most of my close colleagues in the ABA Forum on the Construction Industry and in the American College of Construction Lawyers define good contract language much the same way.

How to Say Yes, How to Say No

the risk of losing all goodwill before the contract is even signed. Instead of making the contract terms the focus of discussion, you may want to sit down with the owner and find out what prior experiences the owner has had with design and construction or with architects and contractors, that created such a harsh, one-sided contract.

One architect received such a contract, and indeed some of the language in this chapter comes from that contract, hence that architect's (and client's) name shall remain undisclosed. He was beside himself. A solid contract analyzer and negotiator, he had no idea where to begin. "Don't bother to begin," said I. "Take the contract back to the owner, put it on the table, sit down, and ask empathetically, 'What happened on your last project that you felt such a need to draft a contract as rigid as this? Tell me. I'll keep track of the problems, and then, instead of negotiating words, let's discuss what I can do and what you can do to make sure those problems don't happen on our project.' Then listen and deal. If, after you two talk, you both feel comfortable in signing a contract, sign one that reflects your collective decisions and supports the project. But if one or both of you are still nervous, and if you still want the project, then think about suggesting that you sign an agreement on an hourly basis just to cover scope development. That way, you can try each other out in predesign services and build the solid working relationship you both will need to get through the entire project." Two days later, the architect called back. "We talked, and I told him that, after what he told me, I wouldn't trust architects or contractors either. So we signed a contract to develop scope and the project delivery process.

And he referred to me one of his colleagues who needs an architect."

There is a lesson here. *Negotiating contracts can build goodwill.* We're more used to the opposite—the antagonism and loss of goodwill when the negotiation process turns sour, particularly if you negotiate a poorly conceived contract word by word. At the end of the process, you may have a contract, but you may also have overstayed your welcome. After all, if chemistry will get you through your first problem with the owner, leaving the negotiation table without goodwill is foolhardy at best.

So how do you negotiate a contract and remain a trusted advisor and designer? You use everything you learned in the first seven chapters, and you prepare hard for negotiation. That means you do your homework so you can come off as the competent, candid, and concerned architect you are. When preparing, of course, you will have to read the contract and understand it. The following may help you in that process.

Ava's Rules of Contract Interpretation

Any trained lawyer will tell you how to interpret a contract, starting with the rule that the specific overrides the general. For example, "three days" overrules "a reasonable time." I don't find that information particularly helpful to teach architects, because by the time you get to that level of analysis, it's too late. I'd rather focus on whether the contract meets the purposes we spelled out for it in Chapter 3, because, if it does, issues like the general versus the specific will never have to be reached. So let us focus on whether the contract is clear, subject only to one meaning, and implementable. Let us ask: Will it make project operations predictable? Will it help the parties achieve their strategic objectives? Does it produce a shared understanding of what will happen, and when? To answer those questions confidently, I suggest you follow these simple rules.

Rule 1: Read All Contracts Out Loud

I read contracts to myself all the time—out loud. The reason I do it is, for me, contracts are intrinsically boring, and, if you don't read them out loud, they can become mere words. Then you are in danger of skipping over details and agreeing to something that you shouldn't agree to because it reads okay, it's spelled correctly, and it seems to make intuitive sense. But if you read contract language out loud *with meaning and emphasis*, it comes alive. Then, suddenly, it is the private law that will control you and the Other, and you concentrate wholeheartedly on the words you are reading, saying, and hearing. That way, it is easier to become aware that *what the contract says* and *what it may mean* are two very different things. Which brings us to Rule 2.

Rule 2: If the Contract Doesn't Make Sense or Has Two Senses, Get a Second Opinion

You aren't in a vacuum on this one, and you need not search far for a second opinion. Your lawyer, broker, partner, or architect buddy can help you out here. So can laypersons, and their help may be even better because they bring no preconceived notions to the table. Ask them, "What does this mean to you?" If they have different interpretations than you have, or additional interpretations, then, whether they are right or wrong, you have a contract that needs to be clarified. Remember, for a contract to be predictable, it cannot be ambiguous. *Only one meaning is allowed, and it has to be shared by both parties.*

Rule 3: If the Contract Still Doesn't Make Sense, Assume It Makes No Sense, and Don't Agree to It

There is a corollary to this rule: Drivel, even if written by an attorney, is still drivel. Both the rule and its corollary stem from one reality: To meet its purpose, a commercial contract must be implementable and make commercial life predictable. If you don't understand it, if it makes no sense to you, you can't implement it predictably. If the owner can help you understand it so it ends up making sense to you, fine. But if you still don't understand it, you can't agree to it. You are not denying the owner anything. You are simply saying to the owner, "You're going to have to help me on this one. The whole purpose of a contract is to make your project predictable, I don't understand this clause, and, if I don't understand it, I can't implement it. And if I can't implement it, I'm not helping you. And if I can't help you, I am a grave disappointment to us both. So let's see if we can find a way of saying what you want to accomplish that speaks to both of us."

Rule 4: If You Can't Objectively Measure It, Redefine It

If the owner is asking you for "the best," "the most spacious," "the highest," your insurance company has probably taught you that you can't agree to the language. It is a guarantee of perfection of sorts and therefore is not insurable. That may be, but assertive practitioners don't think insurance first. They think of the client first. As the whole purpose of a contract is to make commercial life predictable, this contract language fails the owner.

What does "best," "highest," *any superlative* mean to two different people? Most probably, two different things. And then later, when you bring in the contractor, you'll have yet another definer and definition to deal with. As problematic as indefinable terms are, there's no need to fight an owner on this one. All you have to do is *clarify* together the goals of the client in light of their budget and other constraints, and then help the owner define goals that are objectively measurable and achievable. In that way, you can develop an agreement that will help the project succeed.

I can hear some of you saying that objectively measurable language will become a warranty. I address warranties in great detail later in this chapter, but for now remember this: *The value of a contract to both you and the owner rests in its clarity.* The murkier it is, the more likely it is that its major beneficiaries will be not you, the parties to the contract, but the lawyers you both hire to decide what you meant. Decide it for yourselves at the negotiating table.

Rule 5: Don't Get Angry, Get with It: Everything Is Negotiable

This rule is an intentional variation on an old saying, but I use it to stress the need to depersonalize owner requests. I have watched so many architects personalize the contract negotiation process unnecessarily. "Why are *you* (Mr./Ms. Owner) asking *me* (your talented, ethical, caring architect) *this*?" This came home to me when a lawyer colleague of mine called me, shaken. He had drafted a contract for an owner, only to be accused by the architect of drafting "the most unconscionable contract" the architect had *ever* seen. "The architect took everything personally," he complained to me, "as if I was out to get the architect. Would you read this, please?" I did, and, though there were words that I could fine-tune and phrases I might have avoided, the language as a whole seemed reasonable and, where it arguably was not, readily curable. Did the architect have to nuke the owner to arrive at a reasonable end? Assuredly not, and he wouldn't have, had he remembered that everything is negotiable. In America, the rule is: *Anyone can ask for anything at any time, and usually does.* You can say no. You don't have to agree just because the owner asked you to agree. No trial attorney forces you to write your name at the bottom of the contract. The power to contract is inherently yours. Acting affronted doesn't increase it.

There's a pro-architect flip side to this American phenomenon: *You* can ask for anything, too. One owner's lawyer told me, however, that the architects she had worked with, by and large, asked for little and got even less. They worked hard to get the contract as close to standard language as they could, but they rarely asked for retainers and termination fees and the like. I asked her what she would do if an architect asked for these provisions. Her response was simple. "After I got over the surprise,

I would probably say okay to some version. But," she hastened to add, "that would depend on the project." So ask away, if you think it proper. Just make sure that, before you make your request, you think it through using what you have learned about principled negotiations and negotiating ranges.

Rule 6: Every Quid Deserves a Quo

Chuck Heuer, FAIA, a lawyer and longtime documents authority, once said to me that he wished architects understood that, when asked for a concession, they should exact a concession in return. *Quid pro quo. This for that.* As we learned in Chapter 5, expert negotiators use the tit-for-tat process to signal to the Other they are coming to their bottom lines, and they give up nothing without getting something in return, unless their interests dictate some other course of conduct. You learned "your turn, my turn" in nursery school. Play it again. It still works.[5]

End of contract interpretation rules. Now, how do you apply them?

Applying the Rules

As you read owner-drafted contracts, you will discover variations from the AIA's standard documents. (Owners' lawyers may love to hate the AIA

---

[5] This tactic is particularly useful in negotiating burdensome language. Making that language mutually applicable often helps the Other understand its implications. We'll talk about this more when we discuss indemnities.

documents, but they invariably base their contracts on them.) Don't let these variations throw you. Recognizing them and dealing with them will get you started in the right direction. When you come upon one, stop and answer these questions:

> *What does the language say? What does it mean?* Start off hoping for consonance, but keep your eyes and ears open to dissonance and ambiguity.

> *Is the language in my interests? Why? Why not?* Asking this straight up lets you get yourself, your risk aversion, and other anxieties on the table so you can get them out of the way and begin thinking of what's best for the project and your client.

> If you're not sure of your interests, you can double-check contract integration by asking: *With this language, are the exposures, capabilities, responsibilities, and powers rightly aligned?* If they aren't, you can bet your bottom dollar the language will present problems to all concerned—if not today, soon enough—and that, most certainly, is not in your or anybody's interests.

> Now you are free to explore *what is in the project's interests.* What problem do you think the language is intended to resolve? Is the project facing that problem? Does the language resolve the problem? Is there a better way to resolve the problem than this or any contract language?

> Your view of the project and its needs notwithstanding, ask yourself: *Why would an owner want*

this language? What owner interest is it designed to meet? Is there a better way to meet the owner's interests than this or any contract language?

➤ *What do "fair standards," such as AIA standard contracts, have to say about the issues inherent in the contract language?* What is the difference? Will that difference help the owner more? Will it help the project?

The Value of Using Standard Contracts

AIA documents strive to be consensus documents for a consensus project. They are devised by architects with the assistance of engineers, contractors, owners, and everybody's lawyers and insurance counsel. Regardless of the effort all these good people put into the documents, not everybody in the building enterprise does a consensus project, which means you and the owner have to decide what's adequate for the project that you two are contemplating. But AIA docs have been thought out. And they reflect the standard of care at the time they are issued. So, if I were an owner, I would think, "It's risky enough to do a one-time project, why would I want to create a one-time private law?" I wouldn't. I would want to use pretested, standard documents. Does that mean I wouldn't amend the documents? Not a chance. I would want to make sure that what I sign is dovetailed to my project. And, as I said, there is no better place to start than the AIA contracts.

Are the standard documents also good for architects? You assume they are because you're an architect, and they have the AIA eagle emblazoned on them. If you have read this book, you know that's not good enough. You have to think them through for yourself.

All that being said, I urge you not to get into a fight with your clients over the value and fairness of the AIA contracts. It's not in your interests to lose goodwill over them. Moreover, it is not your job to improve people's perception of the integrity of the AIA contracts. It's the AIA's. Let the Institute do it, not you.

Putting the Rules to Work

Now, as promised, what follows is honest-to-goodness owner-drafted contract language. When the owner "titled" the language, I kept the title. When there was no owner title, there is none. We will start with the easiest to analyze and go to the most difficult. Each analysis will follow the same path: architect's view, owner's view, and a cure. In order not to be repetitive, though, I will not repeat the analysis of issues after they have been discussed once, even though the same issues resurface in later contract clauses. Also, I have included extra examples of challenging contract language when they present permutations on themes, for those of you who want extra practice analyzing and strategizing for contract negotiation.

Notice that I said "a" cure, not "the" cure. There are lots of ways to mend bad contract language. After all, where there's a word, there's a way. Regardless of which route the owner and you choose, *if wordsmithing is the solution, I'd try to use as much of the owner's own language as I can.* In that way, I signal to the client that I want to meet them on their playing field; the client doesn't have to come over to mine. But there are other solutions besides words, and we will consider them also. With that, let's look at the first paragraph.

INTERIOR DESIGN
The Architect will assist the interior designer in the selection of furniture, including files, case goods, and seating. The Architect will be responsible for the overall look of the space and the coordination with the designer.

⇓This space is your notepad.⇓

What problem(s) does this language present to you? That's exactly right. One person cannot be responsible for the conduct of another person, unless he or she has power over that person, as people do over their agents and employees. If the interior designer is an independent contractor, you don't have that power. Also, the owner holds the architect responsible for the overall look of the project *and* for coordination with the interior designer. You can't be responsible for the look without the power to select, and you can't be responsible for coordination unless the Other has the responsibility of coordinating with you. In other words, you have three examples in one tiny paragraph of responsibility being assigned without power.

Why would an owner want to construct a project this way? *You don't know.* Maybe the owner isn't aware of the misalignment problems the language creates. Maybe the owner wants a designer who has an ego (or had an experience) such that he or she won't work for an architect. Maybe the owner wants to free both the architect and the interior designer to do their best work and thinks that this language will do it. *You are going to have to ask the owner why.*

Fortunately, most contract language can be cured. How are you going to cure this? That depends on your skills and the owner's answer. If you are not skilled in the interiors arena, you will want no responsibility for it, not even for "assisting the designer." But, if you are skilled, there are options aplenty, depending on the owner's concerns.

➤ If the owner wants the architect to be responsible for the overall look and feel, then the owner should put you in the lead, making you fully responsible for interiors. The interior designer would then serve as a subcontractor to you. That way, you could coordinate activity and results.

➤ If the owner wants the interior designer to lead but fears the designer might place built-ins in the middle of the ductwork, the owner and you have other choices. You can have a contract with the owner making you responsible for exteriors and all things structural, mechanical, and the like. The interior designer can have a contract with the owner designating responsibility for interiors. The interior designer would be required to submit plans to you to provide you ample time for review for interior design consistency with overall structural, mechanical, and other aspects of building design. Ample time for modification, if necessary, would also have to be incorporated into everyone's thinking and schedules.

➤ Alternatively, if the owner wants the interior designer to lead but wants you to keep your oar in as to the look and feel in some undefined way, the owner can ask you to comment on those plans before they are accepted.

➤ Or, if the owner says the language was designed to make you accountable for interior, but not for the procurement process, the owner can require you to review and approve the interior designer's plans. The owner can further require the interior designer to submit the designs to you, according to a schedule that you both devise that gives all three of you the necessary time to review and approve the plans.

The point is, once you and the owner jointly understand an issue, you can jointly draft language to address it, making sure that exposure, capability, responsibility, and power are aligned.

A Brief Aside on Architect As Leader

You may be thinking the architect should always be the leader. But where is that written? The profession can't declare itself as leader and expect everyone to follow. *You have to be worthy of being followed for someone to assign you a leadership role.* You can't assign that role to yourself.

Don't misunderstand me. On my projects, I want the architects to lead, but only when the facts and circumstances indicate that they are the best ones to lead, and they are capable of leading. Sometimes, the contractor should be the leader. Sometimes, the owner. Oh, I know. What contractors don't know about design could fill books. But let me tell you, what some architects don't know about construction could fill just as many books. And what some owners don't know about design and construction could fill a library and a half. But that's the beauty of the building enterprise: People with varying degrees of expertise and skills bring them together to create something bigger and better than any one of them could have created alone. That's why the building enterprise is so complex and, yes, problematic. And that's why leadership in the building enterprise needs to be there and needs to be fluid. Want to improve your leadership skills? Sure, but work on your teaming skills, too, so you know when and how to lead and when and how to follow.

CERTIFICATION
The Architect certifies that the construction of the Project to the date of this Certificate is being diligently prosecuted and the quality and construction of the Project are, in all material respects, in accordance with the approved Drawings and Specifications.

Before we analyze this paragraph, let's talk about certifications and their close kin—guarantees and warranties. Each in some way asks you to promise that something is true and accurate and worthy of the Other's reliance and belief. Can you certify, guarantee, or otherwise warrant that you are an architect? Yes, *if in fact* you are an architect. Otherwise, you cannot. You may want to. You may wish you could. You may feel guilty that you can't, but, unless you can *swear* under oath that something is true without fear of being prosecuted for perjury, you cannot *certify* that same thing as true.

Is refusing to certify something unfair to the owner? *Au contraire.* You want your clients to trust you and rely on you. As you know by now, earning that trust is dependent, in part, on your being candid with your clients. To agree to something when you know that it is not true, or when you have no basis to know whether it is true or not, actively conveys misinformation to your client. You owe your client more than that. So, let's not be afraid of the words "certify" or "guarantee" or "warrant." Let's instead look at the *scope* of what you are being asked to certify, and check to see if you know it to be presently true and accurate. If it is, sign away.

Given what you just read, can you sign off on the certification that begins this section? No, because here the owner is asking you to take responsibility for construction you did not perform, built by someone—the contractor—over whom you had no power. Further, unless you were in every square foot of the site 24/7, you wouldn't know enough or have seen enough to attest to quality and construction in "all material respects."[6] Even if you wanted to sign this certificate, under those facts and circumstances you would have no basis to do so. To sign it is to give your client an empty promise.

Why, then, would owners ask you for this language? They want someone, anyone, you, to guarantee that the contractor did the job and did it well. Think about it. You can't blame them. Construction is *that* complex. Moreover, 10 to 1 if it's a private project, and 100 to 1 if it's a public project, the contractor was hired competitively and primarily, if not only, on price. I, too, would want someone to guarantee that a contractor selected on that basis did right by me. So would you. Now, given this reality and the depth of owner need for construction certainty, how can you cure the paragraph?

Again, you have choices, depending on (a) the facts and circumstances facing you, (b) your capabilities, and (c) the responsibilities and powers you and the owner can agree on. At the macro level, the choices are these:

➤ You can help the owner mitigate the problem that created the owner's need in the first place.

➤ You can expand your services to meet the owner's need.

---

[6] The word *material* always throws me. I know what material means under the Federal Rules of Evidence—important, going to the merits—and I know that silk is a material. Steel, too. But what does the word mean in this context? Beats me. I would clarify what the owner wants your scope of review to be before I agreed or disagreed to anything. Defining "material" in objective or otherwise measurable terms should solidify when and how you should respond and what, if anything, you will be able to certify.

➤ You can limit the scope of your services to meet the interests behind the owner's request.

➤ You can wordsmith.

Let's start from the last option, if only because that's where most architects are taught to start—and stop.

Wordsmithing. Wordsmithing is a powerful tool taught routinely to architects by lawyers and insurance companies. To cure certifications, you can invoke legal weasel words, what I affectionately call "blah-blah." You know the words: "To the best of the architect's knowledge, information, and belief," or "In the architect's professional judgment." And then you insert whatever the owner wants you to certify. Usually, that works. Sometimes you have to do more to make the certification true. Here you might say, "Based on visual observations made during biweekly visits by the Architect, the Architect concluded that, in his professional judgment, the construction seems to have been diligently...." But wouldn't you rather help the owner manage the dilemma that caused the owner to draft the language in the first place? It's that skill that makes an architect valuable and valued. Let's see how that approach works, using this certification language as a guinea pig.

Mitigate the owner's problem. Owners who want you to ensure contractor compliance with your CDs may be signaling they need someone to monitor their contractor. Perhaps they fear they will not choose their contractor well and, hence, look to you to protect them from the weakness of their choice. Instead of arguing over words, why don't you help them out so they don't have the need in the first place? Talk to them about contractor selection and how it can make or break a project. Introduce them to the Qualification Based Selection (QBS)–like templates of both the AIA and the Associated General Contractors of America (AGC). Ask if they want a list of three to five contractors capable of doing their job. Encourage owners to refine the template, and then sit with them as they interview each of the contractors, asking the questions owners need answered. Encourage them also to build partnering into the project and to actively participate in the partnering effort. Maybe you will want to suggest a different type of project delivery approach, such as that described in the IPD system family of documents published by the AIA for the first time in 2008. Whatever your choice, you can make the need for a 24-hour-a-day monitor disappear. This reframing of the issue away from what you cannot do toward what you can do to meet the owner's interests may be just the solution the owner really wants.

Expand your services. Remember quid pro quo? If your owner wants you to certify contractor compliance, step up to bat and *agree if* the owner also agrees to hire you as the design-builder and pays you accordingly for the increased risks and responsibilities. Absent that agreement, you can still help out the owner through expanded services, again *if* the owner agrees to retain you to provide agency construction management services along the lines of B132-2008. Or, if you're not prepared to provide those services, ask the owner to retain you to provide B207-2008 Project Representative services.

In other words, get yourself on the site and help your owner out.[7] If the owner is serious, these negotiations should be easy. If not, there is no better way to determine the real seriousness of an owner's demands than to offer to meet them for a fee.

Limit your scope. If the owner doesn't want to expand your services, yet still wants you to certify something, you can limit the scope of the certification to something you can indeed certify. An example: A Class A, New York–based, nationwide law firm once asked the late Robert Calhoun Smith, FAIA, to certify a plethora of matters from zoning law compliance to contractor compliance, and more. Many of these certifications effectively required him to practice law without a license. Some even asked him to foresee the results of others' conduct that would not occur until far into the future.[8] I suggested he ask the owner's lawyer, preferably in front of the owner, whom he knew well, whether he would allow his own architect clients to sign the certification he drafted. Everyone smiled, and they worked out a scope that Bob could certify. At the end of the project, the

---

[7] *Nota bene* (Lawyer-speak for "pay attention"): This assumes you have the capabilities to provide these expanded services.

[8] Like this one: "The Architect certifies that neither the Project nor the construction of the Project to this date, nor any existing or proposed uses of the Project violates or will violate any existing applicable zoning, building, environmental protection or similar statutes, ordinances, laws, or regulations; and the Drawings and Specifications comply with all existing code and governmental regulations applicable to the Project." Or (and from the same contract) this one: "The Architect certifies that there are no petitions, actions, or proceedings pending or threatened to revoke, rescind, alter or declare invalid, in a manner adverse to the Project or the Owner, any laws, ordinances, regulations, permits, certificates or agreements for or relating to the Project."

How to Say Yes, How to Say No

owner gave Bob a plaque that read, "I, Robert Calhoun Smith, FAIA, hereby certify that I am an architect." Call it what you will—"your turn, my turn" or "what's good for the goose is good for the gander"—*the negotiation tool of mutual reciprocity is yet another way of testing owner need and intention.*

Thinking this way may force you into a new and very different mindset. That's okay. Once you get used to it, I'm betting you find it a most comfortable one. It keeps you focused on your client and on project success, and isn't that why you decided to become an architect in the first place?

RELIANCE

Each certificate is made with the intent that it may be relied upon by the Owner as a condition to payment to the Architect under the Architect's Agreement.

To a great extent, reliance language is but a recent permutation on the certification, warranty, guarantee theme, but it can up the ante big time. In the language here, the big time is that it gives the owner the chance to argue that he or she need not pay the architect, or worse, the architect has to give back all fees paid, if *any* of the certifications made prove not to be true in whole or in part. With a straight face, the owner can make this argument, hoping someone buys it, even if the discrepancy costs the owner little to nothing. Sometimes you have to say no, if only to prove to the owner that you will look out for the owner's interests in the future, just as you are looking out for your own now. But sometimes you can excise bad language by humor or even by silence.

Can you stand another story? A while back, a large multinational bank had the owner modify the then B141 to include language to the effect that "the Architect recognizes that the bank is lending money to the Owner in reliance on each of the Architect's certifications." Now, the humor of a bank lending $30 million to an owner, based upon an architect's certification, is just too great for words. Wasn't the bank interested at all in the owner's financial capacity to repay the loan? Didn't the bank care about its return on its investment? Didn't the bank review the owner's pro forma before it decided to lend the owner a dime? Nah. The bank lent the owner money relying solely on the architect's certification of, say, code compliance. Even the bank officer saw the humor in that one. The reliance language was deleted, but had the architect not spotted the language and called about it, the architect could have ended up serving as the insurance company for a potentially no-fault project.[9]

What You Can Warrant

Insurance companies have so etched into architects' brains the uninsurability of warranties, that it is not uncommon for a lawyer to be asked, "Isn't there

---

[9] Silence would probably have worked, too. You would have used your crackerjack clarifying skills and asked, "You mean the bank doesn't care about your (the owner's) pro forma? It's lending you money based solely on my certifications?" You then sit silently waiting for the absurdity of the language to sink in and for the owner to suggest you both delete it. Another point: A large architecture firm's in-house counsel who read this section said that serving as the owner's or banker's insurance company, because of the reliance language, was the least of his fears. He feared being accused of fraud in the inducement and punitive damages. His reaction brings home the value of having a lawyer review your contracts. Wouldn't you agree?

anything future-oriented that I can promise a client?" Of course, there is. Here are a few things you can warrant:

➤ Something unexpected will happen at some time that could delay the project. I don't know what that something will be. I don't know when it will happen or why it will happen. But it will happen.

➤ Something unexpected will happen at some time that could make the project cost more. I don't know what that something will be either. Nor do I know when it will happen or why it will happen. But it will happen.

➤ My drawings and specifications will not be complete. (No one's are.)

➤ While the project is being designed, I will have limited insight into the materials market. When the project is finally ready to bid, I will have no control over the materials market.

➤ You will change your mind about some aspect of the project, most probably when it is in construction. The cost of that change in both time and money may be large or small, but it is your project, and you will want what you want.

➤ Costs will become increasingly important to you over the course of the project.

➤ You will get angry at me sometime about something. Again, I don't know why or when, but I do know the sooner you tell me you are mad, the better it will be for the project.

Why can you warrant these future events? One, because experience dictates they are quite likely to happen. As important, the mere discussion of these "warranties" opens up a conversation that both of you will appreciate later, as it gives the owner a "heads up" as to the realities of design and construction—a necessity for the seeds of "no surprise design" to root early. ("Remember when we talked about warranties, and I said that ABC would happen? Well, it's happened.") Finally, what's the downside? Have you ever heard of an owner suing an architect because nothing bad happened? Absent the element of damages, they have no case, and that, according to this lawyer, is the true reason we say "no harm, no foul."

Ready for the next one?

COMPLETENESS

All drawings, plans, specifications, and the like prepared by the Architect shall be complete and adequate for construction of the project.

What do you spot right away? The language screams warranty, unlabeled by the owner, but a warranty just the same. The trigger words you spotted that led you rightly to that conclusion are "shall be." You are basically being asked to warrant that the plans you have yet to design will serve as a cookbook for the building. All the contractor has to do is follow them faithfully and—voilà!—a building. The problem is, CDs aren't a cookbook; they can't be, aren't intended to be, and—surprise to many an owner—they *shouldn't* be. Just as important, the owner couldn't afford them if they were.

Before you sign off on those assertions, let's discuss them. When you design a building, you are designing a one-of-a-kind edifice never built before, never to be built again. The only way your CDs could serve as a cookbook would be for the owner to let the building be built, the CDs be debugged, the building be ripped down, and then be built yet again. As that is *never* going to happen; *no CDs, not even those of a Gold Medal winner, can ever be complete.* Moreover, it is often in the owner's interests to save some issues for resolution in the field. That way, the owner benefits from everyone's expertise and the opportunity to see the issue in context. As the issue is resolved and the decision put into place, the closeness of the buying decision to the construction will give everyone a clearer, more reliable sense of costs and benefits.

Why, then, would an owner include such language? One reason comes readily to mind. Owners impliedly warrant to contractors that the design and the CDs are adequate, complete, and constructible. This warrant is similar in thrust to the one given to owners by contractors when they put in a bid.

They warrant that they have read the CDs, understood them, and can build the project as designed according to the designated time schedule and bid, if the owners give them full control over the site and over the means, methods, sequences, techniques, and safety precautions applied by the contractors and their workforces. Now, while you know and I know, and owners and contractors know, that these are more wishes than warranties, courts hold the parties to them. Owners fearing the potential results look to contract language to protect them from those results, at least as regards your designs. Understandable, yes, but wouldn't it be easier to deal with the issues than to gloss over them with feel-good language, particularly language that cannot be realized? A long discussion of the fundamental issues, followed by some wordsmithing commemorating your joint understanding, should do the trick.

CODE COMPLIANCE
All drawings and specifications prepared under this contract shall comply with all applicable laws, regulations, or ordinances and requirements of Government Authorities and Agencies having jurisdiction over the facility to be constructed.

All right, what is the problem, and how are you going to cure it? (You have stopped reading and started analyzing, haven't you?)

First, from your perspective: You know it is your responsibility to design a building that complies with building codes, but you also know that building codes are inconsistent, incomplete, and not tailored to your owner's project. Indeed, that's one of the values you bring to the table—the ability to make sense out of a mishmash of codes and rules. Here, though, the owner is asking for more. The owner wants a warranty of perfection and is not limiting your responsibility for perfect compliance to the building codes that would normally apply to the design and construction of the project. Oh, no. The owner wants you to comply with *all* laws of *all* the government agencies having jurisdiction over the project. Presumably, that means, in addition to building authorities, the owner wants you to comply with "laws" of the Internal Revenue Service (IRS), the whole U.S. Department of Labor (in addition to the Occupational Safety & Health Administration [OSHA]), Health and Human Services (HHS), and who knows what else. Quite simply, you can't do it. You aren't a lawyer trained to know a little bit about a lot of laws. Issues would fly by you. And, even if you could do it, the owner could never afford it. You'd be spending all your time in the law library trying to implement this one clause. More important, it can't be done. The codes that rule buildings and their use have too many inconsistencies within them—obeying one regulation may mean violating another.

Why would owners ask this of you? They want a safe building that complies with building codes.[10] And they have a right to it. You want that, too, so the two of you have common ground to build on in curing this clause. You can rely on that common ground when you explain that your expertise rests

---

[10] They may also be concerned with change orders and other matters. As always, *you are going to have to ask before you can act.*

in producing CDs that comply with normally applicable design codes in place on the day that the CDs are published for bidding and negotiation.

Yet even then, no matter how hard you analyze the situation, codes are up for interpretation. And code officials' interpretations often vary by the code official. They have a tremendous amount of discretion. It is not at all uncommon for the fire marshal to say one thing, one building inspector another, and a third inspector something else altogether different. All you can do is discuss discrepancies with building inspectors, seek variances as appropriate, and resolve whatever issues you can with input from the owner. But when push comes to shove, design is a non-delegable duty, and both of you will have to rely on your professional judgment. Then the two of you can discuss the owner's values and what you can do to manage code issues in light of those values and your professional judgment.

SKILL/JUDGMENT/COOPERATION
The Architect shall furnish its best skill and judgment, consistent with prevailing professional and architectural standards, and shall cooperate with the other members of the Project Team in furthering the interest of the Owner and the Owner's programmatic goals.

If you've read Chapter 3, you should be able to spot the issues here with no difficulty. The owner is trying to set a standard of care for you, requiring you to furnish your *best skill and judgment*, consistent with prevailing professional and architectural standards. The owner is not that far off from the historic and still current standard of care for architects—to act reasonably and prudently as other reasonable and prudent architects would act facing the same or similar facts and circumstances. In fact, the owner might even argue he or she is saying the same thing, just using different words. Is the owner correct? For the most part, yes, except for the word "best." With the addition of that one word, the owner is potentially changing the standard of care.

Note that I do not say *raising* the standard of care. It doesn't do that. Your best could be very crummy indeed. In fact, when one large A/E firm asked me what to do when its big-city airport authority client demanded the firm perform "as well as other national A/E firms that had designed similar airports," I said, "Agree to it. Right now [it was the late '80s], claims for those firms are so out of sight that you can't fail to do as well as they."

Moreover, I think the standard of care for architects, for any professional, is high as it is, and is as high as it can reasonably get. You are retained to exercise judgment, and these days, that's not easy. The building enterprise has become so complex, the number of parties involved in project delivery so numerous, the quantity of materials too many to count and their quality too discrepant to track. Everything designed is, by definition, unique. And the stakes of construction today are as high as its costs, if not higher. When you add to these facts the fact that you are increasingly being asked to answer questions on the spot by people who have never read your owner-architect agreement and may never have seen your contract documents but need answers right away or else, it is a credit to the profession that architects are and continue to be reasonable. To ask for more is to ask either for perfection or for a degree of responsibility and power not delegated by most owners to architects.

INDEMNIFICATION OF THE OWNER
The Architect-Engineer shall indemnify, hold harmless, and defend the Owner, its employees, agents, servants, and representatives from and against any and all losses, damages, expenses, claims, suits, and demands of whatever nature, resulting from damages or injuries, including death, to any property or persons caused by or arising from, in whole or in part, errors, omissions or negligent acts of the Architect-Engineer or its employees, agents, servants, or representatives under this contract.

This is an indemnification clause. You know that because the owner has kindly labeled it as such. What the owner is asking you to do is to serve as the owner's personal bank and insurance company and absorb losses, real or imagined, suffered by the owner.

It is critical to read these clauses *out loud*. They can be very convoluted, and the devil is in the details. Here's a guide: To know whether you will agree to indemnify the owner, you have to read the scope of the promise and decide whether you personally (or with the help of your insurance company) want to take on the risk. If the exposure is one you are capable of managing, and if the owner gives you all the responsibility and the power you need to manage the exposure, you probably will agree to take on the indemnification risk. For example, would you agree to indemnify the owner against injuries caused by your negligence to the same extent as you were proportionately negligent? Sure you would. Why not? As we learned in Chapter 3, being responsible for your own negligence is American common law. But would you agree to indemnify the owner against the contractor's negligence? Of course not, because you have no responsibility for the contractor's conduct and no power to control it.[11] Would you agree to indemnify the owner against the acts of the owner's employees? No, and for the same reason—no capability, no responsibility, and no power to control.

With that said, let's look more closely at the scope of this indemnification, not to cure it word by word—you can't—but to understand the clause in all its glory. Putting the issues in subsets (with the most salient concepts in bold), this is what the owner wants you to undertake—three activities:

> **To indemnify**—To agree to the transfer of the owner's risk from the owner to you and, further, to reimburse the owner for losses after those losses have been determined in negotiation, mediation, arbitration, or litigation

> **To hold harmless**—To agree to protect the owner even from suits by third parties, such as contractors and building users

> **To defend**—To agree to pay all the owner's defense costs should anyone sue the owner, even if this puts you and the owner into a conflict of interest, and even if you have done nothing to cause the suit

---

[11] Under most design-build contracts, your answer would be different if you were hired as "prime" to deliver the project and had the contractor working as your agent and reporting to you.

How to Say Yes, How to Say No

Moreover, the owner wants you to do these three things to *protect five groups of people*: (1) the owner, (2) the owner's employees, whoever they are, (3) its agents, whoever and whatever they are, (4) its servants—and I have no idea what, in this day and age, this group includes, and (5) its representatives, clearly a distinct group of people who are not employees, agents, or servants. And the owner wants you to protect all of these people, regardless of whether or not they are actively involved in the project, and regardless of whether or not you, or anyone under your direct control, have any dealings with them.

As if this were not broad enough, the owner wants you to shield these categories of people (and here is the scope of the indemnification parsed in all its glory, so that you can assess the gravity of what is being asked of you) *from and against: any and all—losses, damages, expenses, claims, suits, and demands—of whatever nature—resulting from damages or injuries, including death—to any property or persons.* This language, coupled with the preceding, has you shielding the owner and the gang of others from whatever comes the owner's way (and paying for all of the group's defense costs in the process, so there is no reason for any of them to settle any time quickly),[12] including protecting them against mere allegations, which is precisely what undecided

---

[12] One A/E professional liability insurer offered its insureds defense outside limits, which made the carrier fully responsible for all legal fees and transaction costs, not the insured design firms. A/Es stopped wanting to settle cases, and legal defense costs soared. "We'll go all the way to the Supreme Court." That coverage soon stopped. Query: Do you think your clients would act any differently than your peers did?

(or unsettled) claims and suits, and mere demands, are.

Now, is this reasonable, given the complexity of design and construction? Let's look at the triggering language. What must you do, if anything, to cause this language to be activated? Again, look at the scope. The loss or mere allegation must have been *caused by or arising from—in whole or in part—errors, omissions, or negligent acts—of the Architect-Engineer or its employees, agents, servants, or representatives—under this contract.* Translating this into English, you need not have been negligent for your purse to become the owner's. Why? Because a mere or a major non-negligent error or omission triggers the indemnity. Had negligent been a prerequisite of error, omission, or act, as in "negligent, error, omission, or act," this clause arguably would have been insurable. Transposing the negligence to limit it to acts made it uninsurable. Moreover, the seeming badness need not be a result of your negligence. It can merely "arise" from it, so that, if the owner can make any argument that takes you in, you get taken. One percent negligent, non-negligent, or 100 percent negligent, with this language, you bought the store.[13]

Owners are not bad people. Why, then, do they ask for this language? Some say it is because of the

---

[13] A lawyer boasted how the language "in whole or in part" saved his client from paying a massive claim. In a deposition of the architect, the lawyer asked, "You mean to tell me you weren't even a little bit negligent, not even a little bit?" The architect's answer? "Well, maybe one percent negligent but nothing, nothing compared to your client." The lawyer had to ask no more questions. The architect may have been one percent negligent, but now he was 100 percent liable.

How to Say Yes, How to Say No

AIA's traditional refusal to include a standard of care in the old B141 contract, on the grounds that common law negates the need.[14] The owner is merely filling the vacuum. *Thankfully, the AIA finally eliminated that rationale by including a standard of care in the 2007 owner-architect agreements.* Others say owner indemnification clauses are an adverse reaction to architects' requesting that owners limit their liability through Limit of Liability (LoL) clauses. Still others point to social causes: People these days don't like taking responsibility for their actions. They want a risk-free life, and, if the Good Lord won't give it to them, they want the next best thing to protect them. On the construction site, that means they want you and your insurance policy, assuming you have one, to protect them from all badness.[15] And some architectural thinkers posit that owners pay so much to put the building up that they need someone else's kitty to cover unanticipatable events. Whatever. These reasons may all be true. The problem with them and the clauses they generate, though, is that *wrongly conceived indemnification clauses hurt the project.*

---

[14] I can't tell you the number of times I have watched architects burn up their goodwill by refusing to agree to language on the grounds that "I am already doing that. Why do we need language on it?" If you are indeed already doing what the owner wants done, why not agree to it in the contract, and get something, in return for that "concession." ("Oh, you want me to agree to *that*? Well, okay, if you will agree to this.")

[15] Don't think going bare will protect you from owners' claims. I've heard too many stories now, and I know that's not true. Also, far too many uninsured practitioners avoid claims by paying to fix things up, even when they are not minimally liable. The amount they pay in acquiesced (or possibly forced) restitution often exceeds anything they would have paid in premiums and deductibles.

Shocked you, didn't I? You expected me to write that crisscrossed indemnification clauses are uninsurable and, thus, empty promises to boot. Well, that's true. You are only insured for your negligence and nobody else's, and, unless you are very rich, you probably don't have the money to live up to the crisscrossed promise exacted by the owner.[16] But remember, we are assertive practitioners. We don't think from the perspective of insurance. We think what's best for our clients' projects, because if we achieve project success, the owner and we ourselves will be taken care of in the process.

In design and construction, to achieve success, all parties must be working on all cylinders all the time. When each person on the construction site puts forth full time and attention to each and everything he or she is doing, the chance of something going wrong plummets. Crisscrossed indemnification clauses, however, induce sloppy thinking and give people permission to hedge. "Oh, why question this? The architect (or the owner or the contractor or whoever) is indemnifying me. If I'm wrong, he or she will be the one to pay. Not me." Sure, some insurance company may kick in, but life is short; who needs the claim in the first place?[17]

---

[16] I was helping a sole practitioner negotiate a $75,000 interiors project for American Airlines. The airline wanted him to indemnify it for $1,000,000, and not only for his negligence, but for theirs also. I said to the lawyer, "That's charming that you would ask a poor architect, a sole practitioner, to insure American Airlines to the tune of $1,000,000 for a small interiors project." I then sat silently and waited. He said, "I'll get back to you." The clause was removed the next day.

[17] I wish I could find the study I read in 1987 on construction claims in Europe. The researchers had interviewed parties to the construction process after buildings had failed. In each case, they found someone

How to Say Yes, How to Say No

How do you cure the clause? Many insurance companies say, "With language as broad and as egregious as this, just walk away if the owner won't agree to less." But why? If you and your client have built a relationship based on common ground and, thus, mutual reciprocity, you probably won't have to. An example: When one large-city airport client asked its architect to agree to absorb its risk by acquiescing to an indemnification clause much like this, the architect merely told them the truth: "The best way to forestall claims is to require everyone to be responsible for their negligence to the extent they are negligent. That way everyone is incentivized to act reasonably and prudently. We don't ask you to limit our liability for our negligence. We stand behind our conduct. We just are asking you to do the same." This mutuality of promises prevailed.

There's the key. *Mutuality*. So next time you face language like this, instead of walking away from a commission or losing goodwill over a wordsmithing session, explore with your client the insertion of mirrored indemnification clauses whereby each of you protects the other to the extent either of you is negligent. If your client won't buy that, you probably have bigger problems than an indemnification clause. Explore them, and then decide for yourself: Is this a client for you?

---

connected to the design or construction process who had come upon what turned out to be the cause of the failure before the building failed, but who had chosen not to speak out for one reason or the other, e.g., fear of stepping out of line, of hurting others' feelings, or just of being embarrassed or wrong. And so, the building failed. Misplaced indemnification clauses may facilitate the same type of self-defeating silence.

MISCELLANEOUS PROVISIONS

The Architect-Engineer shall perform his services in a skillful and competent manner in accordance with the highest standards of the Architectural and Engineering professions and as otherwise specified in this Contract, and the Architect-Engineer shall be liable to the Owner for all costs and damages resulting from defects in design, failure by the Architect-Engineer to perform his contractual services, non-workability of design details, and errors or omissions.

What is this clause? A combined:

- *Standard of care* ("perform his services in a skillful and competent manner in accordance with the highest standards of the Architectural and Engineering professions")

- *Indemnification* ("Architect-Engineer shall be liable to the Owner for all costs and damages resulting from defects in design, failure by the Architect-Engineer to perform his contractual services, and non-workability of design details")

- *Warranty clause* ("liable for all costs" without a requirement of negligence)

- *With a grand catchall clause* ("and as otherwise specified in this Contract" dumped in just in case the owner missed something)

Why am I including the clause in its entirety here? Haven't we just discussed these same issues? There is some value in repetition, but isn't this déjà vu all over again? I included this clause because it is my favorite example of wrong-headed contract language. It comes from the same contract as the twin standard of care and indemnification clauses we just discussed. And the owner tucked it conveniently away under "miscellany." Kind of warms your heart, doesn't it? Third bite at the architect's apple.[18] How hungry can you get? And had the architect negotiated this contract clause by clause, word by word, can you imagine how much enmity the architect would have brewed? Can't you just hear the owner? ("Architects just aren't willing to stand behind their work.") Instead, the architect sat down with the owner and listened to the owner's horror stories that had given birth to the contract, and, in time, the two parties came to "yes." *Nota bene*: You can do this, too.

NO LIMIT OF LIABILITY CLAUSES
Architect agrees that no Subconsultant retained to provide services to this Project by or through the Architect shall limit its liability for negligence.

---

[18] Arguably, the fourth bite, as the contract also included this language: "The Owner may at any time, by written order, require additional work or services from the Architect-Engineer. In the event the Architect-Engineer is requested by the Owner in writing to make changes or additions to work, the Architect-Engineer *shall do so without additional compensation* (my emphasis) unless it is first agreed that such change will materially add to the Architect-Engineer's design work and cost." Demanding additional services without compensation puts the architect into the position of project financier. If the owner uses allegations of architect negligence to justify his demand for additional services, the architect becomes project guarantor, too.

I have a confession to make. This is my language. We include it in all our owner-architect agreements. We do so because we want all players to give our projects their full time and attention and to be comfortable and assured that everyone else is doing the same. Also, I get saddened when an architecture firm becomes the insurer of its consultant, which is what happens when a consultant firm transfers its liability to the architect by way of a Limit of Liability clause and, later, the consultant's sole negligence hurts the owner.

Also, I blame LoL clauses for much of the marginalization of the architecture profession. They have enabled owners everywhere to say that architects run from responsibility. As a result, lots of other professions have arisen, each willing to take on some aspect of the architect's traditional role. I use this clause to persuade architects, one by one, that they can stand up for themselves and their clients simultaneously by taking on reasonable risks and managing them reasonably

---

DEFICIENCIES
Any defective Designs or Specifications furnished by the Architect will be promptly corrected by the Architect at no cost to the Owner, and the Architect will promptly reimburse the Owner for all damages, if any, resulting from the use of such defective Designs or Specifications.

What's the problem here? Spotted it right away, didn't you? There is no requirement of negligence, so this language would have you indemnifying the owner for any defect, real or imagined, large or insignificant, found by anyone at any time. And, as the cost of rectification is going to be only yours, the language makes you the guarantor of the contract documents. No big deal. The language can be cured readily by inserting the requirement of negligence. But there is another issue lurking herein, one of *Betterment*.

Let's take this one slowly because the concept takes a bit of getting used to. In Chapter 3, we discussed that the entire idea of damages in contract law is to give the non-breaching party the benefit of the bargain as if it had not been breached, and the idea behind damages in tort law is to make the injured party whole, to the extent money can undo personal harm or property damage. Under neither concept is the non-breaching party supposed to be better off because of the breach. In other words, *owners should not be hurt by your negligence any more than they should benefit from it.*

Now translate this into architecture. If you are negligent during the design stages, you rectify that negligence at no cost to the owner. That's a given. Common law requires you to be responsible for the consequences of your negligence, and cleaning up a negligently designed contract document at your own expense puts you in compliance with common law. But what if the CDs have already been let out to contract? What then? Here's a lawyer's answer: It depends. The redesign is at your expense always, but only the increased cost of rectification is passed on to you. In other words, if the error is found early and corrected before anything is built, there is no injury to the owner and no additional construction costs to you. The owner would have had to have that part of the CDs built anyway, and they should enjoy no Betterment because of your negligence. Alternatively, if that part of the negligently drafted CDs had been put into place, you would be responsible for the costs of tearing the mistake out. Would you also be responsible for putting the right thing into place? Only if the costs associated with doing that had increased since the time the contractor bid the job. Why? Because of the rules on Betterment: The owner would have had to pay the costs of putting the right thing into place had you not been negligent, so only the *increase in owner costs* that accrued as a result of your negligence are yours to pay. (This explanation, of course, assumes no wrongdoing on the part of either the owner or the contractor.)

So how would you cure the language? Easily, by inserting the twin concepts of Negligence and Betterment, as the two, working together, fully protect the owner. Would owners want it any differently? Oh, maybe in their heart of hearts they'd like to benefit from your negligence, but these two concepts are so logical and sensible that it would be a rare owner indeed who would ever quibble with them.

CONSTRUCTION COST ESTIMATE
It shall be the responsibility of Architect to pay for any sums materially exceeding the construction cost estimate that were incurred without the prior written consent of the Owner.

What have we here? (It is getting easier, isn't it?) Yes, the word "material" needs to be defined, and, yes, the value and reliability of construction cost estimates can cause all parties problems, albeit different ones because of differing vantage points. As architects tend to say, the owner has to be "educated"[19] about the problems inherent in design pricing by noncontractors—that is, architects—when weeks and even months or more can pass between the design stage and the day the goods are bought. And yes, you could be the piggy bank if extras are authorized without the owner's written consent. But give me and all owners a break: Is asking for a "heads up" before our money is spent so much to ask? Of course, it isn't. You would want the same notice if it were your project and your money.

The problem here, though, is that this language is a bit too broadly written, that is, its scope is too wide. After all, once the contractor is brought on board, architects alone don't spend the owner's money. If procedures are followed, though, change orders require owner and contractor sign-off for them to be implemented. That is the key tool available to all the parties to forestall scope creep. Yet this language is written so broadly that you take full responsibility, even if you were not the progenitor of the increase and even if you did not know about it. Moreover, depending on the definition of

---

[19] Just between you and me, does the idea of the architect educating the client smack of arrogance? Yes, there is a real conversation to be had between you and your clients. You need to learn what makes them tick as much as they need to learn what makes you tick. You need to understand how their business operates as much as they need to understand the workings of the building enterprise. So aren't you really *exchanging information* with your clients, you from your vantage point, they from theirs? Isn't that a more accurate description of what the two of you are doing when you sit down to talk? Aren't you sharing data that each other must know, to function effectively together as a team?

"material," requiring owner sign-off on all material increases in cost may slow the project down, which, in turn, could cost the owner money, too.

Speaking as an owner, I can tell you that I understand the impetus behind the owner who wants this language. Controlling costs becomes increasingly important as the project moves along. Personally, I have experimented with varying ways of controlling costs, particularly those caused by change orders. Increasingly, I am relying on the architect and contractor working together *and with me* from the moment the design is sufficiently developed for there to be value in our collaboration.

It generally works. But it has not forestalled all change orders. An example: We once had a small but intricate project, bringing a log cabin built in 1808 back to life. Reader & Swartz Architects developed a smashing design, and Preservation Associates, Inc., experts at log cabin rehabilitation, implemented it. All of us worked together on the building since the design development docs were nearing completion. None of us expected any change orders when we put them out for pricing. Within three months of the start of construction, though, the following happened:

> ➤ The mechanical subcontractor figured out a different way of heating and cooling the building than that designed by the mechanical engineer, one that he was more familiar with and one that he thought he could maintain better and longer for less.

> ➤ The Preservation Associates foreman and his crew thought of an alternative way of securing the loft floor.

➤ I walked into the kitchen and, for the first time, realized how big the windows were going to be—a bit too big for me. (I may be able to read plans with the best of them, but a visualizer I'm not.)

Three change orders in a matter of a month. Is the building better for them? You bet. Would the owner language we are discussing allow them? Except for the owner's changes, not a chance. Everyone would have kept their heads down to avoid the confrontation they feared might result from opening up seemingly closed issues. Had I used this language, we would have been cheated of the expertise of a cadre of individuals—each of whom wanted this project to succeed as much as we did.

The point is, isn't the issue facing you and the owner not the language but how the two of you work together to control costs and minimize the adverse impacts of change orders and other unknowns? If that's the case, welcome this language as an opportunity to address change and change orders up front, before any change takes place, and prove to your owner by your competence, candor, and concern what a wise choice you were.

What to do? Sure, wordsmith the paragraph so that it is clear, unambiguous, and implementable. But there are other choices that need to be explored before you do that. If cost estimating is not your expertise, urge your clients with bottom-line needs to retain a cost estimator to help you both out. Or suggest you bring on the contractor early. Either should help the owner keep costs under control. Additionally, why don't you invite the owner to sit down with you and the contractor and talk about change orders and change directives—before any occur—and the process and values you will all use to control costs. Then it will be easier to work together to make sure those processes are implemented. If controlling costs is the primary impetus behind this language, no owner could ask for more.[20]

TIME LIMITS

The Architect's services shall be performed as expeditiously as is consistent with professional skill and care and the orderly progress of the work. Architect and Owner have approved a schedule for the performance of the Architect's services that recognizes that time is of the essence. Time limits established by this schedule approved by the Owner shall not, except for reasonable cause beyond the control of the Architect or Owner, be exceeded by the Architect.

The owner is sending you mixed messages here. On the one hand, the owner is telling you to act as expeditiously as you can but act reasonably and prudently in the process. On the other hand, the owner is telling you that time is of the essence and that you'd better obey the schedule that you two worked out, or else. This conflict will tear you apart. An example: You wake up in the middle of the night with a new idea that will save the owner money

---

[20] I tell all my yuppie friends that their residential projects will come in at least 30 percent over budget, guaranteed, primarily because their understanding and wants and have-to-haves will grow through the course of the project. Accordingly, I urge them to have a 30 percent contingency fund (at least) tucked away. Alternatively, I suggest they ask their architect to design to 70 percent of their budget. To a yuppie, they have all thanked me for that advice.

but will shove you two weeks off schedule. What do you do? The cause for the delay is reasonable but fully within your control, so should you forgo acting on your idea and proceed as before, rationalizing that the owner already signed off on your previous ideas, so why rock the boat? Or do you risk a lawsuit because your fealty to your owner's bottom line is more compelling than your loyalty to your own? Tough decision, and that is why most architects delete "time is of the essence" language whenever they see it.

Oh, yes, and there are insurance reasons to delete the language, too. Insurance companies assiduously avoid conflict-of-interest provisions where the power rests fully in the insured to trigger the conflict. Asking for claims is not their thing. Moreover, the language here might suggest you are guaranteeing a schedule, and no-surprise design often demands you set the schedule aside to keep the project on track. Agreeing to "time is of the essence" kicks you willy-nilly into claim territory.

What do you do? By now, you could write the answer yourself. *Ask the owner what is behind the language.* What are the owner's interests? What does the owner want? With that information, you can decide for yourself which tactic to take (wordsmith, mitigate the problem, expand services, decrease scope) and if that owner is one for you.

Usually, talking about time issues resolves the problem, if only because time is not of the essence in most projects. Owners just want you to help keep their projects on track and pursued in a determined fashion. A delay of one month or six months won't hurt them. (Annoy them, quite possibly, but hurt them, no.) But sometimes time *is* of the essence. A casino is to open on a certain date, and every day it remains unopened past that date costs the casino at least $1 million. (This is no exaggeration. A Las Vegas architect known for his casino work sat down with us at an ABA Forum meeting and filled us in on casino claims and building economics. Talk about high stakes.) For casino owners, your fee is irrelevant. Their schedule controls. So you are faced with a business decision: Assuming you have the capacity to gin up complicated designs, and assuming the owner gives you all the responsibility and power you need, including fee, to gin up the job, do you accept a commission where fees are no issue, but 24/7 design charretting is? Can you be creative in that forum? Effective? Responsive? Responsible? Only if you can say yes to all of those questions is a time-is-of-the-essence contract one you will want to take on.

TITLE TO DRAWINGS, SPECIFICA-TIONS, AND OTHER DATA

All drawings, CAD files, design, specifications, inventions, improvements, and other data to be prepared by the Architect under the contract shall become the absolute property of the Owner on completion and the Owner shall have the right to make such use of said drawings, CAD files, designs, specifications, and data as it shall see fit, without further payment to the Architect of any compensation other than that provided herein.

Interesting paragraph, isn't it? And hard to analyze, because drivel, even if articulately presented, is still drivel. What transfers document ownership? Completion. Of what? The project? The drawings? A drawing? And what does "make such use as the owner sees fit" mean? Can the owner redesign the project without you, extending your seal's indemnification to design contributions you had nothing to do with? What's the impetus behind the owner's wanting the right to use the documents "without further compensation" to you? Will you see your design cloned across America with nary a royalty payment coming your way? You can't answer these questions without asking the owner what the language was intended to accomplish. And you can't cure this language or know which tactic to take without the owner giving you that information.

Maybe the owner is like my husband's former corporate attorney. When we did our first building, he said he wanted to negotiate the owner-architect agreement for us. "You see," he explained, "construction contracts are tricky. You need an expert at real estate and development law to negotiate them." When I opined that I thought I could do the negotiation myself, he counseled, "Just make sure you own the documents. Architects demand they own them, but nothing screws an owner up more than having an architect walk off the job, leaving the owner with nothing to show for all the design fees he paid in." I told him I would take his counsel under advisement. But my husband's lawyer simply summed up the substance behind some owners' requests to own the documents.

How do you satisfy these owners? Solve their problem. Agree that if it ever comes to pass that they and you no longer want each other, you will take your seal off your documents, give the documents to the owner, and ride off into the sunset *if* (remember quid pro quo?) they pay you *in full* and hold you harmless for any use they make of the documents.

But most owners don't want the documents to stay and you to disappear. Most owners want them so they can maintain the building or build on to it or retrofit it someday in the future. The new 2007 B101 and B103 address their issue head-on with contract language that permits the owner to use the documents for those purposes, provided the architect has been paid for their services, and the architect is released from liability and indemnified against claims and defense costs if the architect is not retained at the time the architect's documents are used.

ADDITIONAL INSURED
The Architect shall add the Owner as an additional insured under the Architect's professional liability insurance policy.

I chose this last clause to end this chapter because, as much as I tease insurance companies about insuring certainty and not uncertainty, I am a strong believer in insurance. *Your practice policy was created to protect you and your firm*, and it will, if you put it and all the other benefits your chosen carrier has to work for you.

But here the client wants *your policy* to protect *them*. Insurance companies will give you salient reasons why you shouldn't let that happen, and I'm always amused by that. Put the client on your policy, for a fee, of course, but make sure your broker explains to them *in writing* that their inclusion means they can no longer sue you, even if you are negligent. After all, one policy's insured can't sue another insured on the same policy. (Can you imagine if your partners could tap your firm's professional liability insurance policy to sue you for negligence?) Even if insureds could sue each other, most owners are not design professionals. Most owners provide no professional design services and, as design professional liability policies only insure negligent design, most owner additional insureds are receiving no protection for the premium they pay, if any. Now, I know some courts hold otherwise, and I also know that, if the insurance market ever hardens, adding owners as additional insureds will be one of the first coverages to go.[21] The conflict of cross-insured suits is just too much and too expensive for most insurance companies (and your post owner-filed-claim premium) to handle. Besides, owners can buy their own policies dedicated to protecting them and only them, if they want. You can offer to have your broker work with your clients to help them get their own coverage. Once the client has that in place, why hook on to yours?

Which brings us full circle to the question "why." It is this most powerful of questions that will give you the information to know how to say yes and how to say no. It is this question that will help you stay riveted on your interests and still move you toward common ground. And it is this question that will help you evaluate the counsel you are given by

---

[21] Some architecture firms will be particularly happy to see the coverage go because they have had their additional insured clients try to use the firm's policy to protect client projects unrelated to the firm.

lawyers and insurance companies. If you use your native curiosity and problem-solving capabilities to discover what is truly important to you and the client, and, if you use your design skills to fashion elegant options to meet those needs, no contract will daunt you. None at all.

When the Best Laid Plans . . .

9

You may be asking yourself: Why, in a book on negotiation, is there a chapter on dispute resolution? Two reasons: First, even the best negotiators in the world have times when the chemistry goes wrong, when one of the parties blows up, when a misspoken word escalates into a full-fledged dispute. They need to use their negotiation skills to try to restore balance to the situation.

Second, no matter how hard you have worked at being a competent, candid, and concerned professional, even in well-managed projects, differences among parties exist, and they will create tensions. When the constraints of time and budget take an additional toll, disputes inevitably arise. That so few construction disputes land in court is a credit to all the parties. It is also proof that negotiation skills are critical assets to have in the design and construction setting. When will you bring the negotiation skills we've covered in this book to bear? Most probably, often and perhaps even daily, though these situations come most readily to mind:

- ➤ When a rift is brewing
- ➤ When you have a confrontation to handle
- ➤ When a change is looming
- ➤ When a claim is in the offing
- ➤ When a lawsuit is pending

Let's discuss them one after the other, in light of what we have learned so far. As you will see, differences—and disputes—can be managed, as long as you can recognize them for what they are: *a rift in expectations between you and the Other*. These rifts usually result from a discrepancy between what a person—could be you, could be the Other—wants or thinks should happen and what they know or fear will happen. A rift. Nothing more. Nothing less.

When a Rift Is Brewing: Recognizing Disputes

The first trick in handling all disputes is to grow "early-warning antennae" to help you recognize rifts when they take place, because it is disregarding rifts that makes a dispute most likely. When a client is quick to communicate, recognizing a rift is usually easy. When communicative clients are unsatisfied or even angry, *they will tell you*. You can then call to task all the communication skills we explored in Chapter 6, Clarifying as necessary until you and the owner can rebuild common ground. Maybe you can do something to ameliorate the situation. Maybe you can't, but at least through Clarifying you can help your clients figure out routes they can take to rectify the problem and identify ways you can help them in the process.

Noncommunicative clients are more problematic. Like some architects, noncommunicators dislike confrontation; they prefer to remain silent and wait for differences to resolve themselves. In the building enterprise, however, as we all know, most differences do not resolve themselves. Unstated problems lead to even bigger ones, and opportunities for action get lost in the silence. Pebbles allowed to build up, mortared with silence and suspicion, too easily become impregnable walls.

Faced with a noncommunicative client, what can you do? You can ask a question and wait patiently until the client is ready to answer. Clients usually do speak up when asked, but, should that approach fail, you will have to rely on the client's nonverbal communication to ascertain client satisfaction.

That is easier said than done, as no one can read anyone's mind, and 10 experts reading body language can come up with 10 analyses. (A study at Xerox Corporation of 10 observers trained in reading body language, for example, showed almost no agreement in their interpretations of the same nonverbal behavior.)[1] Certain *behaviors*, though, do signal possible rifts:

> ➤ Your client returns calls less quickly than before.

---

[1] In fact, there are only two times I am comfortable reading someone's body language. One is when I know the person really well. A noticeable change in their body language will have me testing for understanding. "Is something going on I should know about?" (Note the question. I never assume anything about the Other—not even someone I know well.) The other is during a mediation. I notice the closer people are to agreement, the more likely their bodies will start mirroring each other; e.g., one person puts his hands on his head, the Other soon follows. It is at that point I realize that a settlement is nearing.

➤ You have trouble getting time on your client's schedule to meet.

➤ Client meetings get postponed for seemingly no reason or, in your understanding of your client, for inconsequential ones.

➤ Your client asks you to revisit issues you thought you both had successfully resolved.

➤ Payments come in late and increasingly later and later.

➤ Your client questions or objects to the cost of everything.

➤ Your client reacts to change orders, not with reason, but with anger or, worse, resignation.

➤ Your client's behavior changes in other ways that give you pause.

These behaviors can be read as signals that a rift is brewing and should be respected as such early, before the client feels the need to put more distance between the two of you.

But early-warning signals of trouble don't always come from the client. Oh, sure, they can come from the contractor, but they can also come from you. Are you feeling increasingly uneasy about the project and its progress? Your uneasiness is a signal. Listen to it. No-surprise design means that you shouldn't be surprised any more than your client should be. If you are dreading meeting with your client, rest assured something is afoot. You may not know what it is, but being the competent, candid, concerned professional that you are prompts you to ask the client how they think the project is going. These reality checks will help you pick up client concerns even before your client is in a position to articulate them.[2]

And you *have to* ask, if only because the uneasiness you feel could be yours alone. It could be that *nothing* is wrong. But if you allow your uneasiness to fester, you will increasingly hedge around your clients. You owe them more than that. Your clients need you to be focused squarely and clearly on themselves and *their* problems and fears, *not yours*.

Alternatively, something could be wrong, and if you don't ask, you don't know what action, if any, to take. Maybe there's a problem, but it doesn't rest with you. Maybe the client is having misgivings about the contractor. Maybe the client's business is going slow, making cash flow suddenly an issue, and the client is too embarrassed to bring it up. If you act without asking, if you act on what *you think* is the problem, you may instead be creating problems for yourself and your client. I mean, imagine if you developed a solution to a problem that did not exist? How likely is it that your client would welcome your additional services? So, *when danger signs appear, talk with your clients to find out their view* of project progress, of the quality of your services, or of anything else on their minds. Then decide with them what should happen next.

When the Air Thickens: Handling Confrontations

Okay, so you missed a danger signal or two, or ten, and your client calls you up screaming. What do you do?

---

[2] Some professional liability insurers offer incident reporting coverage to help architects reason through their fears of something being amiss.

Handling confrontations is no easy trick. Your heart is beating faster than normal, your head is pounding, and, depending on your personal proclivities, you either want to fight back or run. Neither approach is hugely effective. If you push back, all you serve to do is create resistance. If you fold, all you do is create resentment, albeit within yourself, but resentment nonetheless.

What, then, are your options? Agreeing for the sake of peace weakens your case, assuming you have one—and you probably do. They don't say there are two sides to every story for nothing. Arguing, making excuses, disagreeing, attacking, and, my all-time favorite, avoiding the issue don't work either. What's the alternative? Try Pulling. As we learned in Chapter 6, asking questions, listening well, searching for common ground, and then building on it is the safest, most accessible way to get to "yes."

In confrontations, Pulling can do wonders. This should come as no surprise to you. As we've learned, Pulling works where win-win outcomes are appropriate. It works with resistant cases, as it draws the Other out and draws the Other in. And, it creates commitment because, if done well, Pulling helps each party speak, be heard, and be understood. Pulling thus helps each party move toward the other. What better solution could you want in architecture?

Now please don't confuse understanding with agreeing. *Pulling requires you to reflect understanding, not to agree.* Just to make sure we are on the same page, let's clarify the two. When you say to the Other, "You are right to be angry," that's agreeing. You have agreed with the Other that the source of their anger is your fault. Understanding is a whole other matter. Here you say to the Other, "I understand that you are angry, and I am sorry that you feel I did wrong." By so doing, you are (a) acknowledging the Other's anger and (b) sharing your regret that they are unhappy with you—without blaming yourself or assessing fault anywhere or with anyone.

Why does understanding work? For a slew of reasons. First and foremost, your understanding, as we just spelled it out, is honest. You *do understand* that the Other is angry, and *you are sorry* that the Other feels that you are the source of their grief. Second, understanding acknowledges and empathizes with the Other, which is what a competent, concerned, candid professional is expected to do. It lets the Other hear that you heard them and shows that you listened and comprehended their plight. And, last, by acknowledging what the Other is going through, you give the Other the freedom to move on.

And understanding helps not only the Other, but you, too. It permits you to extract your ego from the situation. You don't have to argue. You don't have to attack. You don't have to defend. You don't have to make excuses. You don't even have to lower your eyes and wish the entire incident would just fade away. No, none of that. All you have to do is listen, understand, acknowledge, and care. And, in so doing, understanding gives you room to think and react as a professional—not as a target, a contender, or a victim.

But understanding alone is not enough to resolve a confrontation. Your clients want more. They need more. They want action. To handle a confrontation well, once your client (or any angry Other) has signaled to you that they have been both heard and understood, it is time for you to *refocus both of you on action by using all your Pulling skills.* "Tell me how you think the two of us can make things right again." "What would you like to see happen?" "How could we resolve this?" "Would it help if I did . . . ?" are all appropriate ways to refocus the Other's anger away from you and into positive arenas where action can be taken to rectify the problem.

Do you need one more insight to give you the confidence to try this approach? Chapters 4, 5, 6, and 7 taught you how to negotiate when the issues, not anger, are the focus. Those skills still work—and work maybe even better—when people are hot. To that end, *think of confrontations as just noisy negotiations.* Exploit them as great opportunities to build (or rebuild) common ground. Just view the problem as a joint one, work with the Other to build a mutual frontier, and you are both on your way to peace.

This reorientation is not only what *you* want, it is precisely what *your client* wants and expects of you—a professional reaction to a professional problem. Try it next time someone blows up at you, and see if it doesn't work for you both.

If You Are Too Panicked to Listen

Sometimes, when someone is yelling at you, you lose the capacity to listen to—much less hear—what is being said, you are so overwhelmed by the energy and emotion of the person saying it. When that happens, try this trick I learned when I served as an assistant U.S. attorney, prosecuting criminal cases in the District of Columbia: Repeat the last few words of what the Other says, with a question mark. "I don't like this design." "Don't like the design?" "Yes, I told you I want small rooms and these rooms are too big." "Too big?" What does the repetition do for you? It gives you space to breathe while you regain your wits, and it enables you to avoid the self-defeating Defend/Attack scenario described in Chapter 6. What does it do for the Other? It gives them the chance to ventilate uninterrupted by defensive arguments, certain that you are trying to understand their problem. Eventually, you will calm down, and, when you do, you can focus on the Other, comfortably aware that you have done nothing in the interim to exacerbate the situation.

When a Change Is Looming: Managing Change

By now, I am hoping you are fully persuaded that no-surprise design requires you to keep your client up to date on the progress of the project. After all, it is the client's project, not yours.[3] So one of the very first things you will want to tell your client, preferably *before* the contract is signed, is that someday—you don't know when—something—you don't know what—is going to happen to cause your client and you (and, depending on the timing of the change, the contractor, too) to regroup. That "something" could be as minor as a late shipment of a material that holds up construction for a day or two. Or it could be something major, like the government changing codes or zoning. Whatever that "change" is, it will alter the course of the project in some measurable way, maybe even resulting in a change order.

The point to bring home is there are myriad uncertainties inherent in the building process, and these uncertainties can challenge even the best owners, architects, and contractors, and they will happen. Nothing you or the owner can do can stop them. You are going to want to tell the client all this before the contract is signed because then there is a greater

---

[3] If you are still having difficulty with this concept, take it out of architecture and see if it more readily makes sense to you. You are going to have an operation for a brain tumor. Is it your operation or your doctor's? Should you be told what is going to happen to you, or should the doctor keep all that information to herself?

---

chance the client will hear it as the truth it is, and not as a self-serving statement.

You will also want to discuss change with your client, again *before* the first change occurs, because, depending on the nature and scope of the change, uncertainties can increase because of it. And what follows long-pending uncertainties in construction? Conflict. Like night follows day. As change is a given, so is the potential for conflict—even in the best-conceived and best-managed projects. The key to effective project management lies in managing that change so that any resulting conflict is resolved in the best interests of the project.

Now, while you can't tell your client what change is going to take place that will reroute the course of the project, you can share some of the attributes of these course-altering changes:

- The change may occur at any time, but the exact time cannot be predicted, and the reasons for the change may not be preventable.

- Any party to the building enterprise, including the client, may initiate the change.

- The change may be initiated by strangers to the project, such as government agencies or the community in which the project is located.

- The change may require additional, or merely different, architectural services to steady the project. It may also require revisions in the project's budget and schedule.

- Regardless of the specifics, the change will often demand immediate architect and client attention and cooperation, offering the parties less time than either would want to come to grips with the newly change-defined situation.

But you can also tell your client you have a system to handle those changes, a system that will keep the client's needs at the forefront of your thinking and help the client keep the project on track. Then, at least, management of change can be predictable, and a shared approach to it followed. Here is a system I developed when I was at the AIA that, according to the architects who use it, works.[4] It envisions a six-step process to be put in motion regardless of who initiates the change.

Step 1: Inform the Client

The first step to managing change is to involve the client. After all, it is the client's project, not yours, that is at risk. Moreover, informed clients are more likely to be both reasoning and reasonable. So if you are going to forestall a dispute, early action is a priority. *That* you are going to tell the client right away about the change, there is no doubt. If you don't, and the client hears of the change from someone else, you then have two problems: one, the change, and two, the client who has had to rely on a third party to hear the "truth" about what was going on in *their* project. The sole issue, then, is *how* you are going to tell your client about the change.

Take the problem of conveying troubling information out of architecture completely. Imagine you're at a playground and see a child fall and scrape his knee. The mother has two choices: She can smile and say comfortingly, "You're okay. You just went boom." Or the mother can show her angst and cry out, "Are you okay? Ohmygod! Let me look! Maybe

---

[4] In fact, it was reprinted in the newest *Handbook* edition, albeit ascribed to others.

we should go to a doctor! No, maybe we should go to the hospital!" What happens? Within minutes, the mother has either a happy child or a big baby bawling his eyes out. So how do you tell your client about a change? You smile and say comfortingly, "Your building just went boom."

You think I'm kidding you? No, I'm quite serious. No client under stress wants their professional consultant to be stressed. A client wants a competent, candid, concerned professional focused unerringly on them. So when a change has taken place, even one of seismic proportions, take it as the opportunity it is—the chance to prove to your client how wise they were to retain you as their architect.

Step 2: Clarify Client Expectations

Client expectations change during the course of the project, and nothing changes a client's expectations faster than an unanticipated change. A client who tells you at the outset that quality is paramount may decide, when confronted with a changed circumstance, that budget or time is of greater importance. Before you deal with the change, you'll need a reality check to find out whether and how your client is changing.

You'll want to check in for several reasons. First, as a believer in no-surprise design, you are going to want to meet your clients wherever they are. That way, you can be sure that, whatever solution you come up with, there is a near certainty that your client will approve it. (Clarifying client expectations may even surface design options.) Second, your client needs to be assured that the project is theirs, the change notwithstanding. What better way to prove that than by asking the client, "What's important to you now?" And, third, if the client's values have changed, you need to bring that out to verify that you heard correctly, and to make the client aware that *they* have changed directions. With this new understanding, you can work together as a team to keep the project aligned and on track.

Step 3: Analyze Options

Armed with your client's values, you can now go out and analyze options, ever aware that each option involves trade-offs. Some options may be discarded immediately as too contrary to client wishes to be worthy of consideration; others may require the client to reassess priorities; still others may present close-to-perfect solutions in the immediate circumstance but engender even greater changes down the road. And all, more likely than not, will involve either time or money or both.

Whatever options you arrive at, it is always wise to try to develop at least three solid ones for your client's consideration. Think about it: If you go forward with only one option and it gets accepted, who made the recommendation? You did. Who owns the idea? You do. So whose problem is it if anything goes wrong? Yours. A one-option process violates Rule Number One of no-surprise design: It's the client's project, not yours.

Does going forward with two options fare better? Somewhat, but a client still may feel put upon. With three solid options, each of which you can live with, the client has real choice and the chance to maintain control over the project.

Step 4: Present the Options

This step gives you the best opportunity you could want, not only to work with your client to put the project back on course but also to demonstrate visibly the value of your architecture services. In reviewing the options with your client, you will want to relay all the pros and all the cons of each option in enough detail that your client truly understands both the option and its short- and long-range implications for the client and the building. That way, your client can make a decent design and business decision, and you, by your conduct, can persuade them of your commitment to project success and your responsiveness to their needs. During the discussion, you can also learn a lot about your client's perception of project progress and their comfort with your services rendered to date.

The more comfortable the client is with the option-developing process, even if they have to struggle with making a decision, the more likely they are to be comfortable with you and your services.

Step 5: Document the Client's Decision

The best way for a firm to ensure client commitment to a course of action is to remind clients of their decision and the fact that they were the decision maker. That means documentation. Even if your client tells you to decide among the options, their not deciding is a client decision and, as such, should be documented.

But we are assertive practitioners, and to us documentation is not a legal prerequisite. It is a communication opportunity to help you and the owner make reasonable decisions, thus keeping the project on track. If done well, documentation is also a marketing opportunity, a chance to prove to your client—without telling the client—how lucky they are to have you looking out for them.

Documentation usually takes one of three forms:

➤ If the nature of the change demands no client involvement and has no time, money, quality, or scope implications—in other words, a truly technical change—a memo to the file, detailing options and the final decision, is usually sufficient.

➤ If the client was involved—that is, the change has time, money, quality, or scope implications—a memo or letter to the client detailing the options and their implications, as well as the final decision, is appropriate.

➤ A contract amendment may be called for, outlining the changed services to be provided, the compensation to be rendered for those services, and, if necessary, a schedule for service delivery.

There may be circumstances in which you choose to document a decision in more than one form. For example, for particularly tough decisions, you may want to send a letter to your client detailing the rationale, with the requisite change order attached.

Regardless of which form the documentation takes, remember our admonition in Chapter 3: *The purpose of documentation is to keep the project on track*. It also helps you be and prove that you are a reasonable and prudent professional. And, if well done, it is great marketing of you as the competent, candid, and concerned professional that you are.

Step 6: Update the Client

From time to time, and depending on the nature of the change and its scope and impact, you may want to remind the client of the change, their decision, and the progress being made in implementing it. This dialogue gives a client having second thoughts a chance to state them, which gives you the opportunity to reassure[5] the client or to take corrective measures, if any are indicated.

There's Value in Safety Deposit Letters

I received a phone call from a school architect who was troubled. He had spec-ed one lock for exit doors, but the school board, hoping to save money, wanted to downgrade to a second lock. Both locks would work. Both locks were in code. Both locks were aesthetically pleasing. The problem was, the second lock was trickier, so much so that it required training for ease in use. The architect was afraid the training would not take place and that, in a fire, some teacher would not be able to open the door, children would be injured or killed, and the architect would be blamed.

I introduced him to the safety deposit letter. "Documentation gives owners a chance to reconfirm their decision. Give your client that chance. Write the school board a letter, explaining that both locks are fine, but the second one troubles you because it demands special training for ease in use. Tell them you fear that in an emergency a teacher may not be able to open the door, for whatever reason, and a child could be hurt as a consequence.

---

[5] Handling consequences is a science as much as an art form. You cannot minimize them: To the client, they are real. You cannot prescribe solutions, saying, "If I were you. . . ." You are not the client. You cannot pressure the client into resolving them quickly: "Decide today—tomorrow the costs will be even higher still." All you can do is use Pulling to help the client address and resolve the consequences to their own satisfaction.

When the Best Laid Plans . . .

Underscore that, regardless of your fear, there are no code issues. As the building is theirs and not yours, you will implement whatever decision they make." I urged him not to write it as a "CYA" letter, telling the school board of his fear for his own liability, or as a "gotcha" letter. Assertive practitioners share only client-oriented fears with their clients, and I encouraged him to be assertive. "Think first and foremost about your client and their long-term safety needs. No client and no jury could want more. And if, as a result of your letter, the school board takes all necessary safety precautions, and no one ever gets hurt, you will have nothing to worry about. But just in case they don't, put your letter in a safety deposit box, hoping that you will never need to see it again."

Why does this process work for you and your clients? Remember back to Chapter 3: Architects must exercise *reasonable* care. This process assures you and your client that you are exercising reason, recognizing problems, jumping on them right away, analyzing available options in light of client expectations, and then working with the client to select and implement the client's chosen course of action.[6] It also keeps you and your client on the same track, comfortably knowing that, bumps notwithstanding, the project is on track, too.

When a Claim Is in the Offing: Managing Claims

Unresolved conflicts are likely to result in claims—that is, demands for additional money, time, or services. These demands may be in the form of lawsuits or, more likely, in the form of a letter or a phone call demanding that you "just fix it." In the best of all possible worlds, no client-initiated claim

---

[6] Just so there is no misunderstanding between you and me, going below code is never an option available to an owner.

would come as a surprise to the architect. But when the claim is a surprise, lawyers advise that the architect respond to the client's concerns but not admit liability. They suggest this simply because clients whose complaints are ignored become angrier still, and an angry client is often a claim looking for a place to file. But we are assertive practitioners. We know that liability is not the issue, client satisfaction is. So we don't admit liability because it is irrelevant. We look for ways to manage the dispute.

The easiest (and safest) way for you to respond to a claim is to take these steps:

> *Thank the client for bringing the problem to the firm's attention.* I mean this genuinely. You *should* be thanking your client for calling you. After all, the client could be calling a lawyer instead. And thanking a client for calling should protect you from the horrid Defend/Attack spiral we discussed in Chapter 6.

> *Tell the client the firm will look into it and get back to the client.* Nothing is more comforting to an angry client than the reassurance that they have been heard, understood, and will be cared for. And nothing is more disarming to a troubled client than the promise of professional action. That's what you get paid for. That's how you earn the big bucks. Step up to the plate and go out and find out what is going on and what options are available to put the project back on track.

> *Discuss the options with a buddy.* For example, talk to a member of your firm, your lawyer, or your insurance company. When you are under assault, a second opinion is always valuable,

and, if you have professional liability insurance, a necessity for coverage to adhere. Think through the problem with someone who has nothing at stake but helping you succeed with your client.

> *Respond to the client.* You told your client you would look into the matter and get back to them, so you have to do it. But what do you say to your client when you get back to them? You smile comfortingly and you say, "Your building went boom." And you handle the client, the situation, and yourself as if you were just handling a change, albeit an urgent and consequential one.

If all these steps are taken, the sole expectation your clients will have is that you will take their allegations seriously and will respond to them. You can then design the specifics of that response with assistance from your key advocates, without undue client pressure, and present yourself as the competent, candid, and concerned architect that you are and that your clients want you to be.

A Word about the Law[7]

It is easy to stereotype the law as something superimposed upon architects by a "they" who are unaware and unappreciative of the complexities of the building enterprise, but it is not so. The law is composed of three components, and the architect can influence and, at times, control all three of them: evidence, equity, and the law itself.

(continues)

[7] Reprinted with permission from an article I wrote for the twelfth edition of *The Architect's Handbook of Professional Practice.*

(continued)

Evidence. A legal proceeding is like a blank piece of paper. Nothing exists until a lawyer puts it into evidence. Evidence can consist of a person's testimony, a piece of paper, a videotape, a recording—anything that relays relevant information and helps the arbitrator, judge, or a jury reach what they view as a just decision.

Architects' evidence is 100 percent within their control. An architect's memory of what occurred, as well as verbal testimony to that effect, is certainly evidence, and the fact finder will surely want to hear it. But memories fade over time and invariably conflict with others, or else there would be no dispute.

To help shore up their clients' memory, credibility, and confidence before and during a trial, lawyers seek what they call real or demonstrative evidence from their clients—that is, physical evidence that documents the truth of what the client says.

The value of such evidence should come as no surprise to the architect; if there is any profession that understands that a picture is worth a thousand words, it is the one that relies on design to communicate. Fact finders especially value evidence that was created when no dispute existed. Because lawyers know this, they will want to see the architect's contract and all records pertaining to the project.

In this context, "all" will be defined expansively. Taken together, these documents will bring the dispute to life. Scribbled telephone messages ("Client X called. Go ahead with phase 2. No problem.") and correspondence ("Dear contractor Y: What do you mean it will be two more months before you can deliver? You told me three months ago it would be ready in nine weeks.") can make all the difference in a close case. Clearly, it is in the interests of the architect to document actions and decisions relating to a particular project and to archive those documents with care.

Architects should recognize, however, that documenting has an even more important role during the life of the project than it has during the life of a dispute. The law requires the architect to be reasonable, not perfect and error-free. Documenting forces the firm to think, to make choices, and to communicate. What better way has a firm to check the reasonableness of its decisions than to document them for firm review? In short, as important as documentation may prove to be in a court of law, the architect should keep in mind that its primary utility rests in the firm's business arena—and the architect is the only one in charge of that.

When the Best Laid Plans . . .

Equities. The architect is also in charge of the equities, or the fairness of the situation. When the law, as applied to the facts, can cut either way, a jury more often than not resolves its dilemma based on the equities as it perceives them. No one controls the architect's business but the architect. It is the firm that handles day-to-day operations professionally, openly, and responsibly, or not. It is the firm that sets the tone, and it is the conduct of its staff that determines the result.

The law. Again, the architect is measurably in control of the law—for what is the primary law in the case if not the contract freely entered into by the architecture firm and its client? The formation of this "private law" is fully within the firm's purview because, once signed by both parties, the contract establishes the roles and responsibilities, the rights and obligations of the parties. No one but the firm decides to commit the firm to it. No one but the firm is responsible for what it says. Moreover, this "private law" need not be static. If the project changes, the contract can be modified to reflect that change. Indeed, one purpose of change orders is to amend the contract governing the project.

When a Lawsuit Is Pending: Negotiating Disputes

This is not a book on trial tactics, so we are not going to discuss the ins and outs of arbitration and litigation here. Rather, we are going to assume that, despite the possibility of a claim, you and your client still have some type of relationship that makes negotiating a resolution to that dispute the preferred outcome.

And you will want to resolve it, if only to minimize the transaction costs of fighting it out, but also because people fare so badly in court.[8] But, as true as that may be, isn't that passive thinking? Assertive

---

[8] The September 2008 issue of the *Journal of Empirical Legal Studies* reported that most of the plaintiffs who decide to pass up a settlement offer and go to trial end up getting less money than if they had taken the offer.

practitioners settle cases because they have better things to do with their time and money than sit in a closed room fighting over who shot John. Also, they like to maintain their business relationships and professional reputations. Settling a case *with class* lets them preserve both.

Full disclosure is called for before you get too far into this chapter. I've been a litigator. I've been an arbitrator. I've been and am a mediator, and my preference over all forms of dispute resolution is mediation. Mediation gives the parties maximum power over their own dispute to decide it any way they choose. And it is private. After a successful mediation—and some 80 percent of mediated cases settle—no one will ever know who was legally liable. No one will ever know what amount, if any, was paid in the settlement. No one even has to know there ever was a dispute. Confidentiality is the rule of the game. All that can be assumed, if anyone ever hears of the dispute, is that the parties determined that the quickest and least expensive way to resolve the dispute was to settle it in mediation. Even insurance companies love mediation. It keeps transaction costs low and affords them a chance to work directly with their customers—you. So be prepared to mediate, and when you do, know that you are talking settlement.

Handling Guilt

Let's get real. Lawyers tell you never to admit liability because it makes defending you a much harder and more expensive task. Also, you may indeed *not* be liable. You may be wrong about what caused the problem or even whether there is a problem supporting the client's complaint. To admit liability or assign blame without an investigation of some type is to judge without basis. As assertive practitioners don't victimize themselves, you won't do that.

Even if you have some sense of causality, that sense will be skewed. Without comprehensive investigation, you are in danger of placing greater emphasis on the strengths or weaknesses of your contribution, if only because that is what you know. This is so even though the contribution of others may have caused the problem.

But when you are accused of badness, isn't the real issue facing you one of guilt? Architects are taught to view themselves as the protectors of the common good. To have done badness is hence shameful. But I ask you: Is it human to feel guilty? Sure it is. But is it professional? I submit not. And I offer this alternative: *Instead of stomaching angst, investigate and then act.* Do what William J. LeMessurier did when he was told he might have blown his Citicorp column calculations. He looked into it. He investigated, and, when he found out he'd erred, he called in his "buddies"—his lawyers and insurers—devised a strategy with them, and then met with his client. The rest is history. If LeMessurier could act assertively when the future of the then seventh-tallest building in the world and his practice was at stake, you can act assertively on any project.

Now this is a book about negotiation, nothing else, so the question is, how do you negotiate a settlement? *The same way you negotiate everything else.* You prepare. You figure out your interests and the Other's, and you develop several strategies to build common ground, using everything you have read about setting ranges and about developing and assessing BATNAs. Then you walk in, and you listen to the Other's view of the problem, and you hear, and you convey understanding to the Other. And you do it in such a way that you become a competent, candid, and concerned professional once again in the eyes of the Other *and the mediator*, and not some bungling or mean-spirited person from the Evil Empire.

As with any negotiation, to negotiate well, you will want to determine your options before you sit down at the table. As informal as mediation may appear, it has most of the attributes, save formality, of a well-run settlement conference. You will need to determine negotiating strategies and best- and worst-case alternatives ahead of time. In particular, you will need to know where you and the Other will bend and where you and the Other will break, and how to use those insights to your best advantage. Most important, you will have to be prepared to settle the case.

Easy for me to say; I'm not under attack. Well, neither are you. Projects are complex, and sometimes they crumble before the eyes of good people trying their hardest to keep the project on track. If you are an assertive practitioner committed to no-surprise design, that's all that happened to you.

How do you deal with it? First, focus on your interests, as plumbing them will give you the power and influence you need to propel you to a good outcome. How do you do that? Go back to the CARE (capability, authority/power, responsibility, exposure) package we first discussed in Chapter 3. Flip it and apply it retroactively by asking yourself:

- ➤ What were the bad things that happened on this project—the *Exposures*—for which the Other wants recompense?
- ➤ Were you *Capable* of preventing the harm?
- ➤ Was it your *Responsibility* to prevent the harm?
- ➤ Did you have the *Authority/Power* to prevent the harm?

If the answers to the three questions involving capability, responsibility, and authority are a resounding, uncontroverted, and unambiguous "yes," then, most likely, you will have this as your strategy: pay up fast and get out. That, most probably, is what is in your interests. If the answers to the three questions are an equally resounding, uncontroverted, and unambiguous "no," you will probably want to explore ways to help the other parties and the mediator realize that they should settle the case without you. Failing that, you may have to resign yourself to paying up something just to get out of a nuisance suit.

I hear you screaming, "Unfair!" Listen, the results of mediation are business decisions, not legal decisions. You don't have to pay if you think you shouldn't. You can keep on paying your lawyer. You can keep on fighting the Other. No one is stopping you. But why would you want to do that, when you could go back to practicing architecture instead?

How does applying the CARE package work? An example: You have signed a traditional B101-2007 agreement with your client. A construction worker gets severely injured on a day when you are on the construction site but nowhere near the injured worker. You are off in a corner discussing an owner-initiated change order with the general contractor. Will you be brought into the suit? That's not the issue. *Anyone can be sued by anybody for anything, in this day and age.* Scattershot lawsuits happen in no small part because of the lawyers' standard of care, which requires them to sue all possible defendants and decide during discovery who should be let out, else they may be committing malpractice themselves. So the issue is not *can* you be sued, but can you be sued *successfully*?

Here, the answer is no. You were not *capable* of protecting the worker from the harm. You were nowhere near the worker. You had no *responsibility* for construction-site safety: Means, methods, sequences, techniques, and safety precautions are the sole prerogative of the contractor alone. You had no *authority* to intervene either: You are in no position to tell a contractor how to perform his tasks, any more than he can tell you how to perform yours. So should you volunteer to settle this case for anything more than a pittance? Not a chance, and claims data bear that out.

Change the facts. You are standing next to an unshored trench, a phenomenon *you know* to be patently and intrinsically life-threatening. A worker is in the trench. You stand there, next to the foreman, thinking, "Boy, this is dangerous. Why isn't the foreman telling the worker to get out?" The trench collapses. Will the injured worker win in court? In many jurisdictions, no. But should you settle? As fast as your feet can carry you. You were *capable* of preventing the harm. You knew beyond adventure that the situation was dangerous. All you had to do is say, "Get out," and the worker could have taken steps to get out of the trench. Was it your *responsibility* as an architect to tell the worker to move it? Under your contract, no; but was it reasonable for you as an architect to stand there silently, knowing the situation was life-threatening? Arguably not. Arguably, a reasonable architect facing the same circumstances would have taken upon himself the duty to warn. Did you have the *authority* to speak up? Again, under your contract, no. The owner did not assign you authority over the construction site. One could argue, though, that in a patently life-threatening situation, at the minimum, you could have turned to the foreman and questioned the situation.

But most cases are even more gray—having neither clear reasons to fight nor clear reasons to settle. And that's where interests, strategy, lawyers, and claims specialists come in. Remember, just as a project is the owner's, not yours, a dispute is yours, not the lawyer's or the insurance specialist's. They make recommendations. You make decisions. So introduce them to the CARE package and Ava's Cheat Sheet and, by all means, think through both of them with your "buddies" so you can get the benefit of many thinkers. But devise a negotiating strategy you can live with. Because you'll have to.

Pulling It All Together

10

In 1987, I was invited to lecture the pro-practice class at the University of Illinois on risk management. I was doing my usual: "The project belongs to the client, not you. The problem belongs to the client, not you. The budget belongs to the client, not you. You make recommendations, but it is the client who makes decisions." Suddenly, an arm shot up and just stayed there. I turned to the arm and was met by a young, clearly angry student. "Clients, clients, clients," he sputtered. "That's all you talk about. What about me and the integrity of *my* design?" To make a point, I lodged my answer right between his eyes. "I realize that there are some architects who view their clients as unavoidable impediments to the accomplishment of their design objectives. But you are not designing for yourself. If you were, you would be a mere artist. You are designing for clients who asked you to bring your skills to bear for *their benefit*. It is *their problem* they asked you to solve, *not yours*. And as long as they are paying you to resolve their problem, they have a right to expect that your loyalty will go to them, not to you."

Snazzy answer, but it bothered me then, and it bothers me still. The student's question was a good one. Between the duty architects owe their clients and the duty they owe society's health, safety, and welfare, what duty do they owe themselves? I suppose there is a legal answer to it, but the question at its essence is not a legal one. But I ask you, when you design a building, don't you juggle the competing and conflicting demands of your clients, their needs, their budget, your fee, the demands of place, and the realities of costs, of constructability, of codes and standards, and of material availability, to name but a discrete few, in reaching your design recommendations? Why isn't your concept of design integrity just one more element of the design puzzle, which, if juggled well, produces design excellence? Does your sense of design have to be an element unto itself, to be considered and weighed alone by you and your colleagues? Isn't good design just one more issue you have to negotiate? Isn't it an issue you have to work out with the Other, keeping your own interests clearly in mind, but keeping yourself Other-focused in order to develop common ground? Given that, isn't the issue for this chapter: How do you bring all the skills of this book to bear on yourself and your practice, broadly defined, as we have broadly defined practice throughout this book?

Let's focus on you first, but let's make that easy on you. What makes a good client? Go ahead. Use the space. It may be the last chapter, but you still have to work.

What makes a good client?

This is what 250 architects attending one of my seminars at AIA's convention came up with:

- They pay on time.
- They cooperate.
- They trust you.
- They're fair.
- You can have an intelligent conversation with them.
- You're on the same wavelength.
- They're experienced.
- They know what's up.
- They're secure.
- They don't change their mind all the time. Or, if they do, they take responsibility for changing their mind.
- They open up the process. They involve other people so they get the best of everyone's thoughts, not just those of one person.
- They're competent.
- They're worthy of belief.
- They're reasonable.
- They're accessible.
- They empower people to function at their best.

Any characteristics that you disagree with? None? Okay, now ask yourself, is there any difference between the qualities you just agreed make a good client and the attributes of a good architect? Okay, a good client delivers a "good" check, on time, but a good architect delivers good services on time, so I submit to you there is no difference. Absolutely none.

Let's flip it. What's a bad client?

What makes a bad client?

This is what the group came up with:

- They don't pay you.
- They change everything all the time.
- They don't listen.
- They don't communicate. They don't tell you what's on their minds. They expect you to guess.
- They're not accessible. They don't return your calls.
- They have no idea what you're really doing, and they don't know how to find out.
- They're untruthful.
- They're impatient and want everything yesterday.

Is there any difference between a bad client and a bad architect? Again, no, except that a bad client fails to perform by not paying or by paying late, while a bad architect fails to perform by not delivering good services or by delivering them late.

Why am I going through all this? To bring one lesson home: *People like to work with people who are easy to work with.* You do, and so does the Other. This is true in the world of practice as much as it is true in the world of design.

Please don't confuse being *easy to work with* with being *easy*. No one is telling you to be a pushover. No one is telling you that you need to give your clients everything they say they want. Indeed, my only near claim occurred when the architect took our budget as a bottom line without exploring its implications with us, and designed an HVAC system within budget that we had to replace after one year. Would that the architect had told us our budget was too tight.

How do you make yourself easy to work with? *You practice no-surprise design.* You start where your client is, asking questions—including the hard ones—and you listen well to what is being said and what is not. Then, keeping your focus unerringly on meeting your client's goals, you juggle all that architects have to juggle, maintaining yourself as the creative problem solver that you are, and, in so doing, you build common ground.

Practicing no-surprise design is a skill, but one you can readily pick up. It may help you to remember that the sanctity of a design or a design solution may or may not be in the Other's interest, any more than someone's concept of good practice may be in yours. It's fluidity of thought and flexibility of approaches in the problem-solving setting that make someone easy, even fun, to work with, and it's those attributes that you will be called on to tap when you negotiate. You may be a tough bargainer when you negotiate; that's okay. Being difficult is not. If you want repeat business, in the long run, being difficult gets you nowhere. *It's unrelenting competence, candor, and concern, unsullied by seeming self-interest, that will get your clients to invite you back.*

That's a high calling, I agree, and I hear you asking, "What about the owner? Isn't the owner supposed to bring goodwill and fair dealing to the table?" Sure, and most will, but some won't. The reality is you cannot tell an owner how to behave. You meet owners where you find them, and if you don't like their location, *it is you who has to pass* on accepting the commission. In other words, you can't, under any circumstances, control the Other. You can only control yourself. That said, by the way you conduct yourself, you can show others how to deal with you. If you listen, you set up an atmosphere where they are encouraged to listen. If you communicate, you set up an environment where they understand they should communicate. If you deal openly and forthrightly with problems, you set the stage for everyone to be just as open and just as forthright. And isn't that arena where the best architecture is designed and built?

I know architecture is competitive. I know there are people out there eating your lunch. I know you will have nothing to negotiate unless you are sitting at the table. And I know being easy to work with alone will not get you an invitation to sit down. The invitation comes only to those who provide value, *but the invitation gets reextended most often to those who couple high value with no-surprise design.*

Look. Architecture has always been competitive, and present indicators suggest it is becoming even more so. One crucial element of success will be repeat business and referrals. Both depend on one thing: satisfied clients. If history is prologue, in difficult times the difference between outstandingly successful firms and struggling firms is that the former get referrals from satisfied customers. How do you get referrals? Not from negotiating contracts well, but from providing high value unstintingly to clients who routinely feel their projects are under control because of your commitment to no-surprise design.

How do you provide your clients high value and no-surprise design? You commit yourself to becoming an assertive practitioner, and you commit your firm to assertive practice. This is not as hard as it sounds. Having worked with architects these past many years, I have no doubt you can do it. And though an entire book could be written just on assertive practice, here are a few tips to help you on your way.

Increase your own value, and value the result. Owners today want so much from architects that no one stint in architecture school can prepare you to meet their demands. You are going to have to take charge of your education and, on your own time, acquire the skills and knowledge that owners seek.[1] You may be a crackerjack designer, but you are going to have to learn more about construction and constructability, and more about your clients' business and their building economics, for you to help them get the return on investment they are looking for. But when you do, you will be worth ever so much more, and your fees should reflect that.

---

[1] The Appendix is a good place to start your research for additional resources on negotiation and practice.

And do value your increased effectiveness for the owner. You can do this in small ways—for example, by ensuring your billing makes visible the value you create. You can do it in large ways—say, by tying incentive fees to your accomplishing realistic performance measures for you and the buildings you design, and then meeting them. (You have to be very thoughtful in doing this, of course, to avoid unaccomplishable, and therefore uninsurable, warranties.) You can do it everyday by keeping your focus on solving the client's problem and solving it so that all involved benefit from your solution.

You can do it as long as you make friends with risk. The more you recognize that risk is intrinsic to all projects, and the more capable you are at managing it, the more valuable you will be to your clients, society, and even yourself. Risk and reward go hand in hand, so the next time you find yourself confronting a risk, think of our CARE package, reason it out, and act strategically and well for the benefit of your client's project.

And do realize there is risk in everything, even in negotiation. In negotiation, for example, there is the patent risk of not getting to "yes." There is also a hidden risk of opportunity costs, and that risk has to be managed, too. Negotiation costs you time, time you could be using creating value for other clients on other projects. You can value that time by budgeting for negotiation and withdrawing when it's clear that you're going to break that budget with no agreement in hand. It is one way to manage the risk of opportunity costs.

You can do it as long as you value the Other. People matter. They make a difference, and how you interact with them can help make that difference for the better or for the worse. The more you appreciate and convey the fact that everyone has something to offer, the easier it will be for the people around you to offer up their best. In that environment, people will find it easier to begin viewing each other as joint problem solvers intent on finding mutual gain, not blame. And, when, despite your best efforts, things go wrong, as they sometimes will, all parties can more readily join forces to concentrate not on what went wrong, but on making things right.

You can do it as long as you look out for the Other, maintaining yourself as the competent, candid, and concerned professional you are. Architecture and the building enterprise enjoy good times and suffer bad times more than other professions and industries, due to the cyclical nature of the economy. As I am writing this book, we are entering difficult times, which may put a premium on your ability to be Other-centered. If you pick your clients well, it should be easier to do it.[2] And, you will have to look out for the Other to achieve our agreed goal of negotiation—the design of enticing options that meet the critical interests of disparate parties in special and appropriate ways. That's how you negotiate a contract, of course, and isn't that also how you negotiate your way *through* a project?

Which brings us full circle. As exciting as the new information in this book may be to you, and as eager as you may be to put it to use, do yourself a favor: Choose the one skill you want to acquire first, and then practice using that one skill in a safe

---

[2] And do continue to pick your clients well, even in the worst of times. Your client selection skills can make all the difference to your—and your client's—bottom line.

environment until you get it. Try it out on your spouse and children. Watch and understand its impact. Then, when you are quite comfortable with your new skill, put it to use in your practice. Then, focus on picking up your next chosen skill.

I have written this book to be an easy read because I want you and your clients and your colleagues and counselors to read it and put it to work. It is my hope that, in so doing, you and the next generation of architects and all of your clients and peers in the construction industry will have an easier time in the rough-and-tumble of the construction site. But the material here is sometimes tough to implement. The skills of expert negotiators are often counterintuitive and sometimes even run contrary to what we are taught at home and in schools. So take them step by step. Build success into your negotiation endeavors. All the time. Every time. You can do it—and you will.

One Final Story

It is one thing to collaborate on a small project, such as our award-winning log cabin, to bring the owners, the architects, the engineers, the contractors, the subs, and the neighbors together to build common ground and then the project. But, no matter how masterfully the parties listen, no matter how effectively the partnering works, no matter how special the result, no matter that it was accomplished on time and within budget, some of you are probably thinking, "It may have been a big deal to you, but it's small potatoes in the scheme of things. Anyone who works hard enough at it can pull off a small project." So on behalf of you doubters, I ask:

Can principled negotiation and no-surprise design work in the hands of a collaborative group of owners, assertive practitioners, and professional contractors in a high-stakes setting?

You bet.

Witness INVESCO Field at Mile High, the Denver Broncos' stadium—innovatively designed and built 14 days earlier than scheduled and $5.5 million under its $364.2 million guaranteed maximum price, to the satisfaction of the Broncos, the stadium's primary tenant; the owner, the six-county Metropolitan Football Stadium District; the surrounding governments; the neighbors; and the fans.

How did they do it? HNTB Architecture Inc. and Turner Construction decided early that, unless they formed a design-build team and asked for and received high owner involvement, they would never meet the owners' multiple goals of delivering a well-designed and constructed, accessible, safely built, noisy, world-class stadium on budget and in time for the football season. The owners agreed, and with all parties firmly committed to no-surprise design, HNTB and Turner with their many consultants and subcontractors were off and running.

"It was an enormous challenge to us," said HNTB's project manager architect Lanson Nichols, "to successfully negotiate which elements of the project were our responsibility and which weren't. We had to think hard about our value and expertise and everyone else's so we could structure the project for success. Managing the project was harder still, but we all dug in together to pull it off. Constant open communication and follow-up was key."

And everybody who could build success into the design and construction effort was invited in. Even OSHA was asked to come to the table. It did, and with the help of the Associated General Contractors of America (AGC) and Colorado State University, the design-build team (hereinafter called the Team) devised and implemented a site safety plan. It was followed, and no serious injuries were suffered as a result.

"Owners"—and there were many stakeholder-owners, as you can well imagine on a project as public and as complex as a sports stadium—worked just as hard as the Team, reviewing options, asking tough questions, anteing up extra money for special studies, and making tough decisions when tough decisions had to be made. Real-life models of suite types were built so the owners could experience place and determine which finishes and configurations would maximize fan satisfaction.

In other words, everyone did all in their power to make sure decisions were made openly, intelligently, reasonably, and consciously to minimize disruption, dissatisfaction, and waste.

Was the process always peaceful as a result? Is there an Easter Bunny? As Charles Thornton, Turner's project manager, told the ABA Construction Forum, "Never have I spent so much time in meetings. Yes, there were arguments, but there was also respect. We all worked together to get changes captured early enough so there were no impediments to our success. When we needed a decision, the owners made a decision, and we all moved on."

I know I promised you one last story, but I hear you asking, "Do the skills in this book work with

IPD and BIM?" You bet they do, and the best way to drive home the point is to tell the story of a real project. Let's listen to Scott Simpson, FAIA, LEED AP, and Managing Director–Cambridge of KlingStubbins:

> In 2004–2005, we were engaged by Novartis, one of the world's top biotech firms, to convert the former Necco candy factory in Cambridge (550,000 square feet in all) into world-class research laboratories. The schedule was extremely aggressive—only sixteen months from start to finish, and construction actually began on the top floors while candy was still being manufactured below. We formed a fully integrated team with the owner, with all the key players (architect, engineers, CM) on board from day one. Meetings were highly interactive and conducted on the basis of "decision ready information." We worked closely not only with the city agencies, but also the National Park Service, since the building had landmark status. During design everyone used our office as the base, and during construction we all set up shop on site in order to facilitate on-the-spot review of submittals and shop drawings. The design was very innovative and won not only "Lab of the Year" honors but also the *Business Week/ Architectural Record* design award plus the Cambridge Historical Preservation award. The client was so appreciative that they awarded the entire team a very generous bonus at the end of the job. Novartis/Necco is a great example of "assertive design," and proves that quality design, budget control, and schedule acceleration can indeed happily co-exist with the help of IPD and BIM and capable, committed players. In my book, this is the only way to do business.

Now if principled negotiation, buttressed by no-surprise design, in the hands of assertive practitioners can work on buildings as tiny as our log cabin, as monumental as the Broncos' stadium, and as complicated as the Novartis/Necco laboratory, can it work for you and your clients? Absolutely. Try it. You'll see.

Appendix: Building a Support System

There are two professionals you will want supporting you as you practice: a lawyer and an insurance broker. To be truly effective, each should know the ins and outs of design and construction, and each should be committed to helping you be an assertive practitioner. When you choose these counselors, it is important to invest enough time in the selection process so that you can establish the continuing and healthy professional relationship you will need to flourish and profit.

Like architects, lawyers and insurance brokers make choices in establishing their practices. Many choose general practices that offer a wide range of services. Others choose to specialize: lawyers, in particular aspects of the law, such as criminal law, negligence, labor relations, tax law, intellectual property, or antitrust law; and insurance brokers, in commercial, residential, and professional liability coverage.

Most architects establish a business relationship with lawyers and brokers in general practice who can handle a broad range of common concerns and can refer the architect to specialists when necessary. Because it may take time for a general lawyer and typical broker to understand fully the technical aspects of architecture practice, a growing number of lawyers and brokers are now specializing in design and construction law and coverages. You can find construction lawyers through the American College of Construction Lawyers, www.accl.org, and the American Bar Association, Forum on the Construction Industry, www.abanet.org, as well as through your insurance agent. You can find insurance brokers through insurance companies and your local AIA chapter. Please remember when you select your insurance support system that all agents work on commission and that some agents have exclusive ties and obligations to the insurance company they represent. Others are more free to represent only you.

On Selecting Your Lawyer

Regardless of where you look, here's some advice about selecting a lawyer. I use the masculine pronoun for simplicity; in all cases, she or he is implied.[1]

> ➤ Juxtapose the lawyer's specialties with your needs. If the lawyer is to review your contract documents, make sure he has a demonstrated knowledge of the industry and is familiar with construction law in your state.

---

[1] I thank the AIA for permitting me to reprint this section on lawyer selection from its *Handbook of Professional Practice*. When I first wrote it in 1986, for what was then the *AIA MEMO*, it was considered by many to be radical. I thought then, and I think now, it just makes good sense.

➤ Ask the lawyer what makes architects sue-able. If you don't understand the answer (or you do, but he doesn't understand architects), keep looking.

➤ Ask a legal question. (For example: "What is negligence? How does it differ from breach of contract?") If he can't answer your question in plain English, find someone who can.

➤ Ask the lawyer how many architects and engineers he counsels. Ask for references; *then check them out.*

➤ Ask the lawyer what his limitations are. If he says he knows everything, find another lawyer.

➤ Ask the lawyer how he handles problems that arise in areas in which he has limitations. A good lawyer will tell you he will consult someone who does know that area of law. (He should also tell you that you will pay for that guidance.)

➤ Ask the lawyer what he expects of you, and listen for his expectations and his understanding of architecture and how he can help you.

➤ Talk about money. Ask him how much he costs, how he controls his costs, and how you can control his costs. If you're uncomfortable during this conversation, think twice about retaining him. If he's uncomfortable, walk out. Straight talk saves time and money.

➤ Trust your instincts. Even if everyone tells you the lawyer is the "best," if you are uncomfortable with him, he's not the best for you. Mutual respect and trust is necessary for the lawyer-architect relationship to succeed.

➤ Remember: Lawyers have an expertise worthy of respect. So do you.

A Word to My Legal Colleagues

My late husband, a police officer, used to say that the best way to control traffic at an intersection was to get out of it. There is wisdom in that advice for us. If we truly want to help our clients negotiate construction contracts, no matter which party we represent, we do that best if we empower them to negotiate the contracts themselves. That means we have to stop looking at contracts as words for us to finagle, and start designing them as the flexible legal schematic they need to be to support our clients and the myriad negotiations they will have to hold, over the course of their contract, for their project to succeed. It means we have to become true counselors to our clients.

Accordingly, as important as developing front-end alignment knowledge and skills is to our clients, it is clearly in the construction bar's interest that we lawyers develop them, too. Being able to assist our clients effectively in meeting their strategic goals and objectives is just the antidote to the nascent commoditization of our profession. Besides, once we get good at counseling, it is also fun. So where does a lawyer begin?

Here are six solid steps to becoming an effective front-end counselor to an assertive practitioner or owner:

1. *Educate yourself about design, construction, and building economics.* The more you know about how projects get conceived and built, the

easier it will be for you to help your clients build an effective team approach to the project. Additionally, the better you will get at foreseeing the problems that might arise during its course of implementation.

Even more important, that knowledge will let you think about the project's interests and not just your client's interests, when you negotiate the many problems that arise. Most likely, those interests require: (a) the project to be completed on time, on budget, and claims-free, with quality and safety, *and* (b) each party to make a reasonable amount of money in the process. Working from that "shared base" will give you more options and a standard against which to measure them. For example, in the contract negotiation stage, you will be thinking, "For the project and the parties to succeed, as just defined, project risks (and, subsequently, rewards) must be aligned and assigned to the party best able to manage the risk, or, having no one able to manage the risk, the owner." That way, the parties will be maximizing their expertise, enhancing the chances for project and personal success.

2. *Get involved in your clients' projects early, early, early.* This is easier said than done. Clients are acutely aware of legal fees, and an offer of earlier service can all too easily be misinterpreted. Nonetheless, the earlier your client involves you in project setup, the easier it is for you both to build success into the project. Also, your getting involved early may save your client money later in the project.

You may have to introduce your clients to front-end alignment and the value it brings to all parties. For some of them, front-end alignment may already be their standard operating procedure. For others, though, most probably the first time they consider some of the major "claims preventer" factors is the day they start reading the proposed contract. That's too late. For those clients, introducing them to the need to align the project before they (or you) focus on words may encourage them to bring you in early in their deliberations.

3. *Help your client fill out the negotiation cheat sheet included in Chapter 5.* Whether you negotiate a contract or a predicament for your client, or whether your client negotiates for himself, there is no better way to prepare for the negotiation than by completing the preparation sheet together. It affords you insight into your client and his business, insight that should prove critical in identifying common ground and building on differences. It gives you the opportunity to up-tick your client skills. It gives you both the opportunity to build a working relationship, and it gives you the chance to demonstrate your value.

4. *Consider encouraging your client to take the lead in the negotiation process.* Just looking at the chart of the 20 "claims preventer" factors tells you why.

The following would best be brought to closure during the contract negotiation process: site responsibilities; risk/reward allocation; construction contract administration; scope, schedule, and budget; dispute resolution; parties' values and orientation; documents review, key issues; key staff; construction schedule; owner decision-making process, and materials/product investigation procedures. *Most of these are not legal issues.* Yet each of them must be decided before the contract is signed. Let your client address them with the Other.

5. *Stop thinking of contract language as the primary, if not sole, method of handling risk.* There is no way even the best of lawyers can insulate their clients from risk. Nor should they try, because, in America, people who take on reasonable risks and manage them well make money. People who try to avoid reasonable risks don't, and most clients of most lawyers want to make money. So the next time you jump for your favorite hold-harmless clause, ask your client instead, "Is this a reasonable risk for you, and, if not, how should it be handled or aligned so it is a reasonable risk for someone, maybe even you?"

In the same vein, stop thinking litigation every time your client feels or is threatened. Think conciliation whenever possible. As you and your clients become increasingly adept at front-end alignment, your clients may find they have more "repeat work" with others with whom they have worked before. Successful projects, after all, breed new opportunities. As a result, the business relations they form will become increasingly important. Litigation will fade as an option when disputes arise. Conciliation and mediation will be their first choice. Your ability to be a creative problem solver will become ever more valued.

6. *Increase your client's experience base.* The fact that experience contributes so strongly to claims prevention is one strong incentive for your clients to boost their Experience Quotient (EQ). The easiest way to advance EQ is through continuing education, which happens to be very much in vogue today. (It is a prerequisite for AIA membership, for example.) This should give you a special entrée to ask your clients if they would like your assistance in helping them meet their experience needs through continuing education.

Serving as a counselor to an assertive practitioner has its challenges, but the professional satisfaction that comes with it—for both you and the client—makes the entire effort worth it.

If You Want to Learn More

There is a tremendous amount to read out there, but if your time is limited, start here. (I have put asterisks ** next to the four I would read first, if I had time only to read a few.)

On Negotiation

> *Getting to Yes: Negotiating Agreement Without Giving In.* Roger Fisher and William Ury (Boston: Houghton Mifflin, 1981).**

The Harvard Negotiation Project is constantly issuing new books on negotiation. This was its first, and many would say its best. Some find the book tilted toward concepts and theory, and light on practical advice and examples, but, as the book provides the negotiation framework most discussed today, it is one you will want to know.

> *Beyond Winning: Negotiating to Create Value in Deals and Disputes.* Robert H. Mnookin, Scott R. Peppet, and Andrew S. Tulumello (Cambridge: Harvard University Press, 2000).**

This is the textbook I use with my class at George Washington University Law School. Unless you have read *Getting to Yes* or my book first, it is a bit advanced and for some a conceptual struggle. Yet the insights it gives into the process and the tips it includes for dealing with competitive negotiators make it well worth the effort.

> *The Lawyer's Guide to Negotiation: A Strategic Approach to Better Contracts and Settlements.* X. M. Frascogna, Jr. and H. Lee Hetherington (Chicago: American Bar Association, 2001).

Of the many books written on negotiation by lawyers for lawyers, this is one of the most accessible to the lay reader. Read it to learn how your lawyer is taught. You'll see he is taught principled negotiation also.

> *The Fast Forward MBA in Negotiating and Deal Making.* Roy J. Lewicki and Alexander Hiam (New York: John Wiley & Sons, Inc., 1999).

> *Bargaining for Advantage.* G. Richard Shell (New York: Penguin, 2006).

These two books try to popularize negotiation theory, and they do it well. Both are easily accessible and lay out negotiation vignettes in many settings.

> *Women Don't Ask: Negotiation and the Gender Divide.* Linda Babcock and Sara Laschever (New York: Princeton University Press, 2003).

These authors researched why women do less well in negotiations than similarly situated males, and found out that women don't ask for what they want. For all those architects who are loath to ask, regardless of gender, this book is for you. It addresses reasons you may be reticent and gives suggestions on how to increase your assertiveness.

The Harvard Negotiation Project, www.pon .harvard.edu, gives courses on negotiation throughout the year.

On Sales

> *SPIN® Selling.* Neil Rackham (New York: McGraw-Hill, Inc., 1998).**

If you are going to buy one book on sales and persuasion, this is it. It will help you form the best questions with the most impact, keeping you client-centered throughout the sales process. At the end of this book, you will no longer think selling is telling. You will know selling is about understanding.

> *Major Account Sales Strategy.* Neil Rackham (New York: McGraw-Hill, Inc., 1989).

If you get most of your business through responding to requests for proposals, this book will give you insights into what your potential clients are going through and what that means for you.

On Communication

> ➤ *Difficult Conversations: How to Discuss What Matters Most.* Douglas Stone, Bruce Patton, and Sheila Heen (New York: Viking Penguin, 1999).

While not focused purely on negotiation, this book, written by members of the Harvard Negotiation Project, takes negotiation skills and applies them to tough everyday situations.

> ➤ *That's Not What I Meant!* Deborah Tannen (New York: Ballantine Books, 1986).
> ➤ *You Just Don't Understand: Women and Men in Conversation.* Deborah Tannen (New York: HarperCollins Publishers, Inc, 1990).

These two books by Tannen will give you new insights into everyday speech. You will listen differently. You may even speak differently. In time, you may find why some say communicating is an art unto itself.

On Collaboration

> ➤ *How to Make Meetings Work.* Michael Doyle and David Straus (London: Little Brown and Company, 1976).
> ➤ *How to Make Collaboration Work: Powerful Ways to Build Consensus, Solve Problems, and Make Decisions.* David Straus (San Francisco: Berrett-Koehler Publishers, 2002).

These two books are classics. *How to Make Meetings Work*, for example, has sold over 800,000 copies and is in print in eight languages. *How to Make Collaboration Work* is similarly popular. But that is not the only reason that I chose the books. Michael Doyle and David Straus graduated from Harvard's Graduate School of Design and practiced architecture before they turned their focus to collaboration. Now you have two more reasons to see why I wrote that negotiation and collaboration are the architect's cup of tea. By the way, Interaction Associates, www.interactionassociates.com, the company started by Doyle and Straus, gives courses on collaboration and facilitation throughout the year.

On Professionalism

> ➤ *The Trusted Advisor.* David H. Maister, Charles H. Green, and Robert M. Galford (New York: The Free Press, 2000).**

If you want to learn how to be an effective and trusted counselor of your clients, this book is a must-read. It is substantive and practical.

> ➤ *True Professionalism.* David H. Maister (New York: Simon & Schuster, 1997).

If you have time for a second book on professionalism, give yourself a treat and read this one, too. The section on firm management is worth the cost of the book.

> ➤ *The Consultant's Journey: A Dance of Work and Spirit.* Roger Harrison (New York: Jossey-Bass Inc, 1995).

Boyce Appel introduced me to this book. He said it made him the successful consultant he is. Try it, and see if it doesn't work for you, too.

The American Institute of Architects, www.AIA.org, offers continuing education courses geared to increasing architect professionalism.

On Game Theory

> ➤ *Predictably Irrational.* Dan Ariely (New York: HarperCollins, 2008).

Ariely is a progenitor of behavioral economics, the belief that people do not act reasonably under the facts and circumstances facing them. For a lawyer like me, brought up on the "reasonable person" theory, the book was quite an eye-opener and opened new ways to think about getting to yes.

> ➤ *Thinking Strategically: The Competitive Edge in Business, Politics, and Everyday Life.* Avinash K. Dixit and Barry J. Nalebuff (New York: W.W. Norton & Company, 1993).

This book is a great lay introduction to game theory. You will never think of negotiating, brinksmanship, vicious circles, and bargaining quite the same way again.

On Contract Language

The easiest route to contract language analysis is to pick up your insurance carrier's contract guide. Most have them and give them away free as an insured benefit. But think through the information the carrier provides. Some of the books are extremely risk-averse. Do keep in mind the tenets of assertive practice when you read them.

Most insurers also sponsor their own courses on risk management and claims prevention. You can usually find them through their web sites. And again, keep your evaluation cap on while you are listening. Remember, you are in practice to serve your clients and your bottom line, not to make an insurance carrier even more profitable.

And, of course, you can always reach me at AvaEsq@aol.com.

Final Thoughts

The more architects recognize that each interaction with an "Other" is an opportunity for assertive practice, the more they will use their negotiation skills to effect no-surprise design. That should make life easier, more productive, more profitable, and more claims-free for architects. And, as owners and contractors learn and use those skills by watching architects apply them, all parties to the building enterprise should benefit. At its core, negotiation is problem solving, and the more competent, candid, and concerned architects are throughout the negotiation process, the more adept they will become, and the more productive they and all who work with them will be.

Index

B

Behavior. *See* Communication behaviors
  client attraction, 192–193
  labeling, 190
Best Alternative To a Negotiated Agreement (BATNA), 102,
    152, 305
  development, 113–115
Brainstorming
  usage, effectiveness, 215–218
Brainstorming, problems, 208
Bringing In, process behavior, 219–220
Building
  codes, common ground, 258–259
  economics, education, 328–329
  uncertainty, 291–292
Building Information Modeling (BIM), 52
Buildings, noncompletion (problems), 176

C

Candor, 76, 183
  practice, 191–197
Capability, authority/power, responsibility, and exposure
    (CARE), 144–147, 153, 306–307
Capability, concept, 68, 70, 73
Case law, importance, 57
Certification, 247–253
Chairpeople, group leadership, 222–223
Change
  attributes, 292
  management, 291–299
Cheat sheet, 158–163
  questions, 162–163
Claims
  factors, 18
    findings, 20–25
  management, 299–303
  preventers, 20
  risk, increase, 31–32
  starters, 20
Claims-free firms, security, 23–24
Clarifying, 284–285
  absence, 215–216
  behavior, invitation, 216

Firm stability, 31–32
Firm standards, 55
Front-end alignment, 18
    core necessities, 24
    knowledge, development, 328–332
    necessity, 35
    securing, importance, 38
    usage, explanation, 37–44
Full disclosure, 304

G
Game theory, resources, 337
Goodwill, building, 236
Group leaders, 222–223,
Guilt, handling, 304–305

H
Hard negotiation/negotiators, 97, 100–101
Haviland, David S. (research), 17
Holding harmless, 262

I
Indemnification clause, 261–267
    impact, 265–266, 268
Indirect liability, 60–61
Information, disclosure, 189–190
Initiating
    brainstorming, relationship, 215–216
    communication behavior, 166, 168
        usage, 170–171
Integrated Project Delivery (IPD), 25, 52
Interest-based negotiation, 101
    control, 117–118
Interests
    focus process, 118
    identification, 107–108
    knowledge, 106–110
        importance, 118
    location, 111–112
    projection, 119–122
    secret, problems, 121–122
Interior design, 244
Internal information, reliance, 189

N

Negotiation
architect fear, 94–97
cheat sheet, client completion, 330
collaboration, difference, 206
common ground, 91–92
control, questions (usage), 188
defining, 90–94
facilitation, contract (usage), 65–66
focus, initiation, 130–134
instruction, 4–5
preparation time, 129
process
client lead, encouragement, 330–331
equal investment, 135–136
pushing/pulling process, 179–182
resources, 332–334
strategies, devising, 231–232
types, 105t
Negotiation, insights, 2–3
Nichomachean Ethics (Aristotle), importance, 96
Nonpartisan objective criteria, usage, 123
No-surprise design
assertive practitioner belief, 13
impact, 321–323
practice, 315–320

O

Objective criteria, usage, 122–123
Options
analysis, 295
design, 124
development (assistance), questions (usage),
186–187
discussion, 300–301
presentation, 296
Outcome (seeking), goal, 104
Owner
architect allegiance, 52–53
feedback, impact, 30
indemnification, 261–266
problem
mitigation, 250–251
understanding, 110–113

Pulling
    impact, 218–219
    persuasion, 175
        advantage, 176–177
Pushing, persuasion, 175
    advantage, 176–178

Q
Questions
    alternative, 187
    asking, 184–189

R
Reacting
    absence, 216
    communication behavior, 166, 168
        usage, 173–175
Reasonable risks, 11–12
Reframing, usage, 226–229
Reliance language, 253–254
Responsibility. See Capability, authority/power, responsibility,
        and exposure
    concept, 68, 70–71, 74
Risk
    assertive practitioner friendship, 11–12
    awareness, development, 85–87
    elements, clarity (absence), 83–87
    interaction, 318
Risk management, 12–13, 65, 76–87
    contract language, relationship, 331–332
    procedures, 78–83

S
Safety deposit letters, value, 298–299
Sales, resources, 334–335
Schinnerer, Victor O. (research), 17
Scope, limitation, 252–253
Sequence planning, 139–140
Services, expansion, 251–252
Short-term problems (solution), negotiation (usage), 128
Shutting Out process behavior, 219–221
Skilled negotiators, turn-taking, 189
Skill/judgment/cooperation, 259–261
Soft negotiation/negotiators, 97–99